Finding Footprints

A History of Moira
Co. Down

by

David McFarland

Published by 2hearts Ministries
25 The Hollows, Lurgan, Co Armagh. BT66 7FF
http://2hearts.co.uk
http://moirahistory.uk

Second Edition 2019

© David McFarland 2018

Index

Foreword 5

Battles and barbarism 11

Lords and landlords 29

Linen and limestone 55

Sons and daughters 69

Castles and cottages 85

Roadways, waterways and railways 113

Saints and sinners 119

Their footprints and ours 163

Footprints found 165

Appendix 1. 167

Appendix 2. 169

Foreword

Look behind the incongruous commercial signage on old blackstone facades; look beneath the cultivated meadows and overgrown raths; look under the playgrounds and patios of twenty-first century Moira. You may have difficulty seeing them, for all across this area the wind-blown sands of time have conspired to hide the most remarkable footprints of history.

This small village has had an enormous impact on social, political, religious and military life not only in Ireland or in the United Kingdom but across the world too. This place where villagers live, relax, shop or work was once a place where Knights and Earls had their magnificent estate; where the children of nobility played while the children of the lowly laboured. Yet a lad raised in poverty became a hero in the American War of Independence while another who grew up in the grand environs of Moira Castle was to become largely responsible for the establishing of Central India as part of the British Empire.

In the countryside around Moira, soldiers and warriors from across this island and across the sea fought horrific battles leaving the blood of thousands to drain into the soil which we now cultivate. And it is not just the land in north west Down that has seen bloodshed; Moira has important associations with the Williamite wars and many other violent events in Irish history.

The members of the aristocracy have long since moved on and their footprints have faded but Moira remains a place where a host of ordinary folk have lived and worked and died. They toiled in the homes, fields, waterways and quarries of the district to raise their families, often battling through the most extreme poverty and enduring appallingly difficult times. All who trod the parish of Moira, Lords and labourers, have left a legacy for today's residents to experience and enjoy and hopefully conserve. Yet so much is unknown; so many footprints are hidden.

It is my desire to try to help find those footprints so that some record of life in Moira over the years is preserved for posterity. I want to be honest with you from the beginning. Firstly I am not a real historian - in fact I hated history at school. Learning all those dates of English kings seemed so boring. Now I really enjoy my annual visit to Moira Primary school to tell children something about the history of their village.

My second confession is that I am a "blow-in" of sorts for I have never actually lived in the village but in nearby Dollingstown and more recently in Lurgan. Yet Moira holds a very big place in my heart. From 1995 until illness ended my public ministry in 2003, I was Pastor of Moira Baptist Church and enjoyed fellowship with Ministers and members in other churches in the village - and still do. The Rector in Moira when I first came was Rev. Canon C R J Rudd, now deceased. It was through reading his little book, "Moira - a historical handbook," that I was first inspired to do more research into the history of this village.

What I share throughout the book has been gleaned from the writings of others, from historical records in books by both bygone and contemporary writers, from online articles or listening to stories passed down through generations. As far as possible I have sought in each case to acknowledge my sources and apologise if I have missed noting references to material I have quoted.

In presenting a historical record of life in our village, I cannot tell the history of Moira without some concluding reference to accounts of God at work in Moira throughout history for He is God over all history.

Perhaps you have picked up this book out of interest in local or Irish history; perhaps you grew up in Moira or have chosen to come to live in the village and want to know more about the place. Whatever your association with Moira I hope you find this interesting and informative and even challenging.

I am constantly discovering more footprints so If you want to keep updated on the history of Moira, I invite you to visit my web site http://moirahistory.uk where new articles and images will be posted as further research progresses. And if you have stories you wish to share or information that corrects what is written here, then please get in touch. Verifiable corrections will be posted on the web site and in later editions.

Moira will always have a very special place in my heart. It is my desire that this book will help you know and appreciate Moira even more.

David McFarland

Dedication

To Sophie, Charlie, Archie and Mollie
- my dearest great-grandchildren.

Cover image

"Point me to the skies"
Photograph of St. John's Moira
By David McFarland

Battles and barbarism

On the northwest corner of County Down, Northern Ireland lies a beautiful old village with a street of stone-façade homes, shops and a market house. Narrow carriage archways and cobbled courtyards hint at days long gone; an extensive well-maintained demesne covers what once was a grand mansion or Castle. Over time this village was known on maps and documents by many names, most of which sound similar to how we pronounce Moira today. They include Maighe Rath (AD 634), Muigh Rath (AD 942), Maige Roth (1160), Magh Rath (1350), Mag Rath (1392), Myra (1583), Moyragh (1609), Moyrath (1692), Moyra (1712) and Moyrah (1719). It would seem that the name we use today was first in use about the mid-eighteenth century.

Traditionally the name Moira was thought to have has been anglicised from Magh Rath to mean "Plain of the fort."[1] The large number of forts or raths in the area helped create that assumption. However for the second element in the ancient names to mean fort, the word "rátha" rather than "rath" would be required. There are good arguments for the name to mean "plain of prosperity" or "plain of rivers or fords" but perhaps the most natural translation, since the village was a meeting-point of routes north, south, east and west, was "plain of

---

[1] From Archdeacon Atkinson's Dromore: An Ulster Diocese.

wheels."[2] It is a frivolous thought, I know, but if the old name was being translated today, wouldn't "plain of wheels" be appropriate, given that Moira motorway roundabout branches in five directions like spokes on a wheel?

It is clear from the historical names that Moira is an old community. A local newspaper suggests Moira was flourishing when Lurgan had only a few houses and Belfast was little more than a ford on the River Lagan,[3] though to describe it as flourishing may be just a little fanciful. Certainly a community of sorts has existed for many centuries. Some evidence lies hidden from the view of all but the most knowledgeable, while other evidence is walked upon daily with little understanding of its significance.

Over the years, growth in population and the ensuing development of the land has left little to remind us of early life in area, except for the few earthen raths still visible in and around Moira.

The most familiar and accessible rath is the Rough Fort on the Old Kilmore Road. The overgrown and rather inaccessible rath in the townland of Aughnafosker, just below Glebe Gardens, is called Pretty Mary's Fort. How it came to be so named is a mystery. Because it has more than the normal number of defensive earthwork rings, it is said to be a good example of a multi-vallate ring-fort.

Many other forts throughout the district have long since been levelled. Back in 1872, Maralin parish schoolmaster Robert

---

[2] See http://www.placenamesni.org/resultdetails.php?entry=11007 accessed 7th April 2017 for more detailed information.
[3] Lurgan Mail article 10/11/95.

McVeagh took Dr John O'Donovan to the townland of Ballymackeonan where he pointed out the site of a former fort. "This," said McVeagh, "was one of the finest forts in this parish, but it was levelled some years before I was born to give room to cultivation, for people cannot afford here to pay rent for waste ground and in my own memory twenty-four forts have been levelled within the parish."[4]

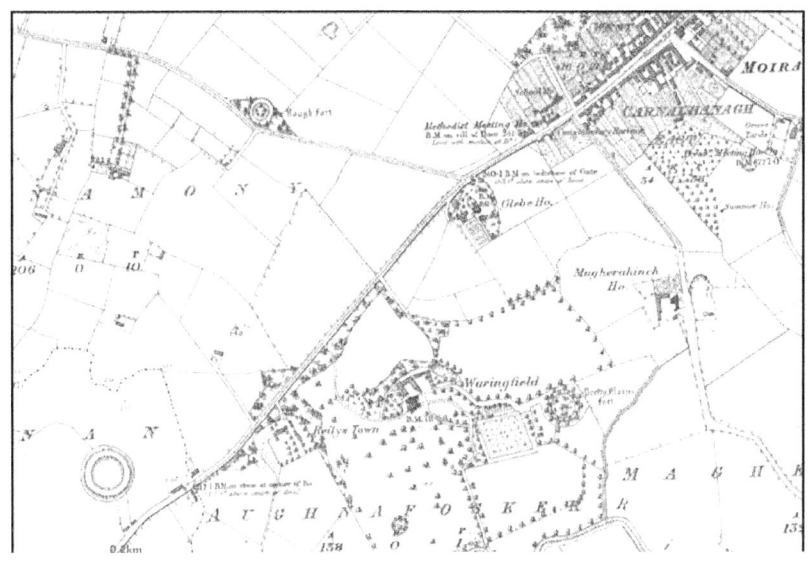

Ordnance Survey map © Crown Copyright 1860

Another fort suffered a different fate. It was an unusually large one and early maps show it so close to the quarry on the Lurgan Road that the western half was gone. Site surveys in 1978 showed no trace and the conclusion was that it had been swallowed up by the quarrying.

In addition to the raths of Moira, there are two other evidences

---

[4] Dr O'Donovan's letters preserved in the Royal Irish Academy, Dublin.

of even earlier life. One has now all but disappeared while the other is very visible but seldom recognised for what it is.

The former is a crannog. They were very early dwellings, sometimes built on stilts, in a lake or bog. Our local crannog was in the townland of Drumbane, on land now bordered on three sides by the motorway, the railway and the Drumbane Road. That area, crossed by road and rail, was once so liable to flooding that it was effectively a lake. An old land survey map of 1780 shows it as a mill dam and turf bog.[5] Virtually all trace of the crannog has disappeared, though the lie of the land still indicates the edge of the former lake.

The henge is a different matter and is visible on land behind the Presbyterian churches and is surrounded by the housing development at Claremont. Henges are from the Neolithic period and Early Bronze Age and were large ceremonial circular earthworks. They are thought to have been meeting places where a tribe congregated at certain times of year for rituals or other gatherings. Interestingly, Edmund Getty described Moira as "one of the classic spots of pagan Irish history."[6]

This circular mound in Moira is reasonably large, being thirty-six metres (almost one hundred and twenty feet) in diameter. Some limited archaeological excavations of the outer ditch in 1977 identified two distinct historical periods. The upper layer showed late medieval activity but by digging deeper, the archaeologists found pottery dating from around AD 500-1100 and showing that there may once have been an underground

---

[5] 'Map of Earl Moira's demean[sic] Moira, Co. Down 1780' by Daniel Mullan. Image T3560/1 PRONI.
[6] Notices of the round towers of Ulster by E Getty. Page 28

chamber which was now collapsed. However, the structure of the mound surrounded by a ditch almost certainly dates it to around five thousand years ago.[7]

Forts and crannogs were means of security in a rural and often barbarous society. The area, being close to Lough Neagh and the River Lagan, was always likely to be visited by those who wanted to dominate or destroy. Over the centuries the Moira area has been the scene of many battles and has endured much adversity before becoming a desirable place to live.

The Romans visited Ireland but did not invade. They believed this island to be a barbaric place. It was "the land where the limits of the known world should be placed" and where the "natives are wholly savage and lead a wretched existence because of the cold."[8] We know the Romans mapped the British Isles. They knew this island called Hibernia, the land of winter, and were familiar with our coastal areas. One of their maps clearly shows Belfast Lough with a river flowing into it. Roman coins and material goods have been found in Ireland providing evidence of scouts and traders exploring up our rivers in search of butter, cattle and Irish wolfhounds. It is possible one of those Roman scouts may have sailed up Belfast Lough and explored the Lagan as far as Maighe Rath. I suggest this because a Roman coin from the time of Vespian (AD 70-79) was unearthed here shortly before World War I and is now in the

---

[7] Ulster Journal of Archaeology, Vol. 42 1979 Excavation of an earthwork near Moira, County Down by N.F. Brannon and the Northern Ireland Environment Agency Rescheduling of a Henge in the townland of Carnalbanagh East, County Down (DOW 013:013).
[8] Strabo – Greek geographer and historian quoted in BBC Northern Ireland - Blueprint series.

Ulster Museum in Belfast.[9]

As we move forward around five hundred years, we discover more barbarous activity. Hordes came to fight in AD 637 and battled for six days. Thousands of them never went home. This Battle of Moira is the earliest historical record of life in Moira.

Congal Cláen, King of Ulster had killed the High King of Ireland in AD 628 but was defeated the following year at the Battle of Dun Ceithirnn in Derry. Congal fled to Scotland and Domhnall of the Clan Connall became the new High King. In Scotland, Congal sought help from King Domnall Brecc of the Dal Riada, a Scottish kingdom that included northern Irish territories. He returned to Ireland with an army of Britons, Scots and Saxons, including a Scottish King and a number of princes.

Perhaps he arrived through Dunseverick (though one writer believes they landed in Ireland at Dundrum). One of the five royal roads from Tara, seat of the Kings of Ireland, ran due north and ended at Dunseverick Castle. That ancient road was known as Slighe Mhidhluachra or High King's Road and it is said to have passed through Moira.[10] Another source says it crossed the Lagan at a fort near Moira – possibly over the ford where Spencer's Bridge now stands. Congal and his troops marched south. Domhnall advanced from Tara, with an army of Irish chieftains and princes.

The two armies, reportedly comprising fifty thousand men on

---

[9] Craigavon Historical Society - Review Vol. 2 No.1 and BBC Northern Ireland - Blueprint series and confirmed to the author by the Museum in 2017.
[10] Colm O'Lochlainn quoted by Rev. Patrick J. McKavanagh in Glenavy, the Church of the Dwarf 1868 – 1968 Printed by IRISH NEWS LTD.

either side, came together at Moira on 24th June AD 637.[11] After six long days of fighting, Congal's army was annihilated; Congal himself was killed as were a number of the Scottish Princes. The battle is described as one of the most bloodthirsty in early Irish History. Sir Samuel Ferguson considered it "the greatest battle, whether we regard the numbers engaged, the duration of the combat or the stake at issue, ever fought within the bounds of Ireland." He wrote an epic poem in 1872. I quote a verse from *Congal: A Poem in Five Books:*

> My sins, said Congal, and my deeds of
> strike and bloodshed seem
> No longer mine, but as the shapes
> and shadows of a dream.
> And I myself, as one oppressed
> with life's deceptive shows,
> Awaking only now to life
> when life is at its close.[12]

The routed armies fled over the Ford Ath-ornagh (Thornford or Thornbrook), up the ascent of Trummery and in the direction of the Killultagh Woods near Ballinderry. This direction of retreat helps the writer to believe that Congal's army had approached the battlefield from the North rather than from Dundrum in the south as suggested by another.

When the Ulster Railway was being built, great quantities of bones were discovered in the cutting close to the ruins of the old Trummery church and tower. It is quite likely that they were those of men and horses killed in the battle. Rev. Henry W. Lett,

---

[11] It has been suggested that The Battle of Moira was not fought at Moira but near Newry. For more information and links see Appendix 1.
[12] Congal: a poem in five books by Sir Ferguson, Samuel, 1810-1886 Publ. 1978.

writing in 1800s, says:

> At Mr Waddell's lime quarries have been found quantities of the actual bones of the natives long ago. This was their graveyard and the mode of sepulture[13] was some form of cremation. After the corpse had been burned, the ashes and bones were placed in a small pot or urn made of the plastic clay, so well-known by the excellent bricks and tiles now manufactured with it, and turned mouth downwards on a flat stone in a hole in the ground about half a yard deep. And just below the kilns, exactly where it was possible to ford the Lagan River there stood a mound which a few years ago was discovered to consist almost entirely of human remains, bearing marks of calcination, evidently of those who had been slain in some great battle.[14]

One thousand two hundred years after the battle, one old resident of Moira parish said, "In all directions bones are picked up when the ground is ploughed deep."[15]

Some of the names of the townlands in the area originate from this battle - particularly Aughnafosker, which means the "field of slaughter" and Carnalbanagh - the "Scotsman's grave." There was once a pillar stone in Carnalbanagh with crude crosses and circles on it, marking the graves of the Scottish Princes. Sir Samuel Ferguson in his poem writes about that pillar-stone.

---

[13] An archaic word for burial or interment.
[14] Quoted by Eileen Cousins B.A. in "Like and Evening gone" - a history of Magheralin Church.
[15] Quoted in Antiquarian Jottings by Right Rev. Monsignor James O'Laverty M.R.I.A. Ulster Journal of Archaeology. Volume XI. Publ. 1905.

> The hardy Saxon little recks
> what bones beneath decay,
> But sees the cross-signed pillar-stone,
> and turns his plough away.[16]

At the end of his book, Sir Samuel added a note concerning this stone.
> I learn with deep regret and some shame for my countrymen of the north that this memorial exists no longer. It has been destroyed by the tenant. I saw it and was touched by the common humanity that had respected it through so many ages, when I walked over the battlefield, accompanied by the late John Rogan, the local antiquary of Moira, in 1842.[17]

Inside the cover of a copy of The Battle of Magh Rath, a book which at a time belonged to one called Edmund Getty, is a note that appears to be by John O'Donovan:
> March 27th 1848. This evening I walked with John Rogan of Lady's-bridge over the supposed site of the battle of Moira. He showed me the part of the hill where the pillar-stone once stood, supposed to be erected over the grave of one of the heroes. It commands a splendid view. The Mourne mountains are seen over the hilltops; the Lagan winds in the valley, and on its banks is seen a rath. Another rath is higher up, near a ford … [18]

O'Donovan refers to a letter he received from the same John Rogan, in which he was told that the farmer who removed the stone "was named Green. He is not long dead."[19]

---

[16] ibid.
[17] ibid.
[18] ibid.
[19] ibid.

Another ancient pillar-stone commemorating the battle once stood on the hill near Trummery old church. It was believed to have been erected over the burial place of Congal Cláen. In 1834 Mr Rogan described it as having been encrusted,

> with gray moss, and measuring about four feet eight or ten inches in height; on the side facing the north were four crosses neatly executed, three of them being within a circle. On the opposite side a large cross was observable, also encompassed by a circle. With regard to the time, or by whom erected, tradition is quite silent; but, that on some occasions this had been used as a place of interment, there cannot be any doubt, as human bones in a very decomposed state were often turned up. Report says that a former proprietor caused it to be carried away and used in the arch of a limekiln; but a mortality which exhibited itself amongst his farm stock having been attributed to this cause, the stone was restored to its ancient site.

Some years later Rogan adds,

> a few years subsequent to writing the above, this interesting relic was wantonly, perhaps I should say maliciously, broken to fragments, and spread on the entrance into a field.[20]

For one thousand years after the Battle of Moira, there are few records of life in the area. It is believed that Vikings were nearby for a time. In AD 839 they reached Lough Neagh through the Lower Bann and wintered there. Confusion over the name Linn-Duachaill led historians to assert that the Vikings

---

[20] The Round Towers of Ulster Source: Ulster Journal of Archaeology, First Series, Vol. 3 (1855), pp. 292-300. Published by: Ulster Archaeological Society Stable URL: http://www.jstor.org/stable/20608774 Accessed: 29-04-2017 08:50 UTC.

had used the area around Maralin as a base to plunder churches in the north of Ireland - particularly Armagh. John O'Donovan had originally believed this but later corrected his assertion.[21] Linn-Duachaill was in County Louth. However the Vikings were as close as the southern shore of the lough for Oxford Island is said to be a Viking name - Ost-Fjord, East inlet - and Viking treasure was unearthed near Aghalee in 2013.[22]

Around the time the Vikings were in Ireland, a King came to Moira as a visitor and not to fight! Murtagh McNeill wrote a poem called "The Circuit of Ireland." He traced the progress of the King of Aileck through Ulster in the tenth century and listed the places where he stayed the night. The list includes Moira.[23]

Moira was never far from bloodshed. Just down the road, near Glenavy, is the scene of further battles between the descendants of those who fought the battle of Moira. The battlefield was at Cráeb Tulcha or Crew Hill where on both occasions, in 1004 and 1099, the native Irish were victorious, even if they still did not gain full control of the East of Ulster for another three hundred years.

The foremost record of life in the area comes from the late sixteenth and early seventeenth century. Hugh O'Neill, Earl of Tyrone, was engaged in a campaign against English expansion in Ireland known as the Nine Years War. O'Neill had a Fort at Inisloughlin close to a ford on the Lagan.

---

[21] "Linn Duachaill, not Magheralin, County Down as O'Donovan once thought. *Circuit of Ireland note on line 35*. He afterwards corrects the error. *Fragments of Annals P.120 Four M., 1045, p.848.n*" - as quoted in The War of the Gaedhil with the Gaill: edited by James Henthorn Todd.
[22] www.bbc.co.uk/news/uk-northern-ireland-25128242
[23] Ibid. (But see also footnote 8 and Appendix 1, where J W Hanna suggests this also was near Newry).

Tyrone had met the Earl of Essex on 7th September 1599, for a "parley" on the instructions of Queen Elizabeth I at a ford on the Lagan and met him again in November that year. However the meeting is more likely to have been on another Lagan, which forms the headwater for the River Glyde in Co Louth. A truce was agreed but Elizabeth was displeased with Essex. She believed he had allowed O'Neill excessively favourable conditions and had treated him as an equal. She said of O'Neill, "To trust this traitor upon oath is to trust a devil upon his religion."[24]

Over the next couple of years, O'Neill continued pressure on the English and a large reward was offered for his capture, dead or alive. He ostensibly sought pardon while continuing to defend his territory but Crown forces kept up the fight in 1601-1602.

Mountjoy, Lord Deputy of Ireland, reported that,
> Chichester is now undertaking a fort in Killultah, held by Brian MacCartar's[25] men, being a place ... of great strength but exceeding importance, for it is the only den that is left for the rebels in all those and these parts.[26]

Fynes Moryson describes how the fort was besieged and captured on 15th or 16th August 1602.
> The Fort of Enishlanghen ... was seated in the middest of a great Bogge, and no way accessable, but through thicke Woods, very hardly passable. It had about it two deepe Ditches, both compassed with strong

---

[24] Golden Lads: A Study of Anthony Bacon, Francis and Their Friends by Daphne Du Maurier.
[25] This was Brian MacArt O'Neill, nephew of Hugh O'Neill.
[26] Calendar of the Carew Manuscripts edited by Brewer & Bullen. Publ. 1870.

Pallisadoes, a verie high and thicke rampeire of earth, and timber, and well flancked with Bulworkes. For defence of the place fortie two Musketeres, and some twentie swordmen were lodged in it. But after that our forces with very good industry had made their approaches to the first ditch, the besieged did yeeld the place to the Queene and themselves absolutely to her mercy. So a ward of English was left in the Castle, after the spoile thereof was taken, wherein were great store of plate and the chiefe goods of the best men in the Countrie.[27]

O'Neill's power was now greatly weakened. In exchange for help in getting a royal pardon, he granted his land in Killultagh to Sir James Hamilton, who five years later granted the same lands to Sir Fulke Conway.

O'Neill eventually fled Ireland in what was known as the Flight of the Earls and the English settlement in the area began in earnest. James was now on the throne and granted much land in the area to several Irish freeholders, "hoping the same would be better manured and inhabited."[28] The territory of Moira was granted to Murtough O'Lavery.[29] According to Rev. James O'Laverty, the territory included the townlands of Risk, Carnalbanagh, Drumbane, Gortnamony, Ballycanal, Feyney, Leg,[30] Taughlumny, Kilminioge, Gortross and Drumnabreeze.[31]

---

[27] An Itinerary by Fynes Moryson 1908, 199-200. (Spelling as in original quote).
[28] The history of Ireland ... to the year 1245 by John D'Alton. Publ. 1845.
[29] ibid.
[30] Perhaps Legmore (Some spellings have changed over the years and some of these townlands are in the Magheralin area).
[31] An Historical Account of the Diocese of Down and Connor, Ancient and Modern by Right Rev. Monsignor James O'Laverty M.R.I.A. Publ. 1895.

The Plantation of this part of Ulster was underway but the area was still a most challenging place to settle. The Irish woodkerne[32] knew their way through the forests and bogs, and were naturally determined to get their own land back. About 1605 it was reported that "Killultagh by reason of strength of bogs and woods was the shelter and lurking place of most of the idle men, thieves, murderers, lawless kerne …."[33] In 1610 Killultagh and the nearby district south of Lough Neagh were described as "a strong fortress, a den of rebels, and as thievish a country as any in Ulster."[34] Two years later the settlers in County Armagh complained that the kernes of Killultagh were committing robberies daily.

There was another major difficulty to surmount. While the land around us today is open and fertile, it was not always so. We know that Ireland has an abundance of turf-bogs that have passed through the stages of de-forestation and moorland to eventually become fertile fields,
> a remarkable example of which may be seen in the parishes of Blaris, Hillsborough and Moira, which lie towards the banks of the Lagan. The whole district was known as "the Bogs."[35]

Sir George Carew describes Killultagh as "a safe boggy and woody country upon Lough Eaugh"[36] and Sir Henry Bagenal, marshal of the English army in Ireland, speaks of it in 1586 as

---

[32] A robber or outlaw who lived in the woods of Ireland.
[33] Quoted by Rev. W. H. Dundas, B.D. in History of Killultagh. "Lisburn Standard," 28th January 1916.
[34] ibid.
[35] Ulster Journal of Archaeology Publ. 1860.
[36] Quoted in The Ulster Journal of Archaeology Vol. 6.

"a very fast countrey full of wood and bogg."[37] A note on the corner of an old map of Down from 1590 showing the River Lagan reads: "Alonge this river be ye space of 26 myles groweth much woodes, as well hokes for tymber as hother woode, which may be brought in the bale of Cragfergus with bote or drage."[38]

In a poem published in eighteenth century picturing the Lagan in flood, the poet describes Moira and the area:
> But soon thy intermitted rage returns,
> As Donaghcloney opens to thy view -
> Soon Maralin her flooded pastures mourns,
> And soon the nymphs of marshy Moira too.
> Thy bloated form askance Kilwarlin eyes,
> A mass uncouth, misshapen, and impure:
> Maze next beholds thy progress with surprise,
> And Blaris sitting on her sandy moor. *Hafiz* [39]

As the years passed, the appearance of the area changed dramatically. Conway's new settlers cleared the natural forest from the valley floor and surrounding hills. It had been so thickly wooded before then that it was said a man might almost make his way from McArt's Fort on the Cave Hill to Lisnagarvagh[40] on the tops of trees. By 1640 the de-forestation must have been considerable for a shortage of fuel was being experienced at local ironworks.

It is only to be expected that the arrival of the new settlers

---

[37] Quoted in A History of County Down by Alexander Knox Publ. 1875. (Spelling as in original quote).
[38] Ulster Journal of Archaeology, Vol. iii. old series. (Spelling as in original quote).
[39] Hafiz was the pen name of poet Thomas Stott Esq. of Dromore (1755-1829).
[40] Later called Lisnagarvey, then Lisburn.

caused great resentment among those already living in Ulster. This eventually boiled over into active rebellion and in 1641 a Rising spread all over the country. Lurgan was burned and Lisnagarvey was besieged. Both sides perpetrated terrible atrocities but soon the tide turned against the rebels. In April 1642 one of those atrocities was close to Moira. Henry Munro leading the Scots and Lord Conway leading the English joined forces to march on Newry. Their first encounter with the rebel forces was at Inisloughlin Fort and in the Kilwarlin woods. It would appear that the Irish had again seized Inisloughlin, as they had seized so many strongholds across Ulster, and hoped to stop the Crown forces from marching south to Newry and Dundalk. But the Irish were shown no mercy and one hundred and fifty prisoners were summarily executed. Kilwarlin means wood of slaughter.[41]

Lisnagarvey and this whole area had suffered badly and much of the country was left devastated by the rebellion. The manager of Conway's estate wrote to him on 6th November 1657 describing conditions;

> Some people who had leases are petitioning to give them up, having no money to pay the rent. You cannot think what misery is caused here ... corn and cattle bring in nothing; any trade there is, is in butter.[42]

The country was also hit by a widespread cattle disease which, given the description, was possibly foot and mouth disease. Restrictions were imposed on the export of Irish cattle into England and losses of cattle in the Lisnagarvey area were said to be considerable.

---

[41] Ulster Journal of Archaeology Vol. 8. 1860.
[42] ibid.

As the Plantation progressed, much Irish-owned land was confiscated and Ulster was planted with Protestant families from many parts of Scotland and England. The depression continued for some time but at length some improvement was seen. This encouraged the noble Lords such as Conway to devote money to improve their estates. And so the area around Moira slowly began to be a relatively more stable and settled community, with the prospect of better times ahead.

St. John's Church, Moira

Lords and landlords

The foundations of present day Moira were established in the seventeenth and eighteenth century. For one hundred and fifty years the vision, influence and wealth of those who lived in Moira Castle helped cement a community that still exists almost four centuries later. Those builders are the focus of this chapter.

Sir George Rawdon, 1st Baronet Rawdon of Moira (1604-1684)

The first man to put a significant mark on this area was George Rawdon. Rawdon came from West Yorkshire in 1631 as secretary or agent for Edward Conway, 2nd Viscount Conway who had an extensive estate with Lisburn Castle as his home. Conway was largely an absentee landlord and Rawdon had his own room in the castle. George Rawdon deserves enormous credit for the remarkable achievements attributed to Conway in the Lagan valley area in the mid-seventeenth century. He skilfully managed the estate and was a successful farmer, introducing up-to-date agricultural methods that greatly increased production. He began to establish industries such as iron works and the manufacturing of glass, soap, stockings and potash. He encouraged the local manufacture of linen, informing Conway in 1667, "I got four barrels of hemp seed and four of flax from Ostend."[43] A remarkable transformation of a difficult area was realised in the most demanding of times.

George Rawdon added military leadership to his achievements in Ireland. He built the garrison at Aghalee, commonly known today as Soldierstown, getting its name from a troop of horse and two companies of foot soldiers who were stationed there during the rebellion of 1641-2. One source says the garrison was close to the site of the present Holy Trinity Church of Ireland at Soldierstown but it is also possible that property on a farm nearer Moira was the actual site. That house has a date-stone marked 1688.

Rawdon's town of Lisnagarvey was of strategic importance, controlling access on the River Lagan and on the vital communication route between Carrickfergus and Dublin. Rawdon saw it as part of his calling in life to fight like a proud imperialist to retain military control of the town and district.

In the rebellion, Lisnagarvey remained loyal to Charles I. Sir Phelim O'Neill sought to occupy it but George Rawdon, with an army of two hundred Englishmen completely repulsed the rebels. Rawdon escaped death when he was shot in the hand and when his horse was shot from under him. But when the rebels failed to capture Lisnagarvey they burned it to the ground.

By then Rawdon lived in a great house belonging to Conway at Moynargedell (Magheragall) "with a stone bawne about it

---

[43] Quoted in "George Rawdon and Lisburn" by George McBratney.
http://lisburn.com/history/history_lisburn/george_radwon_and_lisburn.html

buylded fifteen foote high."[44] The defences did not stop it being overrun and burned as the rebels retreated, destroying a valuable library of almost ten thousand books and manuscripts belonging to Conway.

With the rebellion quelled, Rawdon did much to promote the early growth and development of Lisnagarvey or Lisburn, as it became known after the rebellion. He became "mayor" of the town with tremendous powers over all aspects of life. He was not afraid to exercise his power to dispense justice; even to sentence horse thieves to death by hanging.

And it was not just within the town that his influence was felt. He was responsible for the beginnings of the road system we have over much of the area today. One traveller, Richard Dobbs, wrote in 1683,
> All the highways within eight or ten miles of Lisburn are very good - not only for the nature of the soil, which generally affords gravel and sand, but from Sir George Rawdon's care, who is, I believe, the best High Way Man in the kingdom.[45]

George Rawdon was truly a remarkable man. Within fifty years of his arrival in Lisburn, the small vulnerable settlement that had been surrounded by wood and bog, had become a centre of civilisation and economic activity, largely due to his untiring efforts. All of these activities made Rawdon so busy, that his wife complained in a letter to her brother (Rawdon had married the Viscount Conway's only sibling, Dorothy), that she

---

[44] An Historical Account of the Diocese of Down and Connor, Ancient and Modern by Right Rev. Monsignor James O'Laverty M.R.I.A.
[45] Quoted in An Historical Account of the Macdonnells of Antrim by Rev. George Hill.

seldom saw him except noon and night. However because Conway was largely absent from his estate, the Rawdons enjoyed a rather high social standing and entertained lavishly.

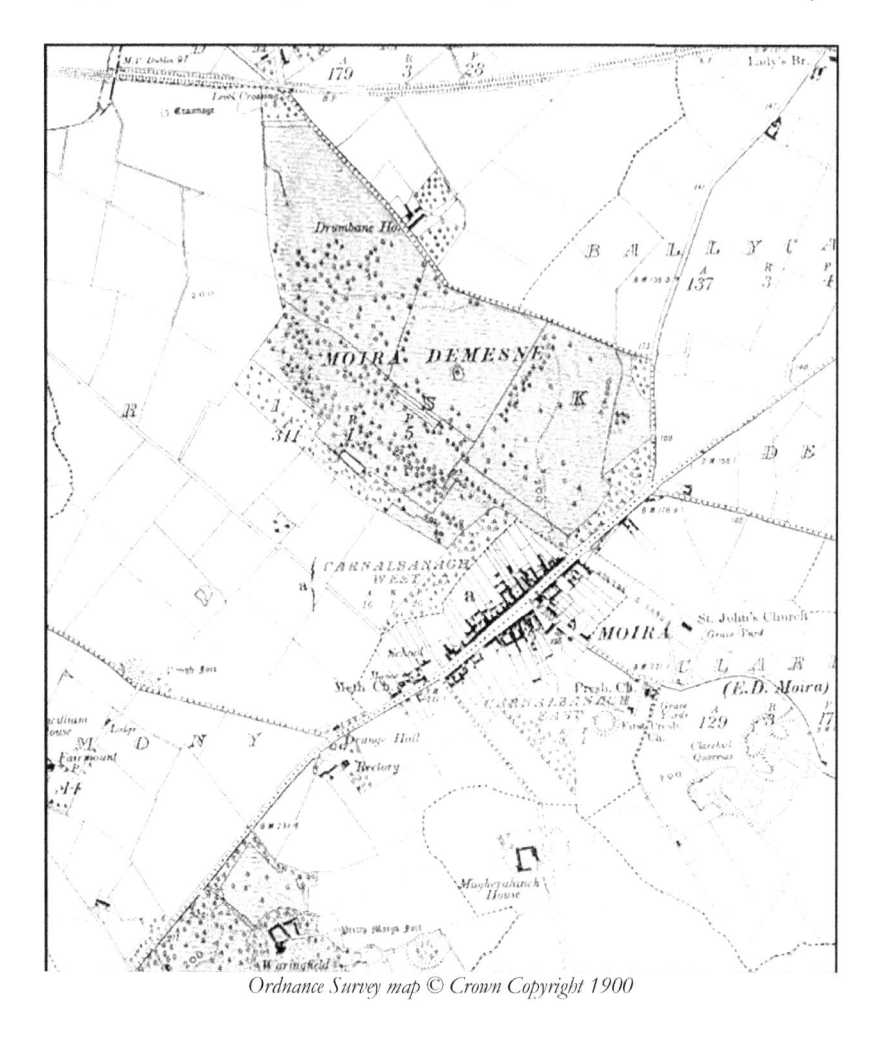

Ordnance Survey map © Crown Copyright 1900

Although Rawdon had such a part in establishing Lisburn, the Rawdon name is now more associated with Moira and Ballynahinch. This is surely due to the influence of the later generations of Rawdons as we shall see, but it was George who first began the development of Moira.

For services to the Crown, Rawdon received property in Dublin and also large grants of land in County Down. Because of the Magennis family's involvement in the uprising, their land was confiscated and since Rawdon was a member of the commission of revenue, he appears to have received a generous part of it. Another to benefit from alienations of land in the area was Edward Brugh who got O'Lawry's land.[46] It is quite probable that this man was Captain Burgh, a military officer serving with George Rawdon.

In the early 1650s, Rawdon became the new owner of a large brick house and estate in Moira. The house had been built by a Major de Burgh who had not occupied it for very long. He is likely to have been the landowner just mentioned for he had bought land encompassing much of Moira in 1639.[47]

Sir George Rawdon was a privy councillor and Irish Member of Parliament for Belfast in 1639. In later years he was Member of Parliament for Carlingford and was appointed the Governor of Carrickfergus Castle. He was made a Baron in 1665.

---

[46] The Plantation of Ulster: War and Conflict in Ireland by Jonathan Bardon
[47] Edward Brugh obtained from Hugh O'Loury of Reske, County of Downe, the towns, lands, sessiaghs, and parcels called Reske, containing 120 acres; Carneallbanagh, 60 acres, Drombane, 60 acres; Gortemoney, 60 acres; League, 60 acres; Kilmonyoge, 60 acres; and Taghlomny, 20 acres. These lands, known generally as Meyrah (Moira) Burgh purchased from O'Laury in 1639 for the sum of £300 – Thorpes' Catalogue of Southwell MSS p.209 as displayed in a footnote in The Montgomery Manuscripts (1603-1706) by William Montgomery. (Note that the name is spelt differently within this short footnote and is used interchangeably in other references.)

Among all his other activities, Rawdon had a great interest in horticulture. He successfully imported and grafted apple cultivars from England, raising a substantial orchard at Moira. Something of that interest would be passed on to his descendants. When George Rawdon died, he was buried in the chancel of Lisburn Cathedral.

Rawdon had made a fortune through serving the Conways and through his marriage. By the time of his death he had become an extensive landowner with estates in Antrim, Down and Wicklow as well as the family seat in Yorkshire. But the appearance of wealth can be deceptive and soon after his death the whole future of the Rawdons in Moira was in doubt because of serious financial difficulties.

Although the Rawdon family would eventually settle in Ballynahinch, George's family home remained in Moira for several generations where they not only established a community but developed it, leaving a legacy that has lasted to this day.

Sir Arthur Rawdon, 2nd Baronet of Moira (1662-1695)

George's son Arthur was born and raised in Moira. He was the youngest of three boys and suffered from very poor health. As an attempt to improve his physical condition, Arthur was sent to France in 1671, when he was just nine years old. His two older brothers were already there but both were tragically killed in separate incidents in 1676. It was a heart-breaking year for the family, for Arthur's mother also died in that year.

When his father Sir George died in 1684, Arthur inherited the

Baronetcy and the estate. He was just twenty-two years old but was immediately faced with a major predicament. It was said that there was not one sixpence of ready money left to pay legacies and funeral costs. To provide for Arthur's unmarried sisters, family properties in Yorkshire were disposed of and the sale of farm stock and other valuables raised less than £100.[48]

Arthur had expected to inherit not only his father's property but Conway's also. He was the "darling" of Lord Conway, his uncle on his mother's side, and since Conway had no children and treated Arthur as his heir apparent, it seemed certain that he would still be a wealthy man. However in 1683, when Conway lay dying, he was prevailed upon to change his will to benefit distant relatives called Seymour. Only Arthur's sisters were mentioned in the will. Arthur was convinced that Conway was not *compos mentis* at the time and went to law against Popham Seymour who had been a witness to the will. However Arthur had lost two previous expensive court cases through what he believed to be judicial corruption and the influence of Seymour in Irish Government circles. He abandoned the suit as long as his sisters received their inheritance. In the event they received only half of what they were due.

This financial struggle might easily have altered the history of this island. A supporter of James II wrote to Rawdon's wife in an attempt to get Arthur to dissociate himself from northern Protestants. He mentioned the loss of the Lisburn estate;

> If your husband was advised by me, he would do as he did in Monmouth's rebellion - offer to raise men to

---

[48] Information gleaned from The Anglo-Irish Experience, 1680-1730: Religion, Identity and Patriotism by David Hayton. page 179. Publ. 2012. The Boydell Press.

serve the King, and by that means entitle himself to Mulgrave[49] and Seymour's estate in Ireland, out of which he was so notoriously wronged. I pray God direct him for the best.[50]

To Lady Rawdon, It was certainly a very tempting offer and correspondence between the two indicates that she was prepared to offer support and certainly appears to "have supplied him with important information respecting the movements of northern Protestants."[51] But Arthur did not abandon his allegiances for financial gain and that decision would have far-reaching consequences for this land.

To add to Rawdon's woes, it was nearly impossible at the time to get rents from Irish tenants because the country was so poor. Arthur wrote to his friend Hans Sloane in 1688 saying, "I believe no country was ever so poor, nor is there any prospect of amendment."[52] Yet somehow through all of these financial challenges, Arthur was to throw what energies his health permitted into three major challenges. He had a passion for horse-racing and tried to establish a racecourse on land at Ballynahinch. It seems to have been a financial disaster. He was more successful in his other challenges. He was greatly interested in horticulture but before he could fully indulge that passion, another issue demanded his attention.

Charles II had encouraged James' Protestant daughter Mary to

---

[49] Mulgrave was the old Lady Conway. She had been previously married to Earl Mulgrave and had been bequeathed the Irish property during her life.
[50] The Rawdon Papers. Letters to and from Dr John Bramhall edited by Rev. Edward Berwick. Publ. 1819. Quote from a letter by Sir Thomas Newcomen to Lady Rawdon, wife of Sir Arthur Rawdon. Dublin January 17, 1688-9.
[51] The Montgomery Manuscripts: (1603-1706) by William Montgomery p. 277
[52] Rawdon to Hans Sloane 10th May 1688. Sloane MS 4036, p. 34-5.

marry William of Orange, to ensure a Protestant heir to the throne. James had converted to Catholicism and married a Catholic. On Charles' death, he was succeeded by James II. Then James had a son who would replace Mary as heir.

In response, William invaded England and ousted his father-in-law who was allowed to exile in France. In 1689 William and Mary became joint monarchs. Arthur Rawdon was a fervent supporter of William.

When James II arrived in Ireland, with help from by Louis XIV, Rawdon determined to stop his attempts to use Ireland as a base to invade England and take back his crown. Arthur had been Captain of a troop of horse while his father was alive and was now appointed Commander of a regiment of dragoons. Despite his health problems, he was a fiercely committed to the Protestant cause and his regiment was often in the thick of military enterprises, though not always successfully. Early in January 1689 he led five hundred men from Moira to Lisburn in an attempt to disarm James' forces and so free Belfast to bring in supplies from England. The attack was aborted and as a result, he had to abandon further plans to attack Newry and Carrickfergus.

The Protestant aristocracy formed defence associations and central leadership was in the hands of a Council of Five or "Junto." One of those five was Arthur Rawdon and their headquarters initially were in his home in Moira, though future meetings seem to have been held in Hillsborough.[53] There is no

---

[53] The Williamite Wars in Ireland 1688-1691 by John Childs. Publ. 2008 by Bloomsbury 3PL. page 35.

doubt Rawdon was an inspirational and effective leader; he was given the nickname "Cock of the North." One historian has described him as "aggressive, impetuous, hot-headed, and messianically anti-Catholic."[54] He became so obnoxious to King James' government that the Lord Deputy Tyrconnel identified him as a threat and made a proclamation against him and a few others on 7th March 1688/9. It stated that he was exempted from Royal mercy because,

> ... in regard he has been one of the principal actors in the rebellion and one of those who advised and fermented the same and inveigled others to be involved therein.[55]

A poem of the time describes "Brave Rawdon."
> Sir Arthur Rawdon's horse rode to the plain
> In warlike order, 'bove a thousand men.
> Some of his men strong polish'd armour bore
> But he himself a silken armour wore.
> Above a thousand men he thither brought
> Who at Dromore against the Irish fought.[56]

Some of this may be fanciful, some perhaps factual, but there is no doubt that the encounter at Dromore was a disaster. James' soldiers took the Williamite army by surprise in South Down and rather than fight, a great number of Rawdon's men fled. It has been known ever since as the Break of Dromore. The Protestant armies were driven north towards Coleraine. It appears Moira Castle and land may have been ransacked as the

---

[54] Ibid. page 34.
[55] The Rawdon Papers page 297.
[56] Recounted in A History of the siege of Londonderry and defence of Enniskillen by Rev. John Graham. Publ. 1873 page 282.

attackers pillaged the properties of Protestants from Down.[57] It would be strange if Rawdon's home escaped since he had such a high profile role in the war and yet, by 1690, the home and grounds were open to entertain troops assembling for the Battle of the Boyne.

Some of William's supporters took the opportunity to flee Ireland from Donaghadee; some surrendered or changed allegiances. Actually it was rumoured that Rawdon had changed sides - but Arthur was made of sterner stuff.

He and what was left of his men reached Coleraine. To try to protect the town from the enemy approaching from Armagh, Rawdon and others were ordered to Moneymore and Portglenone but even that failed to stop the enemy advance.

Despite sheer exhaustion and suffering serious wounds, Arthur survived and eventually retreated to Londonderry. Although illness and injury forced him to end his army role after the battle at Portglenone, he played a very significant role in the events leading up to the siege in that city. This included being one of the signatories of Declaration of Union on 21st March 1688/9, one month before the siege began.

However, all the exertions and injuries had a devastating effect upon him. Some senior officers were abandoning the city and heading to England. Rawdon's friends and physicians persuaded him to leave also and even the troops who felt abandoned by their leaders recognised that Rawdon was

---

[57] Capt. O'Lawry's Letter to Sir Arthur Rawdon, Bart., relative to the ruined condition of the House and Lands at Moy-rah; see The O'Lavery's by The Right Rev. Monsignor O'Laverty P.P. M.R.I.A. (1904)

different. He left Ireland by ship from Lough Foyle just before the siege began. He spent months recovering.

Sir Arthur returned to Ireland just days before the arrival of King William's army at Carrickfergus in 1690.[58] Already stationed in the Maralin and Moira area was a certain Captain Thomas Bellingham, an officer of the King, who was recording preparations for the battle with King James. Throughout June 1690, Captain Bellingham visited Moira and the surrounding towns and villages reporting the arrival of troops preparing for battle. He describes in his diary how on 2nd June he "walk'd in ye afternoon to Moyragh, saw Sir Arthur Rawden's house, and walk'd with Captain Ross to ye conservatory."[59] On 12th he describes being in Moira again and seeing "Jewell's regiment of horse wch is a very good one: but ye Danish regiment of guards is ye best I ever saw. They are an orange colour'd livery fac'd with crimson velvet."[60] He dined in Moira that day and appears to have spent the next couple of days in the village. After dinner on 14th he says, "We fancyd we heard some great guns off, from Bellfast, which we hope are for ye King landing."[61] It was indeed the day of King William's arrival in Ulster.

These visits give us a tantalising glimpse into Arthur's life committed to military affairs and yet at the same time committed to his garden. For several years, despite his heavy military responsibilities and despite the lawlessness in the

---

[58] The Rawdon letters reveal that correspondence addressed to him show that on May 31st Rawdon was still residing at "Congertom, neere Manchester."
[59] Thomas Bellingham: Diary of Thomas Bellingham, an officer under William III.
[60] ibid. (The spelling of words and grammar in these quotes are as Bellingham wrote them.)
[61] ibid.

community, Arthur had been enthusiastically involved in horticulture and botany. He and Sir Hans Sloane[62] were close friends. Sloane had written to Rawdon in May 1687: "Sir, I hope by this you are very much advanced in your garden." Sloane had sailed to the West Indies later that year and in May the following year Rawdon wrote asking him to send seeds from plants growing in the Jamaican mountains, believing they might survive in the colder climate of Ireland.

While still recuperating in 1689, Arthur had commissioned James Harlow to go to Jamaica to bring back living plants. For some time Rawdon wondered if he had been cheated, for he wrote to Sloane in March 1692, "I much wonder what is become of James. I fear he has a designe[63] to cheat me for I cannot hear the least thing from him." But a month later Harlow arrived in Carrickfergus with around one thousand living plants. Many survived, probably under the protection of the hothouse which Rawdon built in the Moira demesne. It is claimed that this hothouse was the first in Ireland.[64] He generously shared duplicate plants with other gardens. In 1690 he employed William Sherard, considered to be the outstanding botanist of his day, as tutor to his family.

Records describe the demesne with its mansion and estate as
> a commodious habitation, surrounded by a wood, which affords beautiful walks, a large lawn extends in

---

[62] Sir Hans Sloane was born in Killyleagh and became a physician. But he also was a noted collector of objects from around the world. By his death in 1753 he had collected over 71,000 objects. Sloane bequeathed his collection to the nation in his will and it became the founding collection of the British Museum.
[63] Spelling as in the original letter.
[64] Some claim it was the first hothouse in Europe.

front, where sheep feed, and is terminated by trees, and a small lough eastwards; the rear of the Castle grounds contains a wood, with large opening fronting the Castle, which forms a fine perspective.[65]

A rather strange entry is made in Bassett's History of Co. Down indicating that frogs were first discovered in Ireland at Moira, probably in those magnificent botanical gardens.

Sadly, Sir Arthur lived only a short time to enjoy the garden he created and loved, for he died in 1695 on his birthday, at the early age of thirty-four. He bequeathed his curiosities and specimens to Hans Sloane. But what a magnificent Castle and demesne he built in such a short time and apparently with such meagre funds! Even in the year of his death he was seeking to put in place measures that would solve financial debts relating to the Rawdon estate.

Arthur Rawdon became known as the "Father of Irish gardening" but after his death the garden deteriorated.

Sir John Rawdon, 3rd Baronet of Moira (1690-1723)

Sir Arthur was succeeded by his son John. He had been born just months before the decisive Battle of the Boyne and suffered from tuberculosis all his life. John barely remembered his father who had spent every moment either obsessed with military affairs or gardening, and died when John was just five years old.

---

[65] Memoir of Gabriel Beranger, and his labours in the cause of Irish art and antiquities, from 1760.

It seems John's mother moved from Moira after Arthur's death and the residence suffered. Helen had a very difficult time managing family debts, in the end using her own inheritance. Somehow the financial situation of the family improved before John attained the age of majority, but by then his mother had also died. He certainly behaved as though he were well off, purchasing many luxury items, refurbishing the house and replanting the garden. The gardens his father had created once again adorned the Castle, though many of the exotic plants had withered and died. John blamed their loss on the carelessness of the servants and the death of Mr Harlow, the gardener.

Sir John followed his grandfather and father into politics and became an Irish Member of Parliament for County Down but he always lived in the shadow of his forbearers' achievements.

However he seemed focused on improving his own community and this required improved properties. He began rebuilding the village with houses and businesses. Nearly three hundred years later, many of those black-stone buildings are still standing with their narrow carriage archways leading to quiet courtyards or modern housing.

Sir John was a much-loved landlord in the village but died at thirty-three years of age. He was recognized as a person of great integrity, piety and charity. In the eulogy at his funeral he was described as

> always ready to do good, employing the poor in works of improvement but did not care to encourage strolling beggars who made a trade by begging.

The clergyman went on to say

> The honour of God was the chief leading principle in Sir John's character. He was first and foremost a

person of true seriousness and earnest devotion in public worship.[66]

The Parish Church in Moira was built by Sir John, though tragically he did not live to see its completion let alone worship in it. He was buried in the vault before its consecration but the funeral service was in the Magheralin Church that he had attended all his life. That church is now an appealing ruin in Magheralin village.

John Rawdon, 1st Earl of Moira (1720-1793)

Sir John's son, also named John, was born in the Castle and inherited the estates at the age of three. He also seems to have inherited his father's character and interests. He is the one normally credited with the development of the village, though if dates are correct, it is more likely his father was the prime developer. It is generally accepted the village was completed in 1735[67] at which point young John was only fifteen years old.

Even as a teenager John took an avid interest in botanical specimens and horticulture. Sir Hans Sloane, who had been such an inspiration and friend to John's grandfather Arthur, wanted to trace specimens of particular plants he knew were in the possession of the Rawdon family. The specimens were from the Moira locality and from Jamaica. Through a mutual friend he contacted John Rawdon. The friend wrote back:

---

[66] from A sermon preach'd at Magheralin on the occasion of the death of Sir John Rawdon, Bart. ... who died, Feb. 1. 1723. By George Wilkins, ... printed by J. Hyde and E. Dobson, for R. Gunne, 1725.

[67] The date stone 1735 on the wall of the Midnight Haunt restaurant is generally regarded as a mark of the completion of the village.

I have accordingly applied to Sir John Rawdon who is a youth between fifteen and sixteen years old and of great hopes - and though he has a great taste himself for gardening and knows most of our plants, yet out of regard to the friendship which has subsisted between your and his family, he is very willing to oblige you with all the plants he has of that kind to enrich your collection.[68]

The same correspondence seems to indicate that John may have been reared by his aunt. The letter concludes with a PS: "Sir John and his aunt present you their respects." John's widowed mother had married Rev. Charles Cobb, later to become Archbishop of Dublin.

This second Sir John was later elevated to the peerage of Ireland as the Lord Rawdon in 1750 and became Earl of Moira in 1762. A letter recommending his elevation says, "I cannot think our House of Lords would be dishonoured by (him). A man with a great estate who pays his debts and commits no act of violence and is well affected to the government."[69] The title had to be changed because of an error in spelling; he was initially called the Earl of Moyra[70] but by then, either the name of the village had changed or he was instigating the change.

The Rawdons lived during the penal times of wretchedness and persecution for Catholics. It was an era when it was punishable by death for Catholics to practise their religion, yet the Earl

---

[68] Sloane ms. 4054, f. 107. British Library, London, Quoted in E Charles Nelson.
[69] Stone, Dublin, to Weston. Public Record Office for Northern Ireland. PRONI Reference: T3019/1012.
[70] ibid

seems to have been a support to Catholics. One instance concerns a bell. In 1178 John de Courcey had sacked the Monastery in Maralin. Many relics were destroyed but St. Ronan Finn's Bell, the Clough Rua,[71] dating from the Battle of Moira, was found on the lands of Magherahinch.[72] It was kept hidden in the community for centuries. Two O'Lavery brothers had possession of it but after a disagreement, the family requested Sir John to give it secure keeping in Moira Castle from where it was later taken to Ballynahinch. After about sixty years, different branches of the family requested that it be returned and placed in the new chapel at Moira.[73] On 20th February 1815, Lord Moira's[74] agent Mr William Hamilton handed it over to Rev. Fr Jennings for the new chapel but according to local tradition that clergyman never received it.[75] It is now said to be in the National Museum of Antiquities of Scotland[76] but others say it is lost again.

But Sir John's attitude to the Penal laws was even more publicly demonstrated in the mid 1730s. His hospitality was extended to Father Tighe of Magheralin parish. It was illegal at the time, but the priest was a regular guest at Moira Castle.[77] This

---

[71] Also called the Clog-Ruagh or Clog Ruadh.
[72] Quoted in Antiquarian Jottings. Ulster Journal of Archaeology Volume XI Publ. 1905.
[73] Newsletter March 14th, 1815. Although it reports that the bell was restored to the priest of Moira, it is doubtful if there was a Catholic church in Moira village at that time. Possibly it refers to the new church at Kilwarlin known as St Colman's, first built 1812. See later in this book - chapter Saints and sinners.
[74] This Lord Moira was John's son who was the second Earl, Francis Rawdon-Hastings and at this time was Governor General of India.
[75] Quoted in Antiquarian Jottings. Ulster Journal of Archaeology Volume XI Publ. 1905. These details also published in the Belfast Newsletter.
[76] Stated in the parish of Magheralin by Kieran Clendinning.
[77] ibid.

hospitality was also extended to his successor, Father Lavery, who is described as an "intimate friend of Lord Moira."[78] As we shall discover, these clergy were not the last "men of the cloth" to be welcomed to Moira Castle.

John Rawdon married three times. His first wife died five years after their marriage. He then married Anne Hill, sister of the Marquess of Downshire – a strange union because he and the Downshires were politically at odds. The Earl was a Whig who supported the Volunteers' agenda of freeing the Irish Parliament from subordination to Westminster. The Marquess of Downshire was a Tory.

But Rawdon's second wife also died without having a family, and was buried in the family vault in Moira. The ghost of this Lady Moira supposedly haunts Moira demesne or some think Lady's Bridge.[79]

The third Lady Moira was Lady Elizabeth Hastings, daughter of the ninth Earl of Huntingdon. They married in 1752. Her mother was a famous follower of John Wesley and was the founder of the Methodist group known as the Countess of Huntingdon's Connection.

By all accounts Elizabeth was a remarkable lady with exquisite taste. She is credited with making Moira Castle a splendid place but even that was outshone by the splendour of Moira House,

---

[78] ibid (If the dates given are correct, then hospitality was by Sir John while he was still a teenager and not yet known as Lord Moira).

[79] Lady's Bridge gets its name, not from a ghost of Lady Moira, but from an old lady who lived nearby in the seventeenth century and who was the owner of a lot of land in that area. Source: An Historical Account of the Diocese of Down and Connor, Ancient and Modern by Right Rev. Monsignor James O'Laverty M.R.I.A. Publ. 1895.

Dublin built by the Earl on the banks of the Liffey in 1752. He decorated and furnished it in the grandest style; the octagonal salon had large windows, the sides of which were inlaid with mother-of-pearl. The Earl's wife was Ireland's leading Whig hostess and just about anyone of importance in Irish history of that time dined there in what was described as a place of constant and magnificent entertainments. On her death in the early nineteenth century her obituary said her home was "the favourite seat of taste and splendour" and describes her as

> a most liberal patroness... her great income was spent in acts of charity and unbounded liberality …. Her Ladyship's death is an irreparable loss to the poor of Dublin, as well as those who daily participated of her splendid board.[80]

It appears Lady Moira may have spent much of her time in Dublin rather than in Moira and some historians suggest that depression or incompatibility with her husband meant them living apart. There are however indications of her in residence in Moira. An example is her reported actions during a particularly unsettled time in the 1770s in Ulster. There was an uprising under the name "Hearts of Flint" (the movement used a variety of names) because of rent levels, evictions and local taxation. Frequently these turned violent and on one occasion the village of Moira was under threat. The warning, later believed by Lady Moira to be malicious, was that the Hearts of Flint had "vowed to hang every Moira person at their own door" unless they joined the protest. Lady Moira was in residence and she wrote in haste to ask for soldiers from Lurgan to come to their aid. Her concern was not that her village people might attack her for she said she was "perfectly

---

[80] The Gentleman's Magazine and Historical Chronicle for the year 1808 page 463.

persuaded the infatuated people who surround me are incapable of doing me an injury." She wanted military support to prevent intimidation of her villagers.[81]
Eventually the Rawdon family's links with Moira were loosened. They moved their seat to Ballynahinch, where in the 1760s Sir John had built Montalto House.

When the Earl of Moira died in 1793, his funeral was said to have been the largest ever seen in Ireland and it took place in Moira. He was buried in the family vault in St. John's, Moira. The funeral was attended by upwards of eight hundred carriages of various kinds, with a train of four thousand people, among whom three thousand hatbands and scarves were distributed.[82]

A sobering and soul-searching obituary marking Lord Moira's death appeared in Heterogenea, quoting words often used on headstones at the time:
> *How lov'd, how valu'd once avail thee not;*
> *To whom related, or by whom begot.*
> *A heap of dust alone remains of thee:*
> *'Tis all thou art! - and all the proud shall be.*[83]

---

[81] The Field Day Anthology of Irish Writing Vol. V. Publ. 2002 by Cork University Press, Ireland.
[82] Samuel Lewis' Topographical Dictionary of Ireland. Publ. 1837.
[83] This verse is a miss-quotation of some lines by Alexander Pope – Elegy to the memory of an unfortunate lady.

Colonel William Sharman (1731-1803)

The Castle was leased to Colonel William Sharman, who was to become a Member of Parliament in Grattan's Parliament. This was the era when the Volunteer movement was growing in Ireland. The Earl of Moira and Colonel Sharman were both original members of the Whig Club. On 8th March 17__ [84] a company was formed in Moira.

The Minister of the Presbyterian Church in Moira at that time was a Volunteer enthusiast. Actually he is said to have sometimes preached in his uniform. Rev. Andrew Craig told how the Moira Volunteers began:

> ...... chiefly by my exertions and advice, and in consequence of an address to William Sharman, which I drew up, he accepted of the command of the company, contrary to the expectations, and perhaps wishes, of some of the neighbouring gentlemen, who took no part in the movement. My situation as chaplain induced me to take an active part in all the concerns of the company, which were a source of activity and pleasure.[85]

Sharman not only was the local Volunteer Captain; he was elected Lt. Colonel of the Union Regiment of Volunteers.[86] By then the Volunteers had begun to pursue Catholic Emancipation. Because of that, Lord Moira (Son of the first Earl) stepped down as Colonel of the Union Regiment, and Sharman took his place. The Volunteers had originally been formed as a defensive force against the threat of a French invasion, but

---

[84] the year is missing – probably 1781. He was a minister in Moira from 1778-1784
[85] An Autobiographical Sketch of Andrew Craig, 1754-1833. Presbyterian Minister of Lisburn, Ulster Journal of Archaeology.
[86] Belfast Newsletter. 24th January 1834. obituary.

they carried their militancy into politics and made it clear to the King's representatives in Dublin that they would welcome the abolition of the restrictions on religious worship, the holding of office, and freedom of trade.

Sharman continued to have a very high profile in the Volunteer movement and was a member of the Volunteer Committee set up to investigate methods of bringing about a radical reform of the electoral system. He was Chairman of one of the famous Dungannon Conventions, a representative at the Volunteer National Convention in Dublin in 1783 and in fact served as President at the Volunteer convention held in the city in October the following year.[87] That year he was also elected as an Member of Parliament for Lisburn. In July 1791 he was president of the Belfast celebrations by the Volunteers and others to commemorate the fall of the Bastille. In 1792 he was reviewing general for the last Volunteer review to be held in the north of Ireland at Dromore.

The Ulster Museum has a portrait showing Colonel William Sharman in full Volunteer Uniform with Moira Castle behind him.[88] A Volunteer Review is taking place. It is possible the portrait depicts the Volunteer review hosted by Sharman in Moira demesne on 16th October 1784. What is astonishing is that the portrait was commissioned by Sharman and painted by Thomas Robinson in 1798. By then Sharman had changed allegiances and had formed the Moyrah Yeomen. This placed him against former Volunteer colleagues who had now become United Irishmen, yet he was reminiscing about his glory days with the Union Regiment!

---

[87] Notes on Sharman from the Ulster Museum.
[88] National Museums NI catalogue number BTLUM U141
linkhttps://www.nmni.com/collections/art/paintings/belumu141

On 12th July 1799 Sharman hosted an Orange Order parade in Moira demesne and took the salute on the steps of his Castle. It was one of the very first "Twelfth" celebrations and is recorded by a visitor from Dublin who was Sharman's guest.

> I spended time here in a most delightful manner until the 12th July, anniversary of the Battle of Aughrim, when the various yeomanry of the country, divided in different bodies, each with their proper ensigns, males and females, adorned with orange lilies and ribbands, marched up the avenues. We went adorned in the same way upon the steps of the Castle, to see them all pass before us; from whence they were to march to the various churches in the environs, to hear a sermon on the occasion, and then adjourn to the public houses, to spend the remainder of the day in merriment.[89]

In the next generation, Sharman's son, William Sharman-Crawford, Member of Parliament for Dundalk, would support Catholic Emancipation. But in 1799 the family was shrewd enough not to antagonize its guests from the Loyal Orders.

William Sharman died in Moira Castle on 21st January 1803 and was buried at Drumbeg.

---

[89] Memoir of Gabriel Beranger, and his labours in the cause of Irish art and antiquities, from 1760 -1780 by Sir William Wylde.

Sir Robert Bateson (1782-1863)

In 1805 the demesne was purchased by the family of Sir Robert Bateson. They were Lancashire people who had settled in Down in the mid-eighteenth century and owned Belvoir Park. The Sharman family still lived in Moira Castle for a few more years, continuing to rent the property from the Batesons.[90] It is suggested that Bateson then used the Castle as a second residence, though it is more likely that it was becoming a ruin by this time. It was the Bateson family which, around 1810, built the Market House we know today in Moira. The facades of the building are adorned by the Bateson crest.

At a dinner given in his honour in April 1825 Bateson congratulated his Moira tenants on the religious harmony and improved conditions on his estates and insisted that he wished to be considered only as "an honest independent country gentleman."[91] He was highly respected for his involvement with various charitable and religious societies.

The Bateson family continued as landlords of the village for many years, though really as absentee landlords. There are no records of them ever visiting Moira let alone residing here.

---

[90] If this statement is correct, it would seem William Sharman-Crawford and his new wife lived for a short time in Moira Castle after their marriage.
[91] The History of Parliament Ref. Volumes: 1820-1832. Author: Stephen Farrell.

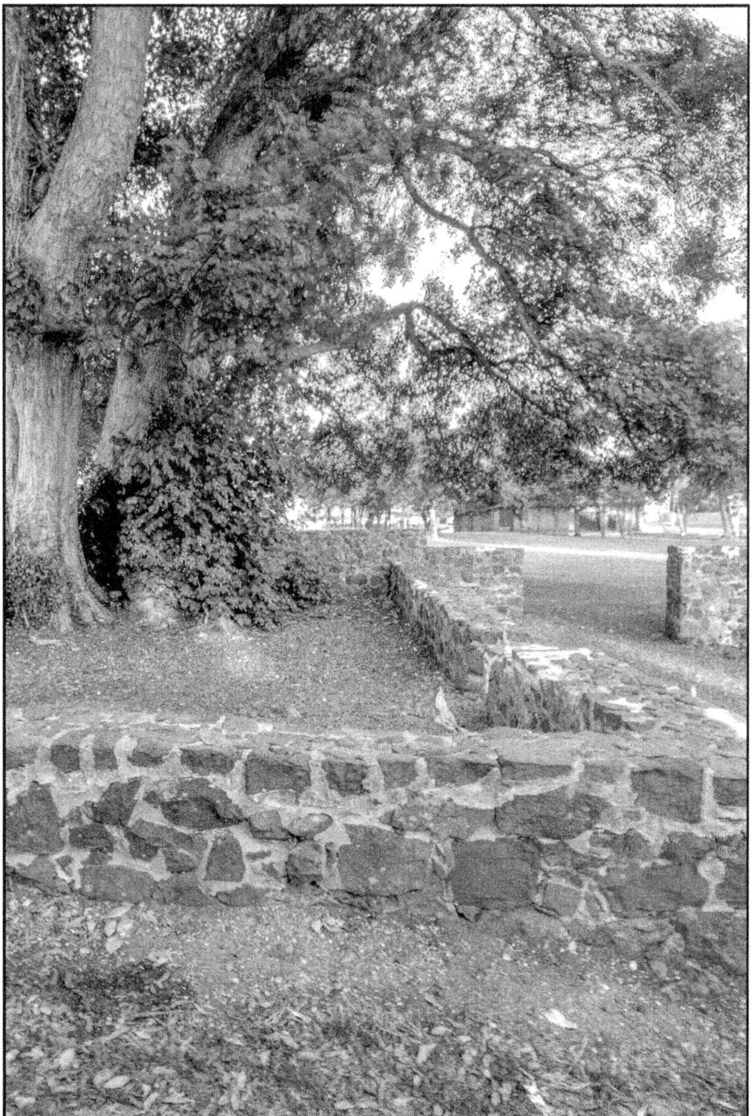

Linen and limestone

The gentry in Moira were responsible for the development of a village only a mile and a half from the considerably older community of Magheralin. As early as 1757, Moira was described as

> a well laid out and thriving village consisting of one broad street inhabited by many dealers who carry on linen manufacture to good advantage. Lately a monthly linen market hath been opened there the more effectively to promote that branch of the trade."[92]

Early in the nineteenth century, one writer says the village "is beautifully situated and inhabited by several opulent merchants."[93]

But someone else known only as E.G.A. wrote "sketches from a tourist notebook rather than a connected tour" and had the account published in a Belfast magazine. On travelling from Belfast to Dungannon in 1814 he passed through Moira and he was not impressed.[94]

> The appearance of the town is not prepossessing; it is the ruins of a town. The late Earl of Moira left this

---

[92] The ancient and present State of the county of Down Publ. 1757.
[93] The Traveller's Guide through Ireland by Rev. Jo. Robertson. Publ. 1806.
[94] The Belfast Monthly Magazine Vol. 12. No. 68 (Mar. 31, 1814) p.192

improved part of his estate and went to reside near Ballynahinch; the town has since ceased to flourish. The house which was occupied by the Earl is now levelled to the ground.

One hundred years after its development, with the Castle now in ruins, a report showed the village had one hundred and thirty-six houses built of basalt or limestone but none of brick. Ninety-three were two-storey houses, seven were three-storey and the remainder were single storey. Thirty had thatched roofs and the remainder had slates. The population of the town was seven hundred and eighty-seven with another three thousand throughout the parish. Almost the final comment in the report was that the streets and houses were very dirty.[95]

Despite the gloomy reports, the town survived. Perhaps this was due more to the working classes who had to work to survive rather than the landlords who could more easily move to more comfortable locations.

A number of industries in the area helped Moira advance in the nineteenth century.

Linen

Linen production in Ulster transformed the province from the poorest in Ireland into the richest and Moira's poorer residents reaped some little benefit from its manufacture. The development of the linen industry in the village was initially

---

[95] Ordnance Survey Memoirs of Ireland Vol. 12. Published by the Institute of Irish Studies in association with The Royal Irish Academy. Publ. 1992.

due to the support of Sir John Rawdon. In many ways he was following in the footsteps of his grandfather George who had been a linen pioneer in the mid-seventeenth century and sought to improve the quality of linen through importing better raw materials.

Sir John saw that the economic situation in the early eighteenth century meant that his tenants were totally stretched financially so increasing rents would be counter-productive. To encourage linen manufacture he obtained grants, purchased flax and spinning wheels and set up a spinning school to train girls. He even gave preference to tenants who would take up weaving. Small farmers, labourers and cottiers supplemented their incomes by working looms from home. The raw material was supplied and weavers got paid for the finished product. In 1740 a monthly brown linen market was established. Large quantities of linen were woven, bleached and sold in the town and neighbourhood. However the venture was not too successful as the price of linen was lower than anticipated.

In the early eighteenth century Richard Bell of Trummery House was one member of an eminent family of linen manufacturers in Lurgan and beyond. The linen boom was not to last. By 1840 the home industry had long been suffering serious decline. The coming of mechanisation eventually had put an end to this income for the locals. New factory looms were invented and each loom could do the work of one hundred hand weavers. Any weavers who lived on uneconomical farms of twelve acres or less, suffered most. Tens of thousands in rural Ulster lost a valuable source of income.

Yet the extent of the local trade, even in its declining years, is seen in the account of a meeting in Moira on 27th September 1842. Clearly there was a lot of resentment in the locality over how those involved in linen manufacture were being paid. A crowd of around six hundred angry men, mostly weavers and linen workers, met in a field in Moira to protest. Such was the perceived threat that the police brought in reinforcements. In the end a magistrate reasoned with them and persuaded them to depart peacefully.[96]

The linen industry in the area declined more rapidly due to population reduction following the great famine that began in 1845. It just about survived into the twentieth century. The last weaver in Moira was said to be Mr James McCoy whose "weaving shop was in a cottage about half a mile from the Lurgan end of the village."[97]

Quarrying and other businesses

Moira was also an important centre for limestone quarrying. There were many kilns continually at work and vast quantities of the stone in its natural state were taken by canal and carriage to distant parts. Evidence of this industry is seen in the recently converted old limekilns on the Clarehill Road. They were built in the 1820s but the industry ceased to function in the middle of the 20th century.

A similar business existed on the Old Kilmore Road close to Legmore House, though a limestone quarry in the vicinity does not appear on old maps in that vicinity. in the early nineteenth

---

[96] Belfast Newsletter 4th October 1842
[97] Very Rev. H Hughes M.A. (Formerly Dean of Dromore and Rector of Moira) as recorded in Review - Journal of Craigavon Historical Society. Vol. 2 No. 1.

century there was a quarry on the Lurgan road with a block of three limekilns just across the road. By the end of the century a new limestone quarry was opened two hundred metres nearer Moira and is the disused one visible today. A tunnel led from that quarry under the road to land behind the present day business premises to what was perhaps another kiln close to the Lagan.

In Kilwarlin there was a major quarry from which large flags of freestone in a variety of colours were cut.[98] Just below Trummery House there was a limestone quarry with kilns on Meadow Road. Stone from McKinley's quarry was said to have been used to construct many of the properties on Moira street. Though the quarry does not appear on maps until the mid 1800s. it is possible that it was the basalt quarry described in some old documents. It is no longer visible, having been built over by the Deramore development.

A brewery and bottling business was located near Palmer's Corner, on the junction of Main Street and Meeting Street. The corner probably got its name from the nearby shop owned by Job Palmer.

The immediate Moira area is not generally known for its mills, whereas upstream on the Lagan at Magheralin there were several. A corn mill was located in the townland of Aughnadrumman, on the north side of the Clarehill Road beside where the Newmill Bridge crosses the Lagan. The bridge dates from the mid-eighteenth century. Ordnance Survey maps throughout the nineteenth century show a mill house on the

---

[98] A Topographical Dictionary of Ireland by Samuel Lewis. Vol. 1 Publ. 1811. It is possible this quarry was close by the junction of Lurganville Road and Grovehill Road.

side of Clarehill Road with millraces and a millpond but none of the maps show a mill. The mill house in those maps is still visible today and has been described as the sick house for the mill, so perhaps it served as a mill hospital.

Historic documents say there is only one mill in this parish describing it as "undershot, diameter of wheel fourteen feet, inconstant supply of water, streams run too slow and have not enough fall of water for mills." In fact there were other mills in the area, for one operated in Legmore and another one further out Old Kilmore Road. George Langtry had a corn mill at Kilmore House. It was said that many mills did not survive because of lack of water.

Tenant farmers

There were many tenant farmers who worked the land, paying their rents to wealthy landowners. For most of them it was a struggle to survive and landlords could be very cruel. Evictions were commonplace. Even Sir John Rawdon was known at times to be extremely aggressive in the recovery of rents and renewal of leases.

We have seen that he offered better terms to tenants who took up weaving but he also showed prejudice in another area. Sir John was a proud "church man" and, like his grandfather George, did not take kindly to Presbyterians. "He had a strong aversion to all separation in matters of religion" and offered leases on favourable terms to tenants who were Anglicans and he is said to have protected Anglicans from what he saw as oppression by Presbyterian landlords.[99]

A later resident of Moira castle, William Sharman-Crawford M.P., was rather different apparently. It was said that he,
> greatly increased the prosperity of the tenants on his large estates by extending and confirming the Ulster custom of tenant-right and the main object for which he strove during his long parliamentary career was to give legal effect to this right and to extend it to other parts of Ireland. The tenant farmers justly regarded him as their champion.[100]

There is an obelisk erected to his memory on the Rademon Estate near Crossgar bearing the following inscription:
> This monument has been erected by a grateful and attached tenantry, and other friends, in memory of one who, during a long life, was ever a most kind and considerate landlord, the friend of the poor, and the universal advocate of tenant right, and of every measure calculated to promote civil and religious liberty.

...

The people who lived and worked in Moira needed support. Life was tough, their children needed to be educated and there was much sickness and disease.

---

[99] Information gleaned from The Anglo-Irish Experience, 1680-1730: Religion, Identity and Patriotism by David Hayton. page 179. Publ. 2012. The Boydell Press. p. 187.
[100] A Compendium of Irish Biography by Alfred Webb. Publ. 1878.

Charity

Evidence from as far back as the mid-seventeenth century indicates the charitable nature of some landlords in Moira. Generally the "religious" gentry thought it necessary to address, or be seen to address, social poverty and the effect it had on society. The Rawdons believed in helping the poor but with a view to enabling them to help themselves.

George Rawdon and his wife were noted for their charitable work and George was anxious that his son Arthur would follow in his footsteps. So much so that even in his will he stipulated that "when he shall come to possess my estate, that he be always very charitable and relieve the poor constantly."[101]

Arthur's wife, "was endowed with extraordinary virtues ... and her charities were numberless to all in distress and will never be forgotten."[102] The Waring brothers of Waringfield House bequeathed a sum of £200 to be distributed by the churchwardens to the poor housekeepers of this parish. The first Earl of Moira bequeathed a sum of money, which, with some other legacies, amounted to nearly £400. The interest on this fund was distributed annually among poor housekeepers.[103]

A memorial tablet to Sir Robert Bateson in St. John's Church, Moira is an example of the extravagant Victorian style of writing, but was apparently a sincere tribute:

---

[101] Copy of Sir George Rawdon's will. 19th October 1683 with codicil 30th July 1684.
[102] The Rawdon Papers by Edward Berwick 1819.
[103] Samuel Lewis' Topographical Dictionary of Ireland. Publ. 1837.

> His hand was open as his heart was tender and on his venerable head were showered the blessings of the poor. His home was hallowed by his spotless life and happy in the sunshine of his cheerfulness, etc.

But the picture is not always as rosy as the monuments and obituaries suggest. Lord Deramore was still evicting tenants from Gortnamoney, Moira in April 1868 because of their inability to pay rent. He was not the first landlord in Moira to be charitable only as long as it did not affect his own pocket.

Schools

The idea of helping the poor to help themselves extended to the provision of education for poor children in Moira. Sir John's grandfather George has been heavily involved in launching a school in Lisburn that became "the foremost centre of education east of the Bann and rivalled the Royal Schools at Armagh and Enniskillen for quality of education."[104] So Sir John sought to do something similar in Moira.

> He erected and endowed an English Protestant school for twenty-four poor children and done (sic) many other acts of public munificence.[105]

Half of the boys were Anglicans and half either Catholics or Presbyterians. Teaching included reading and writing and accounts. Pupils were to attend the established church and would be given apprenticeships with Protestants. Clearly his charitable work had an additional motive.

---

[104] Information gleaned from The Anglo-Irish Experience, 1680-1730: Religion, Identity and Patriotism by David Hayton. page 179. Publ. 2012. The Boydell Press. p.186.
[105] A general History of Ireland by John Angel. Publ. 1781.

The school he erected may have been on the site of the old schoolhouse because a visitor passing through in 1814 did not miss it as he headed towards Lurgan. He was not impressed by the engraving on the front of the building and wrote,

> A school-house in Moira has in front of the building an inscription announcing that the inhabitants are indebted to the Rawdon family for the erection. The inscription conveys some reflections to the mind of the traveller, on the ridiculous and contemptible vanity which leads persons to be so anxious for fame as to induce them to have their benevolent actions engraven on stone and displayed in conspicuous situations.[106]

I think we get the impression this visitor did not like Moira!

In 1837 Sir Robert Bateson supported parochial schools at Moira and Lurganville. Another school was held in a cottage at Ballynock. The Lurganville school was in a cottage at Bottear and may have been the oldest school in the area, having been established in 1777.[107]

Lady Bateson established a school for females in Moira.
> She built the schoolhouse, a large and handsome edifice with a residence for the mistress attached, and by whom also the children are principally clothed; and at Battier is a national school. These schools afford instruction to about two hundred children: in a private school there are about eighty children, and there is also a Sunday school.[108]

---

[106] The Belfast Monthly Magazine Vol. 12. No. 68 (Mar. 31, 1814) p.192
[107] Ordnance Survey Memoirs of Ireland. Vol 12. Parishes of County Down III. 1833-1838 Publ. 1992.
[108] Samuel Lewis' Topographical Dictionary of Ireland. Publ. 1837.

The records of the National School in Moira show that there were one hundred and eight children on the roll in 1906.

Just outside Moira was the Friends Agricultural School opened at Brookfield in 1836. It was a Quaker School primarily for "disowned" children - for those not in membership of the Society. This was at a time when Quakers marrying non-Quakers were automatically disowned. Later the terms of admission were widened to include children of parents in membership, who had limited means. Eventually, carefully selected pupils, not in any way connected with the Society of Friends, were accepted. Children were enrolled from all over Ireland.

The boys were expected to work part-time on the farm, for up to twenty-two hours per week at one point, helping with the crops, looking after the animals, providing vegetables for the school and for sale. The aim was to make the school almost self-supporting in food and at the same time give the boys practical training in agriculture and farm management. Girls were not expected to work on the land but they did the milking, helped in the kitchen, cleaned, churned butter and did dressmaking. Elementary school subjects were taught part-time, but the main objective was "to train the children in a religious life and conversation consistent with our profession."[109] I am not sure how one Master handled that objective! It is said his punishments included compulsory cold baths in mid-winter and forcible lifting by the ears![110]

Around 1877 a separate day school was set up for "the

---

[109] Friends Agricultural School Brookfield, Moira, 1836 – 1922. Journal of Craigavon Historical Society Vol. 5 No. 2 by G R Chapman.
[110] A history of Friends' School, Lisburn by Neville H Newhouse.

surrounding poor" which became Brookfield Primary School on Halfpenny Gate Road. Brookfield Agricultural School closed in 1921 but the final headmaster, Charles Benington, continued a small private school there until 1930. During the Second World War, wholesale drapers Young & Anderson Ltd of 23 Donegall Street, Belfast relocated there for three years or so.

Health

Ulster was stricken by cholera in the mid-nineteenth century and Belfast was particularly affected. But it appears it even reached Moira. Ballunigan House, near Moira (now marooned between the edge of the M1 motorway and the course of the former Lagan canal) was once a Cholera Hospital. A local source says the house was originally built as a manse but had never been occupied and, so the story goes, that no patient ever died in it.

But cholera did bring death to Moira. An old ruined tomb in the graveyard at the Non-Subscribing Presbyterian Church records the death of a well-loved local Doctor. The inscription reads,
>Sacred to the memory of Thomas Simpson of Moira, Surgeon, who fell a victim to malignant cholera on the 29th of December 1832 aged 34 years. This monument has been erected by his friends as a tribute of respect and to mark the estimation in which he was held for the skilful and faithful discharge of his professional duties, his goodness of heart and his worth as a man."

Between 1845 and 1852, the Great Famine and fever raged across Ireland. More than a million people died and two million emigrated. Potato blight spread across Europe in the 1840s and disproportionately affected Ireland where a large percentage of the population subsisted on the crop.

Potatoes had been the staple diet of the paupers and were replaced by oatmeal, buttermilk, soup made from the heads of cows and sheep, and bread. The poorest had porridge for breakfast and supper. There was nothing else. The reasons for the famine being so devastating go much deeper than disease. There were many tragic and avoidable contributing factors beyond the control of the poor victims.

The famine had some impact on Moira. Correspondence of the period suggests that some residents made appeals to English friends for money to help them to provide meals for local children. There were reports of "the destitute condition of the labouring classes" in Moira and a local committee funded both by public subscription and the Government in Dublin was able to provide some food aid to three hundred people.[111]

In 1847 Lurgan Poorhouse was full and people were dying by the score each day. Yet parish records in Moira do not reveal significant distress and loss of life locally. In the following year the Vestry "resolved that each person applying for a coffin shall furnish a certificate of their incapacity to pay." Rev. Hughes, a more recent Rector in the parish, reported that in 1848 the Vestry paid £11.10s.1p. for coffins which he estimated would be enough for about twenty people and in his opinion does not represent a significant increase over a normal year.[112]

---

[111] Some aspects of the great famine in Lurgan Poor Law Union 1845-1847 by Gerard Mac Atasney in Review - Journal of Craigavon Historical Society Vol. 7 No. 1.
[112] Very Rev. H Hughes M.A. (Formerly Dean of Dromore and Rector of Moira) as recorded in Review - Journal of Craigavon Historical Society Vol. 2 No. 1.

The population of the parish reduced considerably in the latter half of the nineteenth century as people moved to larger towns and particularly to Belfast seeking work. In 1834 the population of Moira parish was three thousand, nine hundred and thirty but by 1911 numbers had fallen to one thousand, six hundred and sixty-two.[113]

Of course by the time of the famine, the aristocracy had long since vacated Moira; the Castle was demolished and most of the landowners lived elsewhere. They had built and sustained the village and had given employment but they had the means to move their homes to more secure or more prosperous situations. The future of Moira was to a large degree in the hands of those who continued to live and labour here. It was a struggle to exist but many had nowhere else to go. That we have a village today is due in no small measure to those ordinary men and women for whom Moira was home and who would not give up.

---

[113] From Archdeacon Atkinson's Dromore: An Ulster Diocese.

Sons and daughters

In recording the history of the landlords of Moira, we have already spoken of the children of the Rawdon family who continued to live here and make a name for themselves. Other Moira children, from both sides of the social divide, have become famous for a variety of reasons. Our first and perhaps most famous child of Moira left the village when he was still a young lad.

Francis Rawdon (1754-1826).

Francis Rawdon was born in Moira Castle. His mother was the Earl's third wife, Lady Elizabeth Hastings.

On one occasion when he was ten years old, while playing war games in the demesne, a gun exploded injuring Francis in the leg. He always had an ambition to be a soldier. Francis was educated at Lisburn and Harrow and later enrolled in University College, Oxford but he discontinued his studies to purchase a lieutenancy. He was commissioned on 20th October 1773 and spent the remainder of his life in the service of his country. He may never have returned to Moira except perhaps for his father's funeral but his story is fascinating.

In 1774 he was posted to America and fought in the American

War of Independence. He quickly distinguished himself and later became Adjutant-General with the rank of Lieutenant Colonel. He spent a total of seven years fighting in America and is said to have been one of the most courageous leaders in the whole war. But a combination of fatigue and malaria destroyed Rawdon's health. He gave up his command in 1781 and set off for home. However that voyage proved eventful, for his ship was captured and for a time he was imprisoned by the French. Eventually he was allowed to return to England.

But a great many of his Irish soldiers remained in North America after the war because they were not repatriated by Great Britain. Some are said to have founded a town called Moira in New York State, in memory of his exploits. Many more of his men were relocated to Canada, along with settlers he had rescued in a siege in 1781. There they founded Upper Rawdon, Central Rawdon and South Rawdon in Nova Scotia.

Rawdon's fighting days were not over though. In the French Revolutionary Wars, Francis Rawdon was appointed Major General and fought in the Low Countries in 1793.

While Francis was in America, he had been appointed Member of the Irish Parliament for Randalstown. He also became a Baron in 1783 and when his father died in 1793 he became the second Earl and served in the Irish House of Lords. He was to eventually inherit his mother's titles as well as his father's, and also much of the estates belonging to the Huntingdon dynasty. Francis took on his mother's maiden name and became known as Francis Rawdon-Hastings. He was made Marquess of Hastings in 1817 and Earl of Moira was retained as an inferior title.

The Earl was extremely critical of repression in Ireland and did more than most to expose the misgovernment of Ireland.[114] In a debate in the Lords in 1797, Lord Moira described the horrors he had witnessed in Ireland against the Catholic people. He declared that ninety-one householders had been banished from one of his own estates (it is unclear which estate this was). He asserted that he wished to uphold the Protestant ascendancy in Ireland as much as his accusers but only asked that the poor Catholics be allowed to live in peace.[115]

Wolf Tone was often a visitor at Moira House, Dublin and Rawdon was godfather to Tone's son, Francis Rawdon Tone. He sent his own chaplain, Rev. Mr Berwick to christen the child in 1793.[116] Tone hoped he could persuade Moira "to lead the rebellion in Ireland and so become one of the greatest men in Europe." Francis refused the offer but he did encourage the rebels though without entirely committing himself to them. A major arsenal was discovered on one of his estates. There is no record that this was Moira estate; more likely his estate at Ballynahinch but in Moira, the innkeeper and a guest were arrested.[117]

It seemed the village of Moira was to be just a distant memory. Francis sold his properties in Ulster around 1800 and after his mother died in 1808, he sold Moira house in Dublin too, thus closing his associations with Ireland. Interestingly, in 1916, some of the heaviest fighting of the Easter Rising took place in what was once Moira House, Dublin.

---

[114] An Historical Review of the State of Ireland Vol. 4 by Francis Plowden. Publ. 1906.
[115] The Land War in Ireland by James Godkin.
[116] The Life of Theobald Wolfe Tone - Autobiography 1828.
[117] McGill Faculty of Education, Montreal http://www.mcgill.ca/education

The boy who had played in the demesne of Moira had grown up to move in very high circles. He had a very close relationship with the Prince Regent. In 1797 the Prince initially appeared to support some parliamentarians' proposal that Rawdon be Prime Minister in place of William Pitt. However he was unable to raise enough support to form a government. He had various military postings including Commander and Chief in Scotland (1803-1806), Colonel of the 27th Regiment of Foot (1804-1826) and Master-General of the Ordnance (1806-1807). The Earl eventually married in 1804. His wife was Fiona Campbell, 6th Countess of Loudoun.

In 1812 he was sent to India as Governor General and Commander-in-Chief of one section of the growing British Empire. Rawdon held this post until 1823 and was largely responsible for the establishing of Central India as part of the British Empire. While there he was also involved in the purchase of Singapore for the British in 1819. It was during this time that he was raised to the rank of Marquess of Hastings.

Although Hastings had been mostly engaged in war during his time in India, he also took civic affairs seriously including the building of roads and bridges and digging of canals. He encouraged education among the Indians, founded the Hindu College at Calcutta in 1817 and encouraged the setting up of a printing press and a college at Serampore.

The missionary in Serampore at that time was none other than William Carey, the great Baptist Missionary, known as the father of modern missions. Carey had very close associations with the Earl and Lady Hastings. He dined with the Governor privately and talked of conversations and correspondence he had with him. The Earl even "gave an unequivocal mark of his approbation" for the College at Serampore and became a "patron of the infant institution."[118] Hastings wrote to comfort Carey on the death of his wife. In Carey's will, when he bequeathed his books to the library at Serampore, one of only two books he named was "the folio edition of Hortus Wobournensis (a descriptive catalogue of upwards of six hundred ornamental plants) which was presented to me by Lord Hastings.[119]

His Lordship apparently was a very generous man and much respected. "His ample fortune absolutely sank under the benevolence of his nature"[120] and, far from becoming wealthy as Governor-General, he returned to England in desperate need of employment. He always seemed to have severe financial problems and large debts.

He was later appointed the first Commander-in-Chief of Malta. He died at sea off Naples in 1826 but had left clear instructions that he was to be buried where he fell, if his "adored wife had no objections." But in a bizarre demonstration of his love, he instructed "that his right hand be cut off and preserved, so that it may be put with her body into the coffin when it pleased the Almighty to decree the reunion of our spirits." This "last earthly token" of his and Lady Loudoun's "attachment," he declared, "shall not be an idle lesson for our precious children, to whom I now give my fondest blessing." He was buried in Valetta and his hand was eventually buried, clasped in his wife's hand, fourteen years later![121] A most impressive monument marks Hastings' resting place in Hastings Gardens, Valletta.

---

[118] A Modern Traveller, India Vol. 3. Publ. 1828.
[119] Memoir of William Carey by Eustace Carey. Publ. 1836 pages 572/3.
[120] The Annual Biography and Obituary for the year 1818 page 157.
[121] Francis Rawdon-Hastings by Paul David Nelson.

William Sharman-Crawford (1781-1861)

William Sharman's son, also called William, was born in Moira Castle. He later wrote about his youth, explaining that he was considered a delicate child.

> I spent my infantile years at Moira Castle but every year spending the winter in Dublin during the Parliamentary session. I was inclined as a child to delicacy of health - at least it was thought so by my parents - and I was kept under the most annoying superintendence. I was drugged with medicines. I was made what you would call a crock and a pet. It was alleged I would soon die if I went to school and my Father had an abhorrence of Tutors, so he determined to teach me to read and write; also arithmetic, Latin and some Greek. I instructed myself in history, mathematics, mechanics, geography and astronomy, etc. I was exceedingly anxious to have gone to college but this was prohibited lest my morals should be corrupted.[122]

William's father clearly was terribly controlling of his son. Sharman senior died when William was twenty-two and almost immediately William joined the Yeomanry as captain of the Moyrah Corps. Two years later he married the wealthy heiress, Mabel Crawford of Crawfordsburn, whose surname and Arms he added to his own. Shortly afterwards he "left Moira Castle, the place and estate having been purchased by Mr Bateson."[123]

William Sharman-Crawford became a very notable radical politician and represented Dundalk in Parliament from 1834 to

---

[122] A brief autobiography of William Sharman-Crawford, dated c.1844.
[123] ibid.

1837. In his first contribution, he spoke against the Tithe system for the repair of church buildings. He said

> justice was not done to the Catholic or Presbyterian population in being called on to contribute to the support of a Church to which they did not belong.[124]

He fought hard to protect tenant farmers from eviction and became known as "the father of tenant-right." He was also Colonel of a union regiment of volunteers.

Dennis O'Lavery (?-1781)

Dennis was a native of Moira. His family had been granted land by King James but that was later confiscated because of the Lavery family's support for the rebellion. Dennis grew up in poor surroundings and with little hope. He was recruited by the Army and was shipped off to America with thousands of others from Ireland to fight in the American War of Independence. He never returned to Moira but his name is legendary and deserves its place on these pages.

Denis O'Lavery was serving as a corporal under Francis Rawdon in 1781 and was chosen to accompany a bearer of a highly important despatch. Unfortunately, soon after setting out, both of them were attacked and the one carrying the message was mortally wounded. Despite his own serious wounds, O'Lavery took the despatch from his dead companion and rode off to deliver it. Loss of blood took its toll and soon he too fell to earth. To avoid the despatch falling into enemy hands he hid

---

[124] Hansard. Church of Ireland Committee. HC Deb 03 April 1835 Vol. 27 cc 790-828.

it in his wound. Denis lay for hours, more dead than alive but when found he somehow used his last breath to reveal the hidden message. It was saved but the injury was fatal. The surgeon who examined the body declared

> that the wound in itself was not mortal, but rendered so by the irritation of the paper. Thus fell this patriot soldier. His name was O'Lavery, from the parish of Moira, in County Down.[125]

A verse was written commemorating his heroic actions.
> Within his wound the fatal paper placed
> Which proved his death, nor by that death disgraced.
> A smile, benignant, on his countenance shone,
> Pleased that his secret had remained unknown:
> So was he found.[126]

Sir John Fortescue said that a monument to O'Lavery had been erected in Co. Down.[127] Another military historian believed Rawdon erected the monument. A letter written sometime in the last century says of O'Lavery,

> … in rank a corporal, he was in mind a hero … his country Ireland and his parish Moira in which a chaste monument records at once his fame and the gratitude of his illustrious commander and countryman Lord Rawdon.[128]

The location of the monument has never been established.

---

[125] The O'Lavery's by The Right Rev. Monsignor O'Laverty P.P. M.R.I.A. (1904)
[126] Tales of the Wars - Saturday March 17, 1838.
[127] A History of the 17th Lancers (Duke of Cambridge's Own), by Hon. J W Fortescue. Publ. 1895 by Macmillan.
[128] Journal of Craigavon Historical Society Vol. 2 No. 1 by Very Rev. H Hughes M.A. (Formerly Rector of Moira).

Edward Berwick (1754-1820) [129]

Edward Berwick was born in County Down, almost certainly in Berwick Hall just outside the village of Moira. His father was called Duke Berwick, which has led to some confusion over his ancestry.[130] Edward Berwick was ordained a deacon by the Bishop of Down in 1776 and was the Rector of Tullylish in the Diocese of Dromore from 1776 to 1779 before moving to parishes in the South. In 1793 he baptised Wolfe Tone's fourth son. Two years later he was appointed both Vicar of Leixlip, Co Kildare, in the Diocese of Glendalough, and Rector of Clongish, in the Diocese of Ardagh, holding both parishes at the same time.

He was a great writer and scholar, publishing his own works, scholarly translations of other Greek and Latin works and editing letters including The Rawdon Papers. The Irish novelist George Moore believed that Berwick "wrote the best English prose that ever came out of Ireland." [131]

The bio on Berwick's many publications indicate that he was "domestic Chaplain to the late Earl of Moira and present chaplain to the Marquess of Hastings, Governor General of India &c." He became a friend of the leading Irish politician Henry Grattan in the 1780s and 1790s and of the writer Sir Walter Scott.

---

[129] Some sources say he was born in 1750 but the later date seems more accurate.
[130] It has been suggested that his grandfather was the Duke of Berwick, the illegitimate son of James II who had fought with King James at the Battle of the Boyne. However, a study of the genealogies of the Dukes of Berwick shows that is impossible. Duke Berwick was not related to the Dukes of Berwick.
[131] Quoted by Patrick Comerford.
(http://www.patrickcomerford.com/2015/08/more-about-edward-berwick-but-lady.html)

Anne Lutton (1791-1881)

A less well-known child of Moira was Anne Lutton yet even today her influence is felt in this village. She was born and raised in number 65 Main Street, just below the four trees. She has an interesting ancestry. Two soldiers called Ralph and William Lutton had come to Ireland in 1690 with William III and served as officers in his army. When the war was over, the brothers elected to remain in Ireland - perhaps in Moira. William was an ancestor of Anne Lutton.

Anne's father, Ralph Lutton, was an only son of a prosperous farmer also called Ralph. He inherited much land and property in and around Moira. At the age of eighteen he married his cousin Anne, and became the father of nine sons and four daughters who outlived infancy. Anne was the youngest of these and was born on the 16th December 1791. Later in life, Anne described her home behind the trees that lined the street.

> Conspicuous in this pleasant leafy street stood the spacious, lofty family mansion of the Luttons, lifting its three-storied, many-windowed front close to the sidewalk; its ample garden lay all in the rear.[132]

Mr and Mrs Lutton were both unusually intelligent, though Mr Lutton was partially blind. Anne can hardly be said to have been educated. "Reading, writing, plain and fancy work, household management, and the single accomplishment of dancing," were all that was required of girls at that time. But Anne was a little home-bird. She did not like school at all so the youngest child of the family was spoilt and indulged.

---

[132] Eminent Methodist Women (1889) by Annie E Keeling.

It seems strange that she did not enjoy school for even as a five-year-old she was passionately fond of reading. She wanted to be an author, so she devoured every book she could get her hands on from her father's bookshelves. Her eldest brother gave her a lesson or two in writing; the schoolmaster came to the house each day to teach her arithmetic. When she was seventeen years old she attended a Moravian school, where she learned "a little grammar and geography, as well as satin-stitch and embroidery."[133] She was virtually self-taught.

Public domain image. The Lutton home is the dark three-story building on the left.

In 1811, when Anne was twenty, Mr Lutton and his family moved seven miles away to live in Donaghcloney. The house was so different from the one in Moira. It was a rural location surrounded by lawns and gardens on the banks of the River Lagan. These quiet surroundings were the perfect place for study.

---

[133] ibid.

Anne had always coveted the ability to read languages other than her own and began to study Latin. She had discovered a tattered "Lily's Latin Grammar" on her father's upper bookshelves. The book was rather battered; "schoolboys and worms had combined to outrage and deface it;" but Anne tidied it up and, with only what help her blind father could offer, she studied until she could read the great Latin classics.

Then she did the same with Greek, beginning with the New Testament, followed by Homer, Plutarch, Longinus and Demosthenes. To the classic languages she then added Hebrew, Samaritan, Syriac, Chaldee, Arabic, and Persian; "a little" of Ethiopic, Hindustanee and Irish; and not a little of French, Italian, Spanish, Portuguese, and German. Oriental languages followed and in all, it is said she could understand more than fifty languages and speak fifteen accurately. In addition, she became a musician, an able metaphysician, a mathematician, and a very good poet.

What was the point of all this study? Here was a young woman living in the backwaters of society acquiring the most wonderful education largely self-taught, but it was of little apparent use in Moira or Donaghcloney. But she later saw the purpose. "It was a training process for higher and more hallowed duties," she said. Anne became a highly-respected poet throughout Ireland and Britain. Publications by her or about her include:
    Poems on Moral and religious subjects. 1829
    Memorials of a consecrated Life. 1882

But it was for another reason that she became famous in Moira and far beyond, as we shall see in a later chapter.

Sir John Lavery (1856-1941)

John Lavery is not quite a child of Moira for he was not born in the village. Somehow Moira likes to think it adopted him so I have included him in this chapter.

John Lavery was a Belfast boy whose father was a wine and spirit merchant. They were desperately poor, so his father decided to emigrate to America to set up a new life for his family. But the ship broke up in a gale off the Wexford coast and he perished with three hundred and eighty-six other passengers. John was only three years old at the time. Worse was to follow, for within three months of this tragedy, John's mother also died leaving John an orphan.

His uncle, a farmer from "Trainview," Back-of-the-Wood, Moira took him in. It is almost certain this was where Clenaghan's Restaurant is located, for their former web site gave this information:
> Until recent times this establishment was known as Winnies after Winnie Clenaghan. Her mother was Kate Clenaghan (nee Lavery). She was a first cousin of Sir John Lavery, one of our most distinguished Irish artists and he was reared on this farm as a young boy."[134]

John attended school, first in Soldierstown and then in Magheralin, where it is said he detested arithmetic.

It seems the troubled lad was passed through the families of several relatives and he eventually fled to Scotland. He replied to an advertisement for a lad "good at drawing" and got a job

---

[134] From a previous version of Clenaghan's web site accessed 2015.

as a re-toucher in a studio. With the income from his apprenticeship, Lavery enrolled for evening classes at the Haldane Academy of Art in Glasgow and set up a small studio in the city. Unfortunately, his workshop burned down in a freak accident while he was away in London. However, he used the insurance money to move to Paris to study at the Académie Julian in 1881.

From humblest of beginnings, he rose to be regarded as one of the greatest painters of the late nineteenth and twentieth centuries. In 1888, Lavery received a court commission to paint Queen Victoria's visit to the International Exhibition in Glasgow. It was the year of her jubilee. The prestige of being awarded this commission and the social connections he gained from this one sitting were to benefit him for the next fifty years.

He painted at a time of Edwardian elegance, scandal and the struggle for Irish independence. All of this set against the backdrop of the Great War. In 1918, as an official war artist assigned to the Royal Navy, Lavery witnessed and painted the surrender of the German Fleet! He was knighted in 1918.

Sir John and his wife were indirectly involved in the establishing of the Irish Free State in 1922. They had given their home in London to the Irish representatives during the negotiations of the Anglo-Irish Treaty. When shortly after Michael Collins was killed, Lavery painted him lying in state and in the corner added the title, Love of Ireland.

His other portraits included George V, Winston Churchill, JM Barrie, George Bernard Shaw and Shirley Temple.

We are left with the impression that he knew everyone in high society and every one in high society knew him. He was honoured by many cities in Europe, and received the Freedom of Belfast in 1930. He died in Kilkenny where he had settled at the outbreak of World War II.

Moira Demesne avenue

Castles and cottages

The countryside surrounding Moira has many ancient earthen forts or raths and a henge, all giving evidence of our history. But many of the structures of later generations are now ruins or have disappeared without trace. In or close to Moira, we had at least one large fort, a round tower, a castle and a number of churches all of which are gone from view.

Fort of Inisloughlin[135]

The first reference to Inisloughlin, or Inis-Lochain as it was then called, dates from 1165. Muirchertach Mac Lochlainn entered Ulaid where he "proceeded … to Inis-Lochain, and burned and destroyed the island."[136] Little more is known until Inisloughlin became of strategic importance during the Nine Years War. The Gaelic stronghold was used as a base for campaigning against the English.

Archaeologists believe they have identified the exact location of the Fort of Inisloughlin. It sat on high ground overlooking the

---

[135] There are at least five spellings of this name but all clearly refer to the same place.
[136] O'Donovan 1856 ii, 1154–55 as quoted in Ulster Journal of Archaeology, Vol. 71. 2012. Archaeological excavation at Inisloughlin, County Antrim: identifying the Gaelic fort at "Enishlanghen."

Lagan at Spencer's Bridge on the Hillsborough Road and belonged to Hugh O'Neill, Earl of Tyrone. Historical records describe it situated in a great bog and commanding the pass of Kilwarlin. The Fort was forty yards square with corner bastions. It was conquered in 1602 by Sir Arthur Chichester. Great quantities of plate and valuable property belonging to O'Neill fell into the hands of the English.

Sir Faulke Conway was given responsibility for the fort with a garrison of fifty men. Later he became the owner through a royal grant which included "all of the towns and lands of and in the territory or county of Killultagh"[137] Subsequently he strengthened it by building "a fayre gate at the forte of Enishelaghlin, in Killultagh, where he entendes to build a good house; he hath already at the place 150,000 of brickes burnte, with other materialles."[138]

The fort was levelled in 1803 leaving only the southeast bastion, which still survived in 1837. Today only the fall of ground is discernible.[139] Captain Henry Spencer was Governor of the Fort in 1623 so it is likely the nearby Spencer's Bridge was named after him.

There may have been a castle at Inisloughlin as well. An ancient fortification, also said to have belonged to the O'Neills, stood on the western side of the Lany Road less than half a kilometre from the site of the fort. Records from 1837 also indicate a

---

[137] O'Laverty 1880, 270; Anon 1966, 146, no LXXXVII.
[138] Public Record Office of Northern Ireland (PRONI) ref. no. T/811/3; quoted by O'Laverty 1880, 254, 270.
[139] The Castles of Ireland Compiled by Lee Johnson and Lewis Topographical Dictionary, 1837.

draw well which joined the river through a conduit. In 1978, the location was identified by Rev. Adamson as being on the banks of the Sluggy River which was so named "because it was sluggish."[140]

Trummery Round Tower

At Trummery old church there once was a round tower similar to others in Ireland, except that it was the same diameter all the way to the top. It dates from the early thirteenth century. Records indicate it was sixty feet high and fifteen feet in diameter.[141] Below the cupola-shaped roof were four small windows facing the cardinal points. As usual in such towers, the doorway was several feet above ground level.

It was fairly common for skulls to be found in the floors of round towers and one was unearthed in Trummery. Its interment was different in that it was placed in an elaborate stone chamber under the ground rather than in the soil as at other sites, indicating that the person buried may have been someone of great importance. It was common for chieftains to be decapitated, even by friendly hands to rescue them from indignity and their crania to be given a distinctive interment.[142]

There are many stories about how the tower became a ruin. It was suggested by some that all the excavations hastened its

---

[140] Northern Ireland Sites and Monuments Record. SM7-ANT-067-028.
[141] A topographical dictionary of the British islands by James A Sharpe. Publ. 1852.
[142] Report of the twenty-second meeting of the British Association for the advancement of science held in Belfast 1852. John Murray, Albemarle Street London Publ.1853

collapse. One rather unlikely tradition says Cromwell's soldiers had taken Trummery House while Irish soldiers occupied the church. The English burned the church and killed the occupants. A fairly common belief was that the English soldiers, based in the nearby Fort of Inisloughlin, used the ancient round tower as a target practice for cannon fire.[143] The side of the tower next the church was heavily damaged, but the tower wall was not broken through. Another article continues:

> Nature, as if willing to hide the breach from the eye of the curious, bestowed on it a luxuriant covering of ivy, which gave it a truly romantic appearance. Upwards of thirty years since some person wantonly destroyed the roots of this plant and this once venerable monument of antiquity became a mass of ruins.[144]

Another account of its ruin involves a group of men gathering potatoes nearby when a sudden rain storm drove them into the tower for shelter. Within minutes of them returning to their task, a loud rumble was heard and looking round, they saw their shelter crash to the ground.

Whatever story is true, or partly true, the tower fell in 1828 and nothing but scattered fragments remain.

Moira Castle and demesne

It is such a shame that we no longer have Moira Castle as a landmark in the village. Anne Lutton who was born and reared

---

[143] 1832 Ordinance Survey.
[144] Illustrated Dublin Journal, 1862.

in Moira wrote:
> A hundred years ago[145] the little town of Moira presented to the eye of a stranger something extraordinarily interesting. It consisted of one long street, each side of which was ornamented by a regular row of lime trees. Just where the houses terminated, at the lower end of town, were two gates exactly opposite. Each gate opened into a long avenue of tall trees; each avenue led to a noble edifice. One was the Parish Church, the other the Castle of the Earl of Moira; so that from one majestic pile to the other seemed but one continued avenue, with a lovely lawn of green at either end of it.[146]

We are grateful to Gabriel Beranger, a noted watercolour artist and antiquarian for his two sketches of the mansion.[147] Also a portrait of Colonel Sharman in the Ulster Museum gives an illustration of how the house looked in its setting.

Mark Bence-Jones in A Guide to Irish Country Houses, uses Beranger's paintings to describe the building.
> A large three storey eighteenth century house with a nine-bay front, consisting of a five-bay centre and a two-bay extension either side. Only the roof of the centre section was visible; the roofs on the side bays were either flat or concealed by the massive cornices with which these bays were surmounted. Pedimented and rusticated doorway; curved end bows. The front

---

[145] Anne lived between 1791-1881 and it is unclear when this was written but the scene she describes may have been mid eighteenth Century.
[146] Anne Lutton - "A Consecrated Life" 1880.
[147] These images are used with permission on the History of Moira website - http://moirahistory.uk

was prolonged by single storey wings either side ending in piers with urns.

We are also fortunate to have several older word pictures of the Castle grounds. One writer in 1774 is described as writing
> with luxurious fancy upon the vegetable wealth, the horticultural beauty, the botanical attractions and the tasteful and intricate disposition of the gardens and parks of Sir John Rawdon's demesne.[148]

Rev. Andrew Craig was minister in the Presbyterian church between 1778 and 1782. He describes how William Sharman faced the problems of vandalism in his gardens and indicates the presence of sculptures in the formal grounds.
> .... During a length of time there were nightly depredations on William Sharman's property. At last the windows of the Rock House were broken and the statue of Narcissus thrown into the pond.[149]

Gabriel Beranger described,
> an ancient building on the estate of the Earl of Moira which the Earl got modernised and made a commodious habitation: it is surrounded by a wood, which affords beautiful shady walks; a large lawn extends in front, where sheep are feeding, which is terminated by trees and a small lough eastwards;[150] the rear contains a wood with a large opening fronting the

---

[148] Parliamentary Gazetteer of Ireland 1846. page 781.
[149] Ulster Journal of Archaeology, Volume 14 Issues 2-3 Publ. 1808.
[150] Beranger's illustration would appear to depict "the small lough eastwards" behind the wall on the corner of Station Road. In very old maps a shape drawn at that spot almost certainly is the lough. In periods of sustained wet weather that corner of the meadow floods making it easy to believe that the small lough eastwards was almost certainly located there.

Castle, which forms a fine perspective.
He continued,
> On each side of this extensive lawn are shady walks through the wood, terminated to the east by a long oblong piece of water, surrounded by gravel walks where one may enjoy the sun in cold weather. And to the west lies the pleasure and three large kitchen gardens.[151]

Though Beranger's visit took place in 1799, it seems that much of what he saw must have been planted and designed by Arthur Rawdon. Even a century after the planting of the demesne was begun, the residents still had a pride in the place. Beranger went on to describe a large abandoned quarry on the west of the demesne which

> Miss Sharman got planted and improved and has called it the Pelew. It forms at present a delightful shrubbery with ups and downs, either by steps or slopes and has so many turns and windings, that it appears a labyrinth and contains shady walks and close recesses in which little rural buildings and seats are judiciously placed, with a little wooden bridge to pass a small rill of water. Jassamine, woodbine and many flowering shrubs adorn this charming place.[152]

A topographical dictionary of Great Britain and Ireland published 1833 described the town; "The family of Rawdon, Marquess of Hastings, derive the title of Earl from this place and their ancient and noble mansion is adjacent to this town."

---

[151] The Journal of the Royal Historical and Archaeological Association of Ireland.
[152] ibid.

But another book published in 1837 says the Moira demesne was still very extensive and well wooded, possessing many large and rare trees, with a noble avenue leading to the site of the Castle, long since demolished.[153]

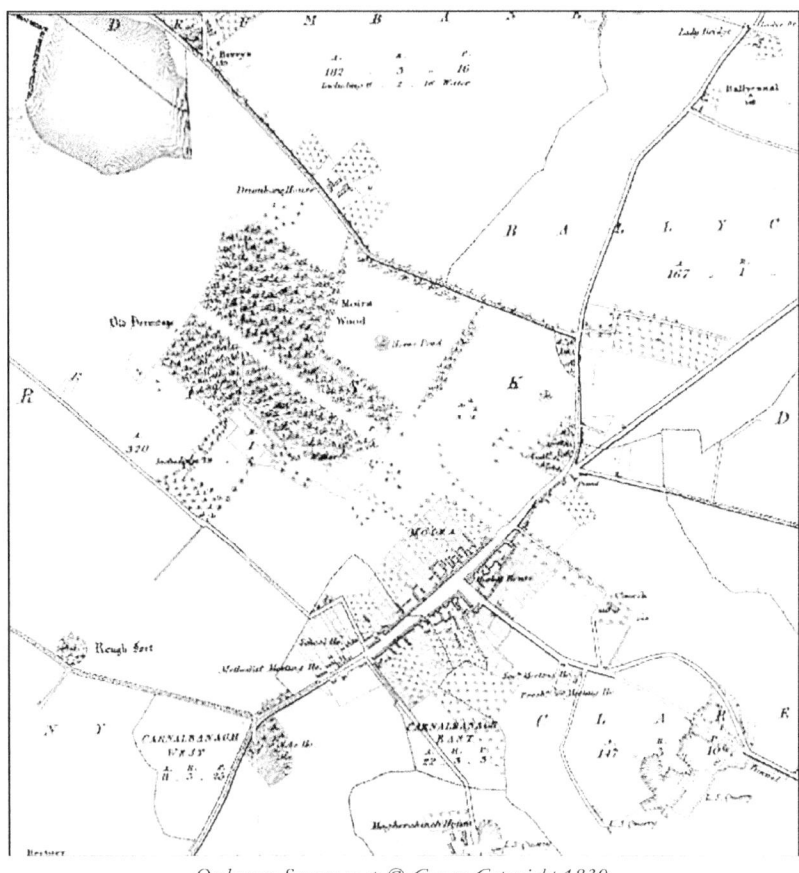

Ordnance Survey map © Crown Copyright 1830

Some sources say the demolition was in the early nineteenth century.[154] This appears to be corroborated by the visitor I

---

[153] Topographical Dictionary of Ireland. Publ. 1837.
[154] McGill Faculty of Education, Montrealhttp://www.mcgill.ca/education.

quoted earlier in this book who said, "the house which was occupied by the Earl is now levelled to the ground." Perhaps after Sharman's death in 1803, the house fell into misuse. Alexander Knox says the house "was taken down after the sale of the property to the late Sir Robert Bateson."[155] Another book published in 1925 says the "gardens and pleasure grounds (were) restored to pasture. The old demesne is now the property of Mr James Douie, formerly agent to Lord Deramore."[156] The Handbook for Travellers in Ireland (1854) says of the village, "near it are the remains of the demesne of the former Earls of Moira." All this seems at odds with the Northern Ireland Heritage Gardens inventory and the Northern Ireland Planning Service, which dates the demolition as happening in 1870.[157] Perhaps the latter refers to demolition of walls or ruins that had been still standing.

Some features are visible today and others long gone. Some walls still stand but it is unclear if these belonged to the house. Some years ago they were higher and hazardous and so were reduced in height and re-pointed.

There was a number of ponds in the demesne. The site of long pond is still visible and a pond is still intact on land beside the demesne. It was called the Horse Pond and now is known locally as the Cherry Island where it provides sanctuary for wildlife. An Ice-house once stood in the corner of the demesne close to where the basketball court is now. A Hermitage was situated just beyond the furthest end of the demesne but all remains seem to have been obliterated under a farm track. The

---

[155] A history of the County of Down by Alexander Knox M.D. Publ. 1875 page 396.
[156] Dromore, an Ulster Diocese by E.D. Atkinson LLB. Archdeacon of Dromore. Publ. 1925.
[157] http://www.ehsni.gov.uk and http://www.planningni.gov.uk.

Dark Walk was a tree-lined avenue, which some say was cut down by the American Military during World War II but is now replaced.

It is a shame so much has been lost but it could have been so very much worse. What is now a beautiful park could easily have become an industrial development!

On 10th December 1957, the Ministry of Commerce at Stormont wrote to W.A. Stewart Esq., at the Royal Courts of Justice, Belfast. The letter said,
> The Ministry of Commerce is interested in Moira Castle Estate as a possible site for industrial development. I notice on the O.S. 6" map, Moira Castle appears in Old English type, with "site of" in brackets underneath and I thought it advisable to enquire if these ruins come under ancient monuments.

The typed letter had two hand-written notes, obviously showing the passage of the letter between different departments. They reveal what might have been. One asked, "Is there any monument at this place? If not, is the site worth investigating before M/Commerce take over?" And the second says, "No archaeological interest." Thankfully someone somewhere took the decision not to proceed with the proposed development. [158]

---

[158] Northern Ireland sites and Monuments Record. http://appsc.doeni.gov.uk Document SM7-DOW-013-010.pdf.

Waringfield House

As one travelled out of the village in the direction of Magheralin, there stood Waringfield House, another notable Georgian building. It was the residence of the Waring family who in 1876 owned more than two thousand acres at Moira. That house is long gone but the perimeter of the walled garden is still visible and included in the residential development now on the site.

Waringfield was clearly a beautiful location and nearby is Pretty Mary's Fort. Rev. Canon C R J Rudd in his book[159] quotes this extract from the poem – "Pretty Mary's Fort" (author unknown)

> I have read about Killarney's Lakes
> I have seen Shane's Castle Hall
> But the beauty of you Waringfield
> You far exceed them all.
> Long may the name of Waring live there
> In this ancient Hall to reign
> And keep an eye unto the poor
> That live round his domain.
> We bid adieu to Waringfield
> With its laurels ever green
> And to the weeping willows
> Down by the Lagan stream.
> And to the Forth and Burns' house
> And pretty Mary's well -
> To describe the beauties of this place
> No human tongue can tell.

---

[159] Moira - a Historical Handbook by Rev. Canon C R J Rudd,

Gabriel Beranger described a visit to Warringsfield[sic] with Miss Sharman in 1799.

> I saw, for the first time, glass bee-houses; they are made conical and covered with cones of straw, to make them dark, otherwise, I was told, the bees would not work. The hives stand in a kind of wooden press, in the middle of a garden. This press had small holes in the doors, to let in the bees, from whence they enter the hives. To show them, the doors of the press are opened, and the straw covers taken off, when I saw the bees at work against the sides. Mr Warring has got the method from France of taking the honey without destroying these useful and ingenious insects.

Waringfield House was destroyed by fire on 10th October 1956 and became a rather exciting and dangerous playground for local youths. It was finally demolished in the late 1980's.

Waringfield Military Hospital

In June 1942, during World War II, the American military constructed a convalescent hospital with nine hundred beds at Waringfield for the British Emergency Medical Service (EMS). It was to grow to one thousand beds the following year. Wounded soldiers from all parts of the world were treated there. Ambulances were always on standby at Maghaberry Airfield awaiting the arrival of casualties to be transported to Moira.

For some time Waringfield was also the base for a Company of

French soldiers.[160] German prisoners of war were also treated there and one man from Moira recalls that as a child at St. John's Sunday School, the Junior Choir was taken to sing carols to the wounded British soldiers and German prisoners. "The Germans using scarce materials made us toys as presents for Christmas, which was brilliant as usually Santa only left an apple and maybe an orange too." He also recalls that those German prisoners who were able enough, were allowed to take regular walks through the village with only a minimum of guard escort. They wore a blue uniform with a white circle on the back which had a red cross within it.

Ten years after the war ended, the hospital was still in use and one MP questioned its suitability. In parliament, the Secretary of State for War indicated that they planned to continue to lease "the site of Waringfield Military Hospital until a new military hospital at Lisburn is completed. Waringfield Military Hospital will then be closed." Captain Orr, MP for South Down, responded,

> Would my Rt. Hon. Friend agree that it is high time that a permanent military hospital was built, and this collection of obsolete shacks and the ground upon which it stands handed back to the original owner?[161]

When the Ulster Military Hospital was eventually transferred to Musgrave Park Hospital, the Royal Army Medical Corps presented their flag to Moira Parish Church. The buildings later became a Chest Hospital and eventually a Geriatric Hospital.

---

[160] Quoted in Like an Evening Gone by Eileen Cousins B.A.
[161] Hansard 29 March 1955 Vol. 539 c186

Trummery House

Trummery House, a short distance from Moira on the Lisburn Road, was built in 1625. It was the home of Captain Henry Spencer, an army officer in 1598 who was granted four square-miles of land in the area under lease from Queen Elizabeth I. He was governor of the Fort of Inisloughlin. Like many grand homes of the time it had an escape tunnel. Some make the rather unlikely assertion that it ran as far as the fort. The Spencer family held this land until 1728 when it was taken over by Jacob Bell whose family held it until 1884.

Early nineteenth century maps show extensive buildings, gardens and avenues but all traces of these are now gone. A tree-lined avenue led from the house to the Hillsborough Road at a point close to Boyles Bridge. To this day a lane follows the line of that avenue. That part of the Hillsborough Road became known as the Avenue Foot and in the last century was a popular meeting place for all ages on a Sunday afternoon.

...

Moira today still has some buildings that give us a flavour of how our village looked nearly three hundred years ago. A number of them date from the time of the Rawdons or their successors.

Berwick Hall

The earliest Moira building that is still occupied is Berwick Hall, the two-storey Planters thatched house on the Hillsborough Road. According to the present owner, the building dates back to 1697 and is Category A listed. It was owned by the Berwick family who lived in the area since the Battle of the Boyne or even earlier. The house is an extremely fine example of a yeoman's home. Members of the Berwick family lived live there until the 1860s. George Wilson bought it in 1861 and his descendants still reside there.

Magherahinch House

Down the lane beside the former Police Station lies the beautiful Magherahinch House. This secluded location keeps this gem well-hidden but it is a very notable building. It affords majestic views down the Lagan Valley to the village of Hillsborough with which it has links.

It is a five-bay two-storey stone and brick double-pile house. The front pile facing east was built in 1838 but the rear pile was built c.1720.[162]

The older part of the house is first mentioned in a will of John Bateman dated 1754, who left his "freehold estate in Magherahinch with my house and gardens thereon" to his dear wife Dorcas and thereafter to his son William Bateman. The house is mentioned in the Post-chaise Companion of 1786,

---

[162] Dept. of the Environment. Historic building Detail Ref. No. HB19/22/054.

"Near Moira and on the west of it, is the seat of John Bateman Esq. standing on an eminence and having a beautiful prospect of wood and the meanders of the River Lagan."[163]

In 1833, the Marquess of Downshire purchased the property and in 1838 he added an additional block on to the front of the old house. A datestone and the Downshire coronet adorn the building. It is suggested that the Marquess used the house as a country retreat though he lived a mere six miles (10 km) away as the crow flies. Over the next one hundred years the house was leased to wealthy farmers including Joseph Green and his brother, Adam Agar and James Turner until, in 1929 the house was sold to Joseph Cresswell for £5000.[164]

Douie House

Number 106 Main Street is now known as Beaufort House and is used for business purposes but the building was once the home and office of the land steward for the Moira estate. It is believed to date from 1760.

Kilmore House

Though a little under three miles out of the village, Kilmore House had a role in one lasting facet of Moira life. The original house was a Rectory built in 1750. Whether this belonged to Magheralin or Moira is unclear but on editions of the Ordnance

---

[163] ibid.
[164] ibid.

Survey map of 1833, this building is labelled as the Old Rectory.[165] The Rectory is long gone but the Langtry family built Kilmore House there in 1854. Its owner was George Langtry, a merchant from Lurgan, who went on to bigger and better things. He bought Fortwilliam in Belfast in 1810 and became a renowned Belfast shipping magnate.

Anne Lutton, founder of Methodism in Moira, loved Kilmore and often visited her friends there. Miss Elizabeth Langtry was a "lady of good social position, intellectual tastes and considerable attainments" and she became a confidante and intimate friend of the young Anne as she began her Methodist ministry in the village and far beyond.[166]

A very different lady had associations with Kilmore House. George Langtry's grandson Edward married Lily in 1874 and she is notorious for being the mistress of the Prince of Wales, later to become Edward VII, as well as having a string of other liaisons.

Rectory

It would seem that Moira once had a Glebe house as well as a Rectory. First edition Ordnance Survey maps in 1833 show a Glebe house where the old Rectory now stands as well as a Rectory marked on the land between Earlsfort and the detached houses on the Lurgan road. The Rectory was not marked on OS Maps dated 1860 so perhaps by then the Glebe house had become home for the Rector. By the time the 1900

---

[165] from Review - Journal of Craigavon Historical Society Vol. 5. No. 3 by Helen Fitzpatrick.
[166] Memorials of a Consecrated life" by Anne Lutton. Pub. 1882.

OS Map was produced the Glebe House was renamed "the Rectory."

The Glebe house had been built in 1799 at a cost of £710.[167] It appears to have been built in stages; a stone above the ceiling in the kitchen is dated 1811 and a bay was added to the south elevation before 1858.

Before the end of the twentieth century the Rectory was sold and a new Rectory erected in the grounds. Although renovated and having lost some of its character, the former Rectory still somewhat resembles its earlier manifestation. It is now converted into a children's nursery.

The Market House

The first market-house was built in the eighteenth century. It was a shared venture by Sir John Rawdon and the Earl of Hillsborough.[168]

On 8th April 1782 in that large assembly room in the Market House, a meeting was convened to consider the Dungannon resolutions. Col. W. Sharman was in the chair. Among the resolutions were:
> That it is the undoubted right of this free people to be governed solely by their own laws.

and
> That next to our liberties, we value our connection with

---

[167] Samuel Lewis' Topographical Dictionary of Ireland. Publ. 1837.
[168] A history of the County of Down by Alexander Knox M.D. Publ. 1875 page 396.

Great Britain, as a blessing on which the happiness of both kingdoms depends; we look forward therefore with a pleasing conviction, that the justice of Great Britain will shake hands with the liberties of Ireland.[169]

The eye-catching building we know today as the Pentecostal church may have been built on the same site as that first market house, though a map of a land survey dated 1780 shows the market house as a free-standing building.[170] The Bateson family erected this new building with its open-arched ground floor around 1810. It is possible that some of the stone used was from the castle which was demolished around the same time. Old photographs show that iron gates secured each arch and that the roof was topped with a small tower and weather vane. The Bateson coat-of-arms adorned each tympanum.

The new Market House had a large assembly room and a courtroom where manor court was held every third week. Samuel Lewis described it as

> a large handsome building, erected by the proprietor, in which a manor-court is held, every three weeks, for the recovery of debts under £5, by civil bill and attachment; petty sessions are also held here on alternate Mondays, and it is a constabulary police station.[171]

---

[169] The minutes of this meeting are recorded in "An argument for Ireland" by John O'Connell. Publ. 1800. pages 137/138.
[170] 'Map of Earl Moira's demean(sic) Moira, Co. Down 1780' by Daniel Mullan. Image T3560/1 PRONI.

[171] Samuel Lewis' Topographical Dictionary of Ireland. Publ. 1837.

Sadly, a rather utilitarian asbestos roof has long since replaced the original slates and the tower is gone but the coat-of-arms remain on the sides of the raised roof.

Public domain image

The building was obviously available for community use and one such is recorded in The Bible Christian of 1838. It describes the Quarterly meeting of the Presbytery of Bangor on 31st July that year and is entitled "Tea Party at Moira."

The Unitarians record that they were joined by "a sample from every religious body in the neighbourhood .... in social intercourse and the cause of Christian Unity." Upwards of one hundred and seventy ladies and gentlemen were served tea followed by many speeches "at very considerable length" and "with so much urbanity, eloquence and address, as contributed very essentially to the gratification and good feeling which universally prevailed throughout the evening."[172] The proceedings closed at 10.30 pm.

The upper floor of the Market House held the Court of Petty Sessions from 1866 until sometime in the 1960s. In 1909 the ground floor became a workshop and from 1929 to 1979, it was used it as a garage and filling station by J. Ruddell & Son.
During the 1960's the upper floor became the Tempo Ballroom, attracting people from far and wide. In 1979 the building was acquired by the "Trustees of Leslie Hale Evangelistic Association" and since then has been the Pentecostal church.

The School House

A school building stood at the entrance to Backwood Road since the days of the Earl of Moira. It was replaced by the Edwardian styled building we see today on that same site. A plaque above the door reads; "Moira Public Elementary School. Erected 1908."

Some credit the building of the school to the Deramore Estate but it seems more likely that it was built by the church. Certainly the terms of its charter stated that when it was no longer used as a school, it should pass to the church. It ceased to be used as a school when a new school was built on Backwood Road in the early 1970s.

In 1975 the old building was opened as a youth hall and a drop-in centre and it is still very much in use.

---

[172] The Bible Christian: designed to advocate the sufficiency of Scripture and the right of private judgement in matters of faith. Publ. 1838 page 283.

The four trees

Moira was always an attractive location. Those lime trees Anne Lutton described down both sides of the Main Street were removed in the early part of twentieth century. Chestnut trees that once lined part of the driveway to the Parish Church unfortunately also had to be taken down.

There were four lime trees in the middle of the Main Street. These two-hundred-year-old trees marked a popular stopping point for the old Dublin stagecoach. In the 1950s Moira Rural Council called in forestry experts to inspect the trees and they were declared unsafe. The Council was advised that they should be felled.

Many residents vehemently opposed the removal of the trees. One resident wrote to the Belfast Telegraph in May 1958 asking "What good purpose can be served by their removal when such wonderful pleasure and happiness can be maintained by their preservation?"[173]

After much debate, a storm in September 1961 brought the matter to a head. One of the trees was blown down and it was obvious that the others would have to follow sooner rather than later. But by 1965 the council could delay no longer. A photograph of the felling operation shows a man with a hand saw sitting on branches high above the road, with no obvious safety precautions, calmly sawing the tree down, branch by branch. Meanwhile a policeman stands on the street warning passers-by.

---

[173] Belfast Telegraph archives. https://www.belfasttelegraph.co.uk/archive/old-pictures-of-moira-from-the-belfast-telegraph-archives-29816136.html.

Public domain image

With the trees removed, the debate continued. Some residents were in favour of replacing the trees and others believed the street was better without them. The local tree lovers prevailed. The Council, after receiving a petition with one hundred and fifty signatures, agreed to plant four new trees.

But rather mysteriously on the night of 1st March 1967, five trees were planted and a sign erected saying, "We shall not be moved." This must have galvanised the council because they planted four copper beech trees on 3rd March! At the time of writing these trees are now fifty years old and hopefully they will stand for generations to come!

The attractive appearance of the streets was lost for a while in the 1970s as hideous barriers lined the street in an attempt to protect property from terrorist bombs. Moira went through "The Troubles" relatively unscathed until 20th February 1998, when a huge car bomb was detonated outside the Police Station. Seven police officers were among eleven people injured and the station was left a mangled wreck. Many properties were destroyed or damaged and at least one beautiful old building was beyond repair.

But that was not the first time that the Police in Moira were fortunate to escape with their lives. In September 1930, the old barracks lower down the street went on fire and upwards of one thousand rounds of ammunition exploded.

The doss house

The outbuilding to the rear of 71 Main Street and fronting onto Meeting Street was originally 1 Pump Row, the end house of a row of nine cottages with village pump was situated at the far end. The remainder of the row was demolished in the 20th century and the building was used as a store for Palmer's shop.

This small outbuilding was originally a doss-house operated by "Sarah" at a rate of sixpence per night and later known locally as 'Dick's shed'. Dick was a local postman who resided there when unable to travel home.[174] And even more significantly, an expert in historic monuments dates "the Doss House" from the latter end of the 1600s which would make it the oldest remaining building within the village boundary.[175]

---

[174] Dept for Communities. Historic Building Details HB Ref No: HB19/22/040
[175] Information supplied by the current owner.

Snippets on other buildings

The parish and village owe their existence to the Rawdon family who were largely responsible for building the houses within the village and for the village's development. The old mud-built houses were replaced with houses built with stone. The Chinese restaurant, Midnight Haunt, opposite the Market House (Pentecostal Church) bears a stone with the date 1735. It is the kind of inscription that usually indicates the date a village was completed

Number 57 Main Street, now trading as The Fat Gherkin, was beside the old police station and for a time it housed the medical dispensary. Across the street, number 54, The Barrow, was a Post Office from the early twentieth century until the early 1970s. Next door, now the doctors' surgery, was once the Presbyterian Manse.

In 1866 numbers 76 and 78 Main Street were referred to as "21 Town of Moira." From the mid nineteenth century, the building was occupied and run as a hotel by John Murphy. Later it was bought by the Ruddell family, who also owned the garage in the Market House. They ran the hotel for thirty-five years until it was bought by Susan Heaney in 1926. It became a temperance hotel, using only the property now occupied by Robert Wilson. The hotel business closed in the 1960s. Mrs Heaney also owned a coal yard at the top of the street.

Number 83 Main Street was once the site of a factory operated by Harry Ferguson Motors Ltd. during the second world war. He had two small production units manufacturing parts for his world-famous tractor and Bofors guns. After the war the factory was adapted by Derg Handwoven Tweeds Ltd to produce fabric.

It is claimed locally that houses in Meeting Street, long since demolished, and some on Main Street used stone from the castle in their construction.

An interesting snippet of information from Moira Rural District Council shows how water was provided for the village in the early years of the last century.

> Lord Deramore has given land on which is situated the well from which it is proposed to supply the village with water, the only condition attached being that no special water rate should be imposed on the inhabitants. The cost of carrying out the scheme is estimated at £450.[176]

Lord Deramore at that time would have been a grandson of Sir Robert Bateson, the last owner of Moira Castle and the man who was said to be "an honest independent country gentleman." It would seem Robert Bateson had passed on those qualities to the next generations.

A century later we take so much for granted with water on tap and all the other amenities that our predecessors in Moira could never have imagined.

---

[176] The Surveyor. Vol. 29. 1906.

The War Memorial

It stands in the grounds of the Parish Church and lists nine residents of Moira parish who fell in the service of King and country in 1914-18 and five who died in the 1939-45 conflict.

Two of the latter were brothers; Isaac and Joseph Walker. Isaac was in the Irish Guards and was killed in action in Tunisia, North Africa on 28th April 1943. He was aged just twenty-one. His younger brother Joe joined the Special Air Service (SAS). He was one of a group who parachuted into France on a special mission but somehow the Germans were aware of their landing site and the men were attacked and Joe was among those taken captive. However they were not treated as prisoners of war should be but were murdered soon after in cold blood by the Gestapo on 9th August 1944 at Beauvais, France. Joe was also just twenty-one years old.

As the inscription on the war memorial says, "These also died in war that we might live in peace." A third brother served in the forces with the Royal Marines and was discharged with honour on 30th November 1944 after seven and a half years of service. We owe so much today to individuals and families like the Walkers.[177]

---

[177] Information from The Second World War in Northern Ireland website. http://www.ww2ni.com/countydownpart5.htm

Roadways, waterways and railways

To live in Moira is to live at the centre of a hub. A transport network fans out from our community to all parts of Ulster. Moira roundabout is a landmark known to just about everyone in Northern Ireland. In bygone days, almost everybody in the southern half of the province, when travelling east or west, passed through Moira. Many, like the author who was reared in the west of the Province, recall the childhood Sunday School trips or the outings to Belfast that brought him through this delightful village.

The beginning of the road network we have today is attributed to Sir George Rawdon. Surveys of the time indicate that all the roads he constructed in his district were very good. From what had been a wooded wet valley with forest tracks, the region developed into a place for agriculture and commerce. New roads linked Lisburn with other towns and the developing villages. Rawdon himself could never have anticipated the highways and transport facilities in Moira district today!

In 1720 coal was discovered in County Tyrone near Coalisland. It was brought to the Blackwater and across Lough Neagh before being carted to Moira and on to Lisburn or Belfast. There was one metalled or paved road in this area available to those coal cart users. Some years ago, when the Department of the Environment put up nameplates, that road was called

Coal Lane but strong objections by locals resulted in a name deemed more polite - Colane Road.

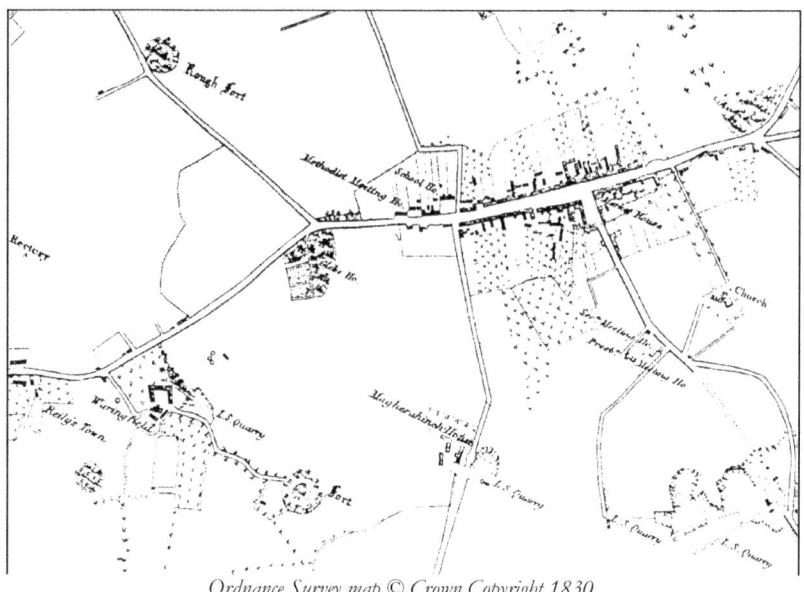

Ordnance Survey map © Crown Copyright 1830

It is only about six miles from Lough Neagh to the River Lagan at Moira. Back in the seventeenth century George Rawdon suggested digging a canal. Well over a century later in 1756, the Lagan Canal enterprise was commenced and was officially opened in 1763. The horse drawn barge, The Lord Hertford, made the trip from Belfast to Lisburn. By 1794, when more money had been acquired through a government tax on beer and spirits, the work was completed on out to Lough Neagh. It was a mighty undertaking.

The route meant it had to cross the Lagan, so a magnificent aqueduct was built high over the river near Spencer's Bridge on the Hillsborough Road. It was a very fine piece of architecture with four arches, three hundred feet long and thirty-five feet high. The sandstone used in construction was quarried in the Earl of Hillsborough's estate in the townland of Kilwarlin. It took three years to build, cost £3,000 and was paid for by the Earl of Donegall. To ensure a solid foundation, the structure was erected on dry ground and then the river was diverted to flow under it. Iron railings protecting the tow-path across the Lagan were removed during the Second World War to aid the war effort. Sadly the aqueduct was later demolished to make way for the motorway bridge across the Lagan.

There are countless interesting stories around the canal. In 1941, at a point on the canal not far from where Moira roundabout now sits, a barge sprung a leak. The sinking vessel was saved when a pound of Killyman butter was brought to plug the hole. How they came to find this during rationing is not clear! And on one occasion a barge waited outside a dock for three weeks to allow a wild duck to hatch her young! What a different fast-paced world we live in today!

However, canal navigation was poor and it was once said that a ship could get from Belfast to the West Indies and back in faster time than it took for the canal lighter to do the round trip to Lough Neagh. Until the motorboat engine arrived, the canal boats were horse-drawn and occasionally poled when empty. There was a towpath all the twenty-five miles from Belfast to Lough Neagh. In 1836 nine hundred vessels worked on the canal. By 1850 the time taken for a canal journey improved to less than a week. Barges carried non-perishable goods from Belfast and returned full of Lough Neagh sand. The trade at Moira was largely servicing the breweries, distilleries and lime works. At its peak over one hundred thousand tons of freight was carried annually. For several years the canal paid its way as a commercial enterprise but it was not to last.

The canal had arrived rather late on the transport scene. The section from Lough Neagh to Lisburn was abandoned on 1st April 1954, and the stretch to Belfast in July 1958.

The Canal managers had been of the opinion that the construction of the Ulster Railway in 1841 would not impact greatly on the canal. How wrong they were! Rail transport arrived less than fifty years after the canal was completed. Within a decade of the world's first rail passenger service, we had a railway in Moira. The section from Belfast to Lisburn was opened for passenger traffic on 12th August 1839. The section from Lisburn to Lurgan was completed just two years later.

Thomas Bateson, later to become Lord Deramore, is reported to have been reluctant to allow the Railway to be built on his land, so that is supposed by some to be the reason why the Station is approximately one mile from the town.

Moira Station, built in 1841, is the oldest surviving operational railway station in Northern Ireland. It was designed by John Godwin and built of stone and brick with stucco finish. It is in Italianate style with a slate roof, tall chimneys and tall, round-headed windows. From the railway level it appears to be a single storey building, but a second storey below platform level was the original stationmaster's accommodation. His entrance was from the yard at the back, which is now a car park. A purpose-built stationmaster's house was later erected on the other side of the track in the 1880s.

Passenger traffic receipts from March to August 1842 (less than one year after opening) show remarkable figures.[178]

---

[178] Industrial Archaeology of N.I. Wm. A McCutchen 1984.

Tickets sold at Moira:
    travelling to Belfast   5,746
    travelling to Lisburn   4,153
    total sold   12,906
    Station Income for those months £376.7s.6d.

And the population in Moira at the time was only eight hundred and twenty-three! That is the equivalent of every resident of Moira making more than sixty train journeys a year! And we think Moira was only a commuter town in the last thirty or forty years! In 1945 fifteen people, including stationmaster, clerks, porters and signalmen, staffed Moira Station.

The railway also brought many visitors to Moira for special occasions such as the 12th July celebration of 1875. The Northern Whig reported:

> The anniversary of the Battle of the Boyne was celebrated here yesterday in the beautiful demesne of Sir Thomas Bateson, Bart., M.P. The little village itself was handsomely decorated for the occasion, there being several very pretty arches through It, composed of orange lilies, evergreens, and flags, which had the effect of giving the place a very lively appearance. The train which leaves Belfast at half-past ten o'clock brought a considerable number of people into the town from that place and the intermediate stations. ... After the meeting ... the entire party, numbering between eight and ten thousand people, left the town immediately and shortly after six o'clock Moira presented its usually quiet and monotonous appearance.[179]

---

[179] Quoted by The Digger in an article in The Ulster Star on Friday 19th July 2013.

You can't think now of Moira without thinking of the M1 motorway. The original plan in 1946 was to build a southern approach road to Belfast which would have by-passed Moira to the South, heading close to Waringstown and south of Lurgan to finish between Lurgan and Portadown.[180] Immediately after the war there was no money to proceed but by 1956 it was decided to build the road to motorway standard, calling it the M1. The route was altered to take the road to the north of Moira.

Because the government agencies owned the canal, following that path was the cheapest route between Lisburn and Moira, resulting in the winding nature of the motorway in that section. The magnificent aqueduct near Spencer's Bridge was demolished and the loss of the canal almost certainly had an impact on wildlife that would not be tolerated today. In 1965 a major junction was created with all the benefits and headaches of tens of thousands of vehicles now using the motorway each day at that point.

A curious urban myth surrounded the construction of the long straight stretch of motorway between Moira and Lurgan. Despite it being not straight, rather undulating and having several bridges crossing it, it was rumoured by some that it was so constructed to be available for use as an emergency runway, supposedly for the United States Air Force in the event of a conflict breaking out with the Soviet Union!

The location of Moira with its infrastructure has attracted many of those who have come to live in the village and surrounding

---

[180] Northern Ireland Roads Site www.wesleyjohnston.com/roads/m1.html

area. There is easy access by road or rail to work, shopping and entertainment. Children can travel easily to school and university. Air and sea travel is within easy reach. But that attraction has brought about much traffic congestion on our main street. Perhaps one day the long-considered by-pass will be built and Moira's Main Street will become a little quieter and return to something resembling its former charm.

Image of the original letter by John Wesley to Lord Moira

Saints and sinners

Time brings changes - demographic, ecological, political and socioeconomic to name just a few. But we are all much more than dwellers in time and space. There is an eternal dimension to life which is why I want to conclude with a look at spiritual life in Moira, considering the formation and impact of the churches in the village and studying a few famous preachers who passed this way.

A legend says St. Patrick came up the Lagan but of course there are so many legends surrounding the man. There is no record I can find of him in the Moira area, though it is claimed he founded a church in nearby Glenavy.

A Bishop called St. Ronan Finn came with Domhall's army in AD 637 and is said to have established a church as well as monastery or nunnery in the area associated with townland of Kilminiogue.

The Right Rev. Monsignor James O'Laverty, M.R.I.A., a noted nineteenth century historian, was able to identify the site of the church of St. Ronan Finn in an area known in ancient times as Corco Ruishen. That area today is divided into three townlands known as Kilminiogue, Risk and Legmore with their names derived from marshes and hollows. Kilminiogue in Irish translates into "the church of my dear Finn," as O'Laverty

explains.
> I should here add that the Irish were in the habit of placing "mo" (my) before the name of a saint, and placing after the name the termination "og" as a term of endearment: hence "Mo-Finn-og" pronounced "Minnog " (my dear Finn).

O'Laverty conjectured that St. Ronan Finn was locally called Finn.[181]

The ancient church was in a field belonging to Charles Byrne, in the townland of Kilminiogue. Cultivation of that field unearthed large quantities of bones indicating the presence of an ancient graveyard. Nearby was a very old well called Tubber.[182] Today there are no traces of this church but it is believed to have been on land that lies between the north-westernmost corner of Backwood Road and the motorway.

Some locals claim that Kilminiogue means "the Church of the young Maidens" supporting the theory that the monastic establishment may have included a nunnery.

Ronan Finn was also associated with Magheralin where there was a seventh century monastery or a nunnery. There is a lane known locally as the "Nun's Walk" in the townland of Ballymackeonan.

Later religious visitors to the Moira district are much better documented, as we shall discover.

---

[181] Quoted in Antiquarian Jottings by Right Rev. Monsignor James O'Laverty M.R.I.A. Ulster Journal of Archaeology Volume XI. Publ. 1905.
[182] ibid.

Village churches

For millennia, a henge has stood on the highest ground in Carnalbanagh overlooking the Lagan valley. Henges were used largely for ceremonial gatherings during the Neolithic and Early Bronze Age periods, around five thousand years ago. Those large gatherings may often have been religious in nature. For the last three centuries and more, the hill that was once a centre of paganism, has drawn villagers each week to worship Almighty God. Four of the six church buildings in Moira stand on that hill.

Moira was originally part of the greater parish of Magheralin and until Moira parish was formed in 1721 Anglicans went there for worship. The Rawdons opposed all other forms of religious practice in the parish

Quite possibly only after George Rawdon's death in 1684 was it feasible for dissenters to worship publicly in the village. George Rawdon had been required to prevent Scots ministers from preaching; his instruction, in a letter dated 16th December 1649, was "that you suffer no Scots ministers to preach in the country again."[183] Rawdon took this responsibility very seriously and boasted that his Scots neighbours "esteem me one of the horns against the Kirk."[184] He was most active in the Lisburn area but even went as far as Ballymena to oppose

---

[183] http://www.education.mcgill.ca/profs/cartwright/rawdon/rawdons.pdf.
[184] The Anglo-Irish Experience, 1680-1730: Religion, Identity and Patriotism by David Hayton. Publ. 2012. The Boydell Press.

Presbyterians and vigorously enforced the Five Mile Act.[185]

The Presbyterians of Lisburn did not apply for a permanent minister until three years after the death of George Rawdon, indicating how much they feared him. It would be another six years before those in Moira could have a minister, for Sir Arthur took the same view as his father of the "rigid Presbyterians" and continually refused requests for a meeting house. His agent told him, "You may expect little friendship from the Presbyterians and other fanatics for they "are all against your interests."[186]

The following accounts are mere summaries of the history of religious life in the village and district since the seventeenth century and are taken in the order of their formation in Moira. Due to the highly unusual juxtaposition of two Moira churches designated Presbyterian, we will look at little more closely at their history.

Presbyterianism

Irish Presbyterianism originated with the settling of Scottish immigrants in Ulster early in the seventeenth century. By 1685,

---

[185] The Five Mile Act 1665 sought to enforce conformity to the established Church and to expel any who did not conform. Clergymen were forbidden from living within five miles of a parish from which they had been expelled, unless they swore an oath never to resist the king or attempt to alter the government of Church or State. They had to swear to obey the 1662 prayer book. Thousands of ministers were deprived under this act.

[186] Edmund Ellis to Sir Arthur Rawdon. 27th June 1689 quoted in The Anglo-Irish Experience, 1680-1730: Religion, Identity and Patriotism by David Hayton page 187.

one year after George Rawdon's death, there was a small meeting house for Presbyterian worship somewhere in the vicinity[187] of Moira and by 1693 records show that the church had it first minister. So the oldest church in the village is Presbyterian. But for much of the next century and for a variety of reasons, Presbyterianism in Moira would go through difficult times.

Significant theological, confessional and church government differences among Presbyterians resulted in disagreement and division within the denomination. Christianity is a confessional religion, having for most of its history an agreed body of faith. For Presbyterians, that confession is summed up in the Westminster Confession of Faith of 1646 to which the Synod of Ulster made subscription compulsory for licentiates in 1698 as a test of orthodoxy.

However many objected saying that mere human words could not form such a test, only the Word of God; though that in turn raised the issue of what any candidate understood the Word of God to teach; particularly about the nature of God the Father, Son and Holy Spirit and the atonement.

Many who opposed subscription said they were contending for the cause of liberty in thought rather than outright disagreement with the Confession. To them it was the practice of subscribing as a test of faith to which they objected, rather than the confession itself, though others were less convinced of the non-subscribers' orthodoxy.

---

[187] Rental of the Estate of Moyrah for the years 1723/4 under 'Tenants whose Lease or Minnets are expired or neared expiring.

In 1725 the Synod of Ulster formed the Presbytery of Antrim consisting of ministers and congregations who were opposed to any form of subscription and Moira was one of those congregations.

For much of the late eighteenth century both Subscribers and Non-subscribers appear for the most part to have got along together, sharing each other's pulpits and being educated at the same colleges but with the non-subscribing view dominant in the Synod.

However that relative peace between the two groups in Ulster was not universal. Disputes and divisions over faith and confessions were still evident in many congregations. That was the experience of Moira Presbyterians.

It would appear that many in the Moira congregation were much like other Presbyterians in Lisburn and Down who found that the "ill-disguised Pelagianism[188] delivered from several pulpits was exceedingly distasteful to the more pious and intelligent worshippers."[189] Some in the presbytery "craved a minister who would preach the Gospel, not in the wisdom of man's words but in the purity and simplicity thereof."[190]

That emphasis attracted them to the Seceders in Scotland, a body which had withdrawn from the jurisdiction of the Church

---

[188] Pelagianism is a fifth century heresy that views mankind as good and morally unaffected by the Fall. It denies the imputation of Adam's sin, original sin, total depravity, and substitutionary atonement. It teaches that man possesses free will which allows him to choose good or evil without God's help and that man has the ability in and of himself to obey God and earn eternal salvation.

[189] History of the Presbyterian Church in Ireland: Volume 3 by James Seaton Reid. Publ. 1867 page 242.

[190] Ibid. page 243.

of Scotland and formed the Associate Presbytery in 1733. These were men of piety and zeal and were just the kind of ministers some in the presbytery craved. So when the Seceders came to County Down, they found a ready welcome among quite a number in the Moira congregation.

By the middle of the eighteenth century there were two Presbyterian congregations in the village because, for some reason, the Moira congregation had been deprived of its place of worship around 1731. The deprived congregation appealed to the Synod of Ulster for help and in 1738 the Synod instructed that a day's collection from all the congregations should be taken, to assist the building of a new "convenient and handsome house for God's worship" in Moira.[191] That year a second church was built on what then was a one-acre site. To this day that site is occupied by two Presbyterian churches.

But two buildings did not initially solve the problem. Years of dispute followed with claims and counter claims over the property. The Seceder supporters, perhaps in the majority in the new building, asked the Scottish Seceders for help in 1747. Moira became a Seceder congregation in the 1750s.

Although there was a new building and an older one on the same site (probably the older building was still serviceable) both groups appear to have claimed the new building for in 1760 it was said "the seceders still had the house." This led to a protracted and expensive legal dispute lasting many years and was only resolved in 1790. A Deed of Partition on 27th May 1790 shows

---

[191] Moyrah Congregation by Kieran Clendinning. Review - Journal of Craigavon Historical Society 1996/7. (though in my view the author incorrectly attributes this appeal to the building of the present Non-Subscribing church building.)

the dissenting and the seceding Presbyterian congregations of the parish of Moira, Co. Down agree to divide equally between them the meeting house and acre of ground on which it stands in the townland of Clare. The dissenting parties to the deed were led by the Rev. David Trotter of Moira and the seceding parties by the Rev. Adam Gilbert of Ballymagaraghan, parish of Moira."[192]

As a result the Seceders retained the building while the acre of land on which the buildings stood was divided in two. The Deed also required the Seceders to give £40 to the dissenting congregation.

A century of division in Moira became permanent in 1830 when Rev. John Mulligan joined sixteen other ministers and withdrew from the Synod. He and the congregation known as First Moira became members of the Remonstrant Synod of Ulster which eventually became the Non-Subscribing Presbyterian Church of Ulster. Since then there have been two Presbyterian congregations in Moira worshipping side by side, still reflecting those diverging theological viewpoints.

Tensions between themselves were not the only issues facing Presbyterians. Although George Rawdon, the "horn of the Kirk," and his son Arthur were long since gone, there were on-going tensions for many years between the Anglicans and Presbyterians in Moira and particularly at the time of the Rebellion of 1798.

Some evidence of those inter-church tensions is found in the

---

[192] Public Record Office for Northern Ireland PRONI Reference: D1038/15

census of the parish between 1776 and 1831. In 1776 the parish was 34% Anglican, 34% Presbyterian and 32% Catholic. By 1831 the Anglicans had risen to 53.5%, the Catholics had 27.5% and the Presbyterians had dropped to 19%. By 1911, the Presbyterian figure was as low as 8%. Miller in the book, Irish Immigrants in the Land of Canaan[193] acknowledges that this:

> may reflect common disparities as in West Ulster between Ulster Presbyterian and Anglican emigration but also reflects the official and unofficial repression in a parish whose Presbyterian inhabitants were notoriously rebellious in 1798.

Miller suggests the reason for the decrease:

> Barring wholesale conversion to the established church, surely only drastic pressure such as post-rebellion changes in landlords' leasing policies …. and favouritism to "loyal" Anglican migrants from other parishes, can account for such dramatic revisions of Moira's ethno-religious composition.

Professor John Barkley in his Short History of the Presbyterian Church in Ireland tells us,

> After the government had succeeded in quelling the rebellion, the people, especially in Antrim, Down, Wexford, and Wicklow were treated with great brutality and cruelty. Many innocent people were put to death without trial, homesteads were burned, and property was destroyed. Hundreds fled to America.[194]

---

[193] Irish Immigrants in the Land of Canaan, letters and memoirs from colonial and revolutionary America, 1675–1815 Oxford University Press 2003.
[194] Rev. Professor John M. Barkley, M.A., Ph.D., D.D., F.R. Hist.S. Published by the Publications Board, Presbyterian Church in Ireland. Church House, Belfast. 1939.

We are thankful to God that there is such a different atmosphere in Moira village today.

Presbyterian Church in Ireland

The Presbyterian building erected in 1738 was replaced in 1829 at a cost of £550. Historic Building records described it as "a free-standing two-storey Presbyterian Church, dating from the early-nineteenth century with later alterations. The church had little architectural or historic interest."[195] The building had been renovated in 1920 and an organ installed.

The oldest stone round the Presbyterian church dates from 1856. However the graveyard has a most interesting box-tomb. Therein lies the remains of former minister, Rev. James Hume who died in 1782. He had not been buried in Moira, despite having ministered there for almost thirty years and having been minister when the Seceder congregation was first established. While ministering in Moira, he had also been minister, first of Lisburn Congregation (Hillhall) and then Magheragall, so he resided at Beechfield, Hillsborough. At the time of his death the property dispute in Moira was still not resolved so it was decided that he would be buried in Hillsborough. However in 1864 his tomb was transferred from Hillsborough to Moira.[196]

After almost one hundred and ninety years of Presbyterians

---

[195] Dept. of the Environment. Historic Building Details. Ref No: HB19/22/043.
[196] In the graveyards of North West Down by Richard S J Clarke in Review - Journal of Craigavon Historical Society Vol. 2 No. 1. It is stated that this tomb in in the Non-Subscribing graveyard but the two churches and graveyards have been confused. The History from Headstones internet site makes clear that Hume's tombstone is in the present Moira Presbyterian Church graveyard and it is visible to this day.

worshipping in the same building, it was demolished in 2016 and replaced by an impressive sanctuary the following year.

Non-subscribing Presbyterian Church

The present Non-Subscribing congregation in Moira may, for much of its existence, have been the smaller of the two Presbyterian congregations but has endured all these years. Rev. Anthony McIntyre kept a diary of his preaching engagements and on 9th October 1853 he preached to "a very small congregation principally composed of young people."[197]

It is agreed the congregation is one of the oldest in Ireland but there is less agreement about the age of the church building. One historian says it is likely that the present Non-Subscribing building was erected around 1860,[198] whereas an in-house publication by the Non-Subscribing Presbyterians speaks of financial help to erect their building in 1738 where "it remains to this day, and still reflects something of the character of a meeting house of the period."[199]

The confusion arises over the location of that 1738 building spoken of earlier which was erected within the boundaries of the acre of land. Recent research undertaken by the Very Rev Dr. W Donald Patton shows that the 1738 building was undoubtedly on the eastern half of the acre of land and was

---

[197] The Rev. McIntyre was employed by the Unitarian Domestic Mission to the poor of Belfast. 1853-6. PRONI D1558/2/3

[198] The graveyards of North West Down by Richard S J Clarke in Review - Journal of Craigavon Historical Society Vol. 2 No. 1.

[199] Congregational Memoirs - Moira by Dryasdust. The Non-Subscribing Presbyterian - December 2002.

granted to the Seceders in the Deed of Partition 1790.

The present church is not a listed building "as the building is not worthy of a full survey." It is a "detached double-height mid-nineteenth century gabled Presbyterian Church, with modern extension to rear ... Simply detailed, the original proportions have been altered by the modern extension."[200]

The church has several historic Moira Presbyterian items including an old Communion plate marked "Moyrah" and a precentor's flute.

Anglican

The parish of Moira was founded in 1721 having been once part of the parish of Magheralin. For some time before the church was built, the congregation worshipped in the Charity school, possibly on the site of the Old School we know today at the end of Backwood Road.

In 1723 the Hill family from Hillsborough gave land opposite Moira Castle for the building of the church and it was so designed that the avenue to the church and the Castle avenue were in a straight line as they are to this day. The Rawdon family contributed generously to the building of the church, although Sir John Rawdon himself died the same year the church was built and before it was consecrated in 1725.

It seems the parish was originally called St. Inn's of Moira.

---

[200] Dept. of the Environment. Historic Building Details. Ref No: HB19/22/042.

Certainly in 1835 it was still called by that name.[201] The name might derive from St. Ronan Finn who founded the old church in Kilminiogue. O'Laverty suggests that the founders of the church of Moira, calling it St. Inn's, did not understand that the " F " of Finn was silent on account of "mo" preceding it.[202] It is suggested however by Very Rev. H Hughes M.A., a former Rector of Moira, that "Inn" is not from the Gaelic "Finn."

> It could in fact be a corruption due to the common practice of abbreviating Latin names when writing. Thus Joannes (or Ioannes) for John became Inns.[203]

The Church building was roofed using shingles or what were locally called wooden slates and the spire was similarly covered.[204] Perhaps those shingles contributed to the loss of the spire in 1884 when it was destroyed in a freak storm. Its replacement is the spire we know today, which is not so high as its predecessor. In July 1884, a quote of £379 for a replacement was considered but the select vestry deemed it too high. A reduced height spire drew a lower quote of £346 "for the erection of a wooden spire coated with copper 50 feet 6 inches high."[205] That was accepted and the spire was replaced and has endured until the present day.

The window just above the west door is not original. A gallery was constructed in 1877 and at the same time the new window was added to give additional internal light.

---

[201] Topical Dictionary of Ireland by Samuel Lewis. Publ.1840.
[202] Antiquarian Jottings by Right Rev. Monsignor James O'Laverty M.R.I.A. Ulster Journal of Archaeology Volume XI. Publ. 1905.
[203] From Review - Journal of the Craigavon Historical Society Vol. 2 No. 1.
[204] A History of the County of Down by Alexander Knox M.D. Publ. 1875.
[205] From a little book published in1972 by Rector, Rev. John McCarthy, to celebrate the 250th anniversary of the creation of the parish of Moira.

An organ was installed in 1903 and required an organ blower. The lady who laboured at the bellows was paid £1.10s.0p. per year! Electricity was brought to the church in 1933 and the oil lighting was replaced and shortly after the organ blower was made redundant. Today the parish church is a Grade A listed building.

Public domain image

One of the most popular talking points about Moira, certainly by local school children, is a tunnel from Moira Castle leading to the church. Some suggest it was used by the Rawdon family and their servants as their means of entry to the church. This writer thinks this is most unlikely, for with both buildings on a hill there would be a large dip in a tunnel which would constantly be damp or liable to flooding, to say nothing of rats and other unpleasant creatures - not very conducive to going to church in Sunday best clothes! And the tunnel entrance to the church, which is said to be under the aisle, would have required a large opening to allow the people from the Castle to ascend a ladder or steps. Not so elegant for well-dressed ladies in full view of the congregation! The gentry in those days liked to travel to church in style in their carriages, with the lower classes doffing caps or curtseying as they passed.

The tunnel was more likely to have been an escape route if the Castle ever came under attack. This was a common feature in grand houses in the past. When work to install sewers, water mains and other services was undertaken, the tunnel was blocked and the mystery of its size and use remains to this day.

There is an unconfirmed report that the first Harvest Thanksgiving services in Ireland were held in Moira Church in 1726 shortly after it was consecrated.

William Butler Yeats, grandfather to the famous poet WB Yeats, came as Curate to the parish in 1831. He was a good horseman and his Rector, presumably Rev. Thomas Beatty, remarked that he had hoped for a curate but they sent him a jockey. In 1836 Yeats became Rector of Tullylish and was there until his death in 1862. He is described by one biographer as being "an easy-going evangelical" but was "uneasy in (Ulster), disliking the temperament of the Presbyterians by whom he was surrounded."[206] His church in Tullylish describes him as "a man of mystery and a complex character."[207] He had nine children and remarkably was grandfather to two of Ireland's most notable artists - Jack Butler Yeats the painter was another grandson.[208]

---

[206] W B Yeats: A new biography by A Norman Jeffares. Publ. 1988.
[207] http://www.tullylish.com/tullylish-historical-society/2806-reverend-w-b-yeats.
[208] JB Yeats was also Ireland's first Olympic Games medallist when he won silver at the 1920 Olympics in Paris. It seems strange now but art competitions were part of the summer Olympics from 1912 to 1948.

An incident from 1798 Rebellion deserves mention. Moira at that time had three church buildings within a stone's throw of each other; the Parish Church and two meeting houses. This proved to be "helpful" to the Seagoe Corps of Yeomanry under the command of William Blacker. Early that morning, with the rebellion in County Down coming to a head, he had been instructed to march with haste from Portadown to Lisburn. It was Sunday 10th June. Blacker tells us what happened.[209]

> We reached Moira while the congregations were in their respective places of worship. There are two Meeting Houses besides the church and at each of the three there were a number of horses, the greater part of them furnished with pillions, on which the farmers of those days carried their dames to prayers, market-cars and jaunting-cars being then unknown. To possess ourselves of the animals was a work of but a few minutes and ere the owners were aware of what was passing, each nag was mounted by one or two Yeomen, according to the length of its back and its extent of saddlery, and many a farmer's wife trudged home in sourness and sadness, despatching their servant-men towards Lisburn to pick up their horses, when it suited us to dispense with their further service.

A very interesting story of church life in Moira in those early years concerns a certain lady parishioner called Abigail. She was wife of D McC. (rather conveniently for him, his full name is not recorded). Abigail was ordered to
> repair to the Parish Church of Moira the next Lord's Day

---

[209] Lisburn and Neighbourhood in 1798 by T G F Paterson. Ulster Journal of Archaeology. Third Series, Vol. 1 (1938), pp. 194-5

and after Evening Prayer, she is, in the presence of Thomas Waring, Rector of the said parish, and some of the rest of the parishioners to acknowledge that she is sorry for the abusive words which she made use of against Sarah, wife of J. C. , in saying that she, Sarah was a ***** to D McC, the said Abigail's husband.[210]

Methodist

As this book was approaching completion, the church building dating from 1822 was demolished to make way for a new sanctuary. The church manse which sat very close to the front door of the church had previously been removed. It was also dated to the early part of the nineteenth century.[211]

In 1837, there were places of worship for both Wesleyan and Primitive Methodists.[212]

The origins of Methodism in Moira can be traced back to visits by John Wesley but it was a Moira woman called Anne Lutton who played a vital role in the early years of Methodism in the village. Her life and work are commemorated on a plaque in the church.

Anne Lutton was not yet born when Wesley first visited Moira in 1756. The Luttons had a home beside the four trees. In fact

---

[210] Dromore - an Ulster Diocese by E D Atkinson L.L.B. Archdeacon of Dromore Fellow of Royal Society of Antiquaries of Ireland page 45. © G. Damien Kerr June 2009.

[211] Department of the Environment. Historic Building Details. Ref No: HB19/22/007.

[212] A Topographical Dictionary of Ireland, Volume 1 by Samuel Lewis 1837.

the family owned several properties in and around Moira. Anne was the youngest surviving child of a family of thirteen, so it was quite possible that, as a boy, her father had witnessed John Wesley's visits and if not converted then, perhaps had the good seed sown in his heart. Interestingly he called one of his sons John Wesley Lutton despite the fact that he had given the name John to an earlier son who had died in infancy.

According to Miss Lutton, her father once entertained a Methodist preacher when he arrived in Moira. Although she was not born at the time, she describes the day Methodism began in Moira.

> It was Sunday; the people were just returned from the morning service in church, and whilst careful mistresses were looking after due preliminaries of the approaching dinner-hour, and younger members of the household were lolling over books, or idly gazing on the occasional figures which flitted past the windows, a stranger rode up to the principal inn, dismounted, gave his horse in charge to the usual attendant, unstrapped a huge pair of saddle-bags, and flinging them over his arm, walked into the house. He was not like any one they ever saw before; plain, but not in Quaker costume. They ran off and reported the matter to their father. He immediately observed it was most probably a Methodist preacher, and as he believed those men were generally very poor, and the stranger might not order a dinner at the inn, he should wish to ask him to come in and share theirs.
>
> Half an hour later the master and mistress of the mansion, two grown-up daughters, a son, and some five or six junior members of the family, sat round the dinner table, with Mr John Grace, the Methodist

preacher, occupying the most honourable place beside the lady.

That memorable Sabbath, when my father invited the Methodist preacher to come in and eat bread with him, was the beginning of days to a household which hitherto sat in darkness. They were all charmed with the winning manners and sweet conversation of their guest. He attracted and held them fast bound by some secret spell they never felt before. He seemed to awaken new powers of mind, and give new subjects for thought and converse. The little circle sat wondering, and delighted to find that religion was not clad in sable, repulsive and exacting. From that day the Methodist preachers were regularly entertained at my father's house; and as no chapel was then, nor for many years afterwards, built in that little town, his parlour and hall were the places where sat the congregation, whilst the laborious and pious men of God sought to save the souls of them that heard them.[213]

The Luttons attended the Parish Church in the morning and Wesleyan preaching on Sunday evening. "Thus I was preserved from extremes; the arrogant exclusiveness of High Church prejudices, and the contracted bigotry of hostile sectarianism," wrote Anne. The Luttons saw themselves as proper Church-Methodists and never entered a Dissenting place of worship until 1813. The Wesleyan preaching they attended on Sunday evenings may have been in their own home, for there appears to have been no Methodist Church building in the village until 1822.

---

[213] Memorials of a Consecrated life by Anne Lutton. Publ. 1882.

The Lutton family became a great witness for Christ in the village. The Moira curate, described as a "mild, scholarly man who just managed not to starve on the poorest stipend," was invited to hear the humble Wesleyan minister. He was "blessed, and made a blessing, finding Christ crucified for himself, and zealously proclaiming Him to others, in the church, in barns, in cottages."[214] Perhaps it was the same curate who is reported later to have helped Anne in her studies of Greek and Hebrew.

But despite the Gospel witness around her, Anne's spiritual interest waned. The family had moved to Donaghcloney where there were no Methodists, so she had no Methodist classes to attend and that pleased her. She felt herself to be upright and holy and encouraged others to live pure lives but she was not converted.

One day a great conviction of sin came upon her. The burden of her sin weighed her down and she longed to find Christ's forgiveness. Then she began to gather together a little class, to meet in her home and persuaded a simple, pious Methodist class-leader to teach. This good man did not fail in urging the anxious Anne to seek and find pardon, without which she could have no peace.

Anne began to think of nothing else. How she longed for peace with God! Despite her yearnings and tears, she could not find it. She felt she was without hope but her father gently pointed her to Christ and assured her that by faith in Him she would be saved. With childlike faith, Anne knelt before God and cast herself on His mercy. Here is her own account of her

---

[214] Eminent Methodist Women. Publ. 1889 by Annie E Keeling.

conversion:

> "Mother!" I exclaimed, "if I do not get my sins pardoned, I shall perish everlastingly!" I went to my own room, knelt down at the bedside, clasped my hands most imploringly, and with streaming eyes said, "O Lord God, I here most solemnly and heartily, with all the faith I know how to use, cast my whole soul at Thy feet, and take the Lord Jesus Christ as my Saviour from this moment, and my Master and portion for time and for eternity, and will henceforth believe I am forgiven for His sake." As I abandoned myself to Him so He gave Himself to me. There was an immediate sense of acceptance. Oh, such a love as never, never had I before conceived![215]

The date was 14th April 1815 and Anne Lutton called that day the commencement of "her happy existence." She was twenty-four years old. "I praised the Lord with a loud voice; I was too happy to keep silence," she said.[216] But that was only the beginning of something remarkable, as we shall see later.

Roman Catholic

There is presently no Catholic Church in the village. Royalists burnt an old church in 1742 but there are no records of it being within the village. With no building, Mass was held under a tree but in 1812 a church was built at Stoney Batter. The Marquess of Downshire had generously granted the land and on 14th September he performed the opening ceremony and laid the

---

[215] Memorials of a Consecrated life by Anne Lutton. Publ. 1882.
[216] Eminent Methodist Women. Publ. 1889 by Annie E Keeling.

first stone. The Marquess was the great grandson of the man who gave the land for St. John's in Moira. A second stone was laid "by the united hands of the Catholic, Protestant and Presbyterian Clergy present."[217] The chapel was a stone whitewashed building with a painting of a crucifix over the altar.

There is an interesting comparison between that new chapel and the much larger St. John's Parish building. According to one survey, the St. Colman's chapel held one thousand people while the church held only four hundred! There were no seats in the chapel but forms were used, so they clearly enjoyed closer fellowship! The building cost was £1,000 but the priest received no salary.[218]

Early in the twentieth century the church was renovated and in 1967 the building was substantially improved but now has lost some of its late Georgian character. It is relatively rare example of an early nineteenth century pre-emancipation Catholic Church with a T-plan layout.[219]

A Topographical Dictionary of Ireland, 1837 lists Moira and Magheralin, saying "in each of which is a chapel."[220] I suspect that might refer to the church at Kilwarlin. Although known as St. Colman's Kilwarlin, it could also have been known as Moira Chapel. An advertisement published in the Vindicator, Belfast on 22nd January 1842 announces a meeting in the Catholic

---

[217] The Protestant Advocate, Vol. 1. 1813.
[218] Ordnance Survey Memoirs of Ireland Vol 12. Parishes of County Down III 1833-8 Publ. 1992.
[219] Department of the Environment. Historic Building Details. Ref No: HB19/22/057
[220] A Topographical Dictionary of Ireland, 1837.

Chapel Moira to be held on Sunday 30th January. The preacher was Father Matthew, the Apostle Temperance, preaching a Charity sermon to encourage temperance but also to raise funds to help build the chapel in Magheralin.[221] The service was held just thirty years after that new chapel was built. The offering must have been substantial for work on the new chapel in Magheralin began later that year and was completed in October 1844 at a cost of about £2,400.[222]

Several other places of worship opened in the village in the last century.

Brethren

A small Brethren hall built in 1930 sits on the Old Kilmore Road. They hold a gospel service on Sunday evenings.

Pentecostal

Pastor David Goudy, who at the time of writing is still the Pastor, founded the church in October 1979. The church meets in what was formerly the Market House built by the Bateson family. The upper floor of the building that had been the Tempo Ballroom is now a place where God is worshipped. Although modernised on the inside to provide suitable church accommodation, it still retains much of its exterior and is a

---

[221] British Newspaper Archive (www.britishnewspaperarchive.co.uk) The Vindicator, Belfast Saturday Morning January 22nd 1842.
[222] Magheralin – an historical notebook by T.N. Hamilton. (from Review –Journal of Craigavon Historical Society Vol. 2 No.2.)

listed building of historical and architectural value.

Baptist

A church was formed in 1987, meeting initially in the Orange Hall and later in a portable building on the site where the present building stands. It was erected in stages beginning in 1995 and the sanctuary completed a couple of years later.

The writer is a Baptist and is fascinated to discover that at one time there was a "Baptist" witness in the area. Andrew Wyke was a Particular Calvinistic Baptist, sometimes disparagingly called Anabaptist. He had come to Ireland with Cromwell and was first appointed in 1651 as commonwealth minister to preach the Gospel at Lisnagarvey. He was not popular in some circles and one writer at that time described him as "void of human learning, never educated in that way, but a tradesman and imprudent."[223] George Rawdon at first held a different view, saying, "a rare treat, a most powerful preacher, so that the congregation at Lisnegarvy[224] is very great, and look upon it as a very great mercy and providence."[225] Three years later Rawdon's wife disagreed and perhaps that is why Rawdon was later influential in having him replaced. Wyke went on to preach in Dromore, Lurgan, Tullylish and Donaghcloney.

In 1659, in response to a petition from the English residents of Magheralin, the Government controversially sent him to preach in that parish too. Some years later he and other non-

---

[223] Quoted in Like an Evening Gone by Eileen Cousins B.A.
[224] Lisnagarvey historically had a variety of spellings.
[225] Quoted by Very Rev. W P Carmody, M.A., In Lisburn Cathedral and its past rectors.

conformists were imprisoned in Carrickfergus. Wyke was eventually forced back to England and it was to be nearly 350 years before a "Baptist" witness returned to the Moira area.

Other Christian influences in the village history

Sunday Schools

Back in the early nineteenth century there were Sunday Schools in the village and area. On 23rd October 1814, a letter was written;

> Dear Sir, I have great pleasure to send you an account of the prosperous state of our Sunday School Institution, which under God's providence has done considerable good in the neighbourhood. About five miles for Hillsborough a Sunday School has been established in the town of Moira, under the care of some charitable Ladies, and is reported to be in a very prosperous state." The following year, the writer was grateful to the society for the books sent but they were "far from adequate to our wants; as the number of scholars have (sic) increased to above two hundred and still likely to increase. We beg a further supply."[226]

Moravians

The Moira area was visited by a number of well-known Gospel

---

[226] Report of the Hibernian Sunday School Society 1810-1837.

preachers in the eighteenth century. George Whitefield[227] preached in Lisburn, the Maze and Lurgan in July 1751. He must have passed through the village but there is no record of him preaching that day in Moira.

John Cennick, the Moravian evangelist and hymn writer, frequently walked from Dublin for a preaching tour in Ulster and a favourite stopping place was Ballinderry. On the 7th February 1751, when there was a dreadful snowfall, he preached in Portmore stables to about one thousand people. On Sunday 7th March he preached at Crumlin and that afternoon at Portmore to around five hundred people. Violet Best writes:

> On the 1st December 1751 Mr Moore, who resided at the Manor House of Lord Conway at Portmore, showed Cennick, after hospitable entertainment, a large hall ninety feet long and twenty feet wide which would hold eight hundred people, another, larger still, capable of containing nearly two thousand persons, also a third, all of which he placed at his disposal. (Portmore Castle was famed for its ivory tables and marble halls, and even the extensive stables had marble fittings).[228]

Here he preached the next day and the throng was so great that fears were entertained about the walls giving way. He remarks:

> I never remember such a thirst for the Word of Life, though the country is not very populous yet we have astonishingly large congregations, people crowding in from Moira and beyond.[229]

---

[227] Also spelled Whitfield.
[228] A History of Ballinderry Moravian Church 1750 - 2000 by Violet Best © Violet Best 2000. Published by Ballinderry Moravian Church to mark 250 years of Moravian work.
[229] Ibid.

But rather strangely there are no records of either Cennick or Whitefield preaching in Moira.

On 20th May 1754 a Moravian settlement was founded at Kilwarlin. The Earl of Hillsborough was most supportive. But by 1834 the buildings were in ruins and membership was in single figures. That changed when Basil Patras Zula accepted a call to serve the Kilwarlin congregation. He was originally from Greece. A new church was built and opened in March 1835. Twenty-six new members joined the congregation on the same day and the numbers gradually grew to more than two hundred.

Zula always lived in fear of reprisals by former adversaries, whether real or imagined. He rebuilt the Kilwarlin Manse and created a number of means of escape, including two doors in all rooms on the ground floor and two staircases to the upper floor. He built another small room with a trap door in the floor giving access to a secret hiding place.

Zula never had to use these and died naturally in Dublin on 4th October 1844. His body was brought back to Kilwarlin for burial. His widow ran a boarding school for "select young ladies" and died in 1858.

A very interesting feature of Kilwarlin Moravian Church is the landscaped grounds that Zula built to represent the terrain of the ancient Battle of Thermopylae in which the Spartan army saved Athens from attack by the Persians. Most of that landscaping still remains and is listed as one of the historic gardens in Parks and Gardens UK.

John Wesley

John Wesley paid his first of many visits to Ulster in July 1756 and during that visit he came to Moira. Anne Lutton who grew up in Moira said:

> One day in the year 1756, the Earl of Moira sent a servant to the clergyman to request the key of the church, so that the Rev. John Wesley might preach to the people. The clergyman declined in giving the key, and was accustomed during the course of a long life, to boast in company that, even to oblige a nobleman, he would not tolerate Methodists. The Earl was greatly annoyed at the Rector's refusal, but determined that nothing should prevent Mr Wesley from preaching; so he sent the bellman through the town, to summon all the people to the lawn before the Castle, and Mr Wesley stood on the top of a long flight of steps before the grand entrance hall and preached to the people.[230]

In his journals, Wesley describes preaching in Lisburn on the evening of Monday 26th July 1756 to "seceders, old self-conceited Presbyterians, new-light men, Moravians, Cameronians and formal churchmen; it is a miracle of miracles if any here bring forth fruit to perfection." He then describes the countryside between Lisburn and Moira as he rode to Lurgan where he preached in the Market house that evening and again the next day, Wednesday 28th July, when he says he had the largest congregation since he left Cork. Although Wesley does not record the visit to Moira, it is clear he passed through here on 27th July and almost certainly is the occasion Anne Lutton describes and should not be confused, as is often

---

[230] "Memorials of a Consecrated life" by Anne Lutton. Publ. 1882.

the case, with his next visit.

The Earl of Moira, who was so welcoming to the Maralin priests, welcomed Wesley also! In fact Wesley carried a letter from the Earl of Moira that was to see him through difficulties he faced in Monaghan in 1762.[231]

Another example of the Earl's openness to spiritual matters and to Methodist preachers comes from 1759. Thomas Seccombe, a Cornishman, was one of Wesley's preachers. His father had disinherited him, but he came to Ireland as a Methodist preacher in 1755. He was a very powerful preacher of the Gospel. Charles Dixon says:
> His preaching was such as I never heard before, for his word was with power. It made me cry out in bitterness of soul - what must I do to be saved.[232]

Thomas took ill with consumption while in this area in 1759. Rawdon took him into his house and treated him as his son. Seccombe asked that the Methodists might come and receive his dying benediction, so it seems possible a Methodist congregation was already gathered in the village or district. Lord Rawdon was present and after Seccombe had addressed the people he lay down and passed away. Rawdon sent an account of his death to a nobleman friend in London adding, "Now, my Lord, find me if you can a man that will die like a Methodist!"[233]

---

[231] Wesley's Journal May 1762.
[232] Narrative by Charles Dixon of Cumberland County, Nova Scotia September 1773 recorded in Discoveries of America: Personal Accounts of British Emigrants to North America during the revolutionary era by Barbara DeWolfe.
[233] Atmore's Memorial, pp.379-80; Crookshank's Methodism in Ireland.

I sometimes wonder what the Earl's new wife Elizabeth (married just four years) thought of Wesley. Her mother was very sympathetic to the Gospel witness and, as a young woman, Elizabeth had listened to many famous preachers of that day, including John Wesley. A biographer tells us Lady Huntingdon's desire for her family was that they

> would one day follow her religious sentiments. It was a battle she lost with her eldest daughter Elizabeth who in 1752 moved out of her influence by marrying an Irish Peer, Lord Rawdon …. It is clear a principal motive for Elizabeth marrying was to escape her mother's religious dominance. Mother and daughter reportedly never met again and there was apparently no contact at all between them during the last 20 years of Lady Huntingdon's life.[234]

Indeed, Elizabeth confessed to her brother that she had married to get away from home and said "I lived a life of duty with my mother. I own it grew wearisome at length and it was a strong inducement to my marrying. My situation in Ireland is happy – extremely so, in separating us so far asunder."[235]

Faith Cook quotes from a letter, which was written by Lady Huntingdon to Charles Wesley in March 1752:

> I am sure it will be a great pleasure to you to hear that Lady Betty was yesterday married to a most sensible and worthy man, Lord Moira of Ireland. He has a very great fortune and above all a man disposed to great seriousness and which, from the respect I have for him,

---

[234] The Countess of Huntingdon's Connection by Alan Harding 2003.
[235] Lady Rawdon to Lord Huntingdon, 13th December 1752 – Huntingdon Library.

I trust will end in true and exemplary piety.[236]

Despite all her protestations, Lady Moira was not totally disinterested in religion and perhaps some of her upbringing was still influencing her. At one point in correspondence with the Bishop Percy of Dromore, she asked him to give the living of Moira to an Irish clergyman. She wrote of "the inferior clergy in England, being certainly a less polished set than those in Ireland," and "between ourselves, my Lord" hints at some delinquency of the Rector of Seagoe.[237] God was at work in Lady Moira and was using John Wesley.[238]

In 1760 Wesley visited Moira a second time. He was apparently a guest of the family at Moira House. (Wesley visited Ireland on twenty-one separate occasions between 1747 and 1789.) Wesley describes the occasion in his journal:

> Thursday 1st May 1760.
>
> I rode to Moira. Soon after twelve, standing on a tombstone near the church, I called a considerable number of people to "know God and Jesus Christ whom He had sent." We were just opposite to the Earl of Moira's house, the best furnished of any I have seen in Ireland. It stands on a hill with a large avenue in front, bounded by the church on the opposite hill. The other three sides are covered with orchards, gardens and woods, in which are walks of various kinds.

---

[236] Quoted by Faith Cooke in Selina, Countess of Huntingdon. The Banner of Truth Trust. Publ. 2001.
[237] The Gentleman's Magazine 1907.
[238] In a letter by Wesley to Lady Moira, he appears to believe she was a backslider and urges her to return to trust in the Lord. See appendix 2.

In Journal No. XII, Wesley writes of a third visit just over a week later on Monday 12th May 1760; that morning he had preached in Ballymena and his comments were;

> I preached in the market house to a large concourse of people and God was there of a truth. I found no such spirit in any congregation since I left Dublin.

Presumably it was in the afternoon that he rode into Moira. A limestone pillar at the front of the Moira Church is said to be near the spot where John Wesley preached. And what had he to say about Moira people? One sentence … "I preached to a very civil congregation but there is no life in them."

Knowing how Wesley preached, he was not merely talking about the people of Moira being passive. His words echo his passion to see his hearers respond to the message of the gospel and come to know God personally. Wesley's favourite definition of Christianity[239] was taken from the title of a seventeenth century book by Henry Scougal, "The life of God in the soul of man." He thought that people of Moira had no such life. Those were to be Wesley's last words about the people of Moira.

But he still had deep concerns for the residents in the Castle and for Lady Rawdon in Particular. She must have weighed heavily upon his heart as he travelled west.

Wesley was now fifty-seven years old, yet the next day he rode fifty-five miles to Coothill in Monaghan. He says, "My horse was thoroughly tired. However with much difficulty, partly riding, and partly walking, about eight in the evening I reached Coothill." No mention of how tired he was! He preached when he

---

[239] Quoted by Dr Martyn Lloyd-Jones in "Saved in eternity" page 128.

arrived and the next morning at 5.00 am and at 11.00 am in the Market house. Then with a fresh horse he rode to Belturbet! By 18th May he was in Sligo and wrote from there to Lord Moira about his spiritual communications with Lady Moira.

> My Lord, I have taken the liberty to speak to Lady Rawdon all that was in my heart, and doubt not that your Lordship will second it on every proper occasion. The late awful providence I trust will not pass over without a suitable improvement. God has spoken aloud, and happy are they that hear and understand His voice.

It was Wesley's belief that Lady Moira once believed on Jesus Christ for salvation but he had great concerns now for her spiritual condition. A few months earlier he had written to Lady Moira.[240] His words to her included this challenge.

> Did not your love of God grow cold? Did not you measure back your steps to earth again? Did not your love of the world revive? Where are you now? Full of faith? Looking into the holiest, and seeing Him that is invisible? Does your heart now glow with love to Him who is daily pouring His benefits upon you? Are not you a lover of pleasure more than a lover of God?

But in that letter from Sligo, Wesley also had some concerns to share with Lord Moira himself.

> In one respect I have been under some apprehension on your Lordship's account also. I have been afraid lest you should exchange the simplicity of the gospel for a philosophical religion. O my Lord, why should we go one step farther than this, "We love Him because He first

---

[240] See the content of Wesley's letter to Lady Moira in appendix 2.

loved us?" I am Your Lordship's most obedient servant.[241]

Rev. John Wesley was in the area on several occasions during the following years, no doubt to continue to urge those in the Castle to seek after God. He passed this way on 26th June 1762 and 14th June 1773 en route to Lurgan from Lisburn. On 6th July 1771 he "spent two hours very agreeably in Mayra" on his journey between Ballinderry and Newry. He visited Ballinderry on several occasions between 1771 and 1778. On Friday 5th July 1771 he dined in Ballinderry House with the good man, his wife, one son and five daughters, all he found "walking in the light of God's countenance." There were about fifty members of the Methodist society in Ballinderry at the time. A much larger crowd however gathered around the house to hear Wesley preach from an upstairs window. Wesley writes of that evening:

> Afterward I prayed with an ancient woman; while a little girl, her grandchild, kneeling beside me, was all in tears and said, O grandmamma, have you no sins to cry for as well as me?[242]

It seems God did a mighty work among children in Ballinderry for Wesley tells of another visit there on 19th July 1773 when he declared "the grace of our Lord Jesus Christ. Many of them experienced this and many felt their wants; several children in particular."

---

[241] "Letters" Volume 4. For more on Lord Moira and his spiritual awareness, see Appendix 2.
[242] Rev. J Wesley's Journal. July 1773.

But despite him being in the vicinity of Moira or even likely to have passed through Moira quite a number of times over the following eighteen years, there is no record of him ever again preaching in the village.

Anne Lutton

Anne Lutton was to become a mighty tool in the hand of God in Moira and far beyond. Not long after she was converted, her mother died. She and her father left Donaghcloney to return to Moira, to a house across the street from where they first lived. Anne took on responsibility for running the home but she also had a growing conviction that she should be "proclaiming to her fellow-countrywomen the love of the Saviour, which was so inexpressibly dear to her own heart."[243]

Despite her great learning, Anne was a shy, retiring woman, yet she resolved to speak for her Lord. When she did, "Roman Catholics as well as Protestants, the intellectual and the wealthy as well as those in humble stations, flocked to hear her, at first perhaps from curiosity, but afterwards from love and reverence."[244]

She was resolute in excluding all men from her meetings, believing that as a woman she should preach to only women.
> Women preachers were seen as itinerant supporters in virgin territory ... and were never accepted as regular preachers to settled congregations. They generally

---

[243] Born to Serve: women and evangelical religion Ch. 7. Evangelical Protestantism in Ulster Society 1740-1890.
[244] History of Methodism in Ireland. Vol. III. by C H Crookshank, M.A.

confined themselves to preaching to their own sex. But by the 1830s male followers of Anne Lutton were reduced to dressing in women's clothing in a vain attempt to hear her preach.[245]

Miss Lutton posted keen-eyed gentlemen at the chapel door while she was conducting a service and on one occasion, when she suspected a man to be present, she paused until the intruder was expelled. A minister once hid in the stairwell to hear her but when discovered he was allowed to stay, "respect for his cloth preventing his extrusion." One young man dressed up as a woman and his disguise was obviously very good, for he gained entrance to the meeting. But through Anne's ministry God spoke to him to turn to God and serve Him. He owned up and told how he was converted. Anne was encouraged to relax the rule she had laid down but even this event would not make her change her conviction that she was called to preach to women only. Her ministry widened and she preached often far beyond Moira in such places as Belfast, Banbridge, Scarva, Tullymore and Bryansford. She is regarded as the founder of Methodism in Moira.

In the Society at Moira, there were men who were mighty prayer warriors and preachers and most faithful class leaders. Rev. Samuel Nicholson tells of remarkable meetings in Moira when he was a boy. He speaks of prayer meetings of great power, where "good, plain men of God poured out their souls' desires to the Lord for their families and the young," and of "the Holy Ghost falling upon old and young, mightily convincing

---

[245] Born to Serve: women and evangelical religion Ch. 7. Evangelical Protestantism in Ulster Society 1740-1890.

of sin, and making plain the path of duty."[246]

He speaks also of numerous and striking conversions in Moira and describes his own conversion.

> Mr Jonny Armstrong was the preacher. He preached short and earnestly, and had great power in prayer. After the sermon, several old men witnessed for Christ first and then followed many others. In a short time, the speaking could not be continued. Men and women rushed forward to the communion rails, weeping and crying out for mercy. In a few minutes, the rails were crowded with penitents. I was in the gallery and saw the people weeping below and heard their cries. Tears of penitence began to flow from my eyes. It was impressed upon my mind that if I would go down to the rails and join the seekers, I should find peace; all my sins should be forgiven me.
>
> I walked down the stairs at once and the burden of guilt upon my heart seemed to get lighter at every step. I kneeled beside the others in heart distress. I was but eleven years of age and had not entered into any open, wilful sin but I was in great distress. No doubt, temptation came from Satan to frighten me from seeking pardon. Soon my mind was directed by the Holy Spirit to the Saviour upon the Cross, nailed there, and dying for me. I thought I saw Jesus in agony and blood transfixed to the accursed tree. It was with my mind's eye. As I gazed, the question arose in my mind "What led Jesus to that cross to suffer and to die?" The reply

---

[246] Irish Methodist reminiscences; being mainly memorials of the life and labours of the Rev. S Nicholson by Edward Thomas. Publ. 1889.

suggested was, "Not to send you to hell, but bring you to heaven. He came there to die for your sin; and in order to pardon your sin and prepare you for heaven." In that moment I believed on the Lord Jesus Christ; and my sins were pardoned and I was reconciled to God. Oh how happy I was! I stood up and I told the people what God had done for my soul. Shame and fear alike forsook me. Afterwards I felt as though all things were changed. Nature itself seemed new and I rejoiced with a joy unspeakable and full of glory. The meeting that day lasted about seven hours.

The conversions of young and old numbered between forty and fifty. The two preachers left the meeting so hoarse from talking to penitents that they could not continue speaking. Several little boys, who were converted on that occasion, became preachers of the gospel in different Methodist Societies. I had two miles and a half of a walk home. I was so happy. [247]

The Jewish preacher

John O'Donovan tells another interesting story from Moira. He travelled this area on behalf of the Ordnance Survey authorities: Extract from a letter dated - Moira, Wednesday, 27th March 1834.

> After having wandered all day through the parish of Magheralin, I returned to Moira about 5.00 pm much

---

[247] Irish Methodist reminiscences; being mainly memorials of the life and labours of the Rev. S. Nicholson by Edward Thomas. Publ. 1889.

fatigued. I went to my bedroom and attempted to write, but sleep overcoming me, I stretched myself on the bed, and fell into a sound repose, during which there was an absence of dreams and thought from my mind. I awoke - looked at my watch. It was six o'clock! But whether six o'clock in the morning or evening, I could not tell. I started up, walked out, and being attracted by a semi-circle of people standing at the sheltry (sic) side of Moira market house, I went down to them. Standing on chair, I saw a venerable old man with a beard hanging down to the middle button of his waistcoat, repeating aloud one of the psalms of David. His long bushy beard, his Abrahamic countenance, and his thick pronunciation of consonants characterized him a Jew. I gazed on him with wonder, thinking I would have an opportunity of hearing him preach the Law of Moses, but I soon learned that he had abandoned the old cause of his tribe, and is now going about preaching the morality and doctrine of Jesus of Nazareth.
Yours truly,
JOHN O'DONOVAN
Moira[248]

The Evangelical Revival

The great spiritual awakening of the 1859 revival across Northern Ireland seems largely to have by-passed Moira, despite years of spiritual blessing early in the century. I can find no record that there was any great increase in attendance or expansion of buildings in local churches as happened in

---

[248] Dr. O'Donovan's letters are preserved in the Royal Irish Academy, Dublin.

communities all around us.

The gallery in St. John's Parish Church was added around 1871 to allow for more to attend church. It is said this increase was due to the expanding households of the various landed gentry and aristocratic families like the Rawdons, Warings and Berwicks.[249] However it is quite likely that most of the gentry had moved away by then; the Rawdons certainly had. Perhaps the Revival ready did have some impact in the parish.

Congregational returns from some Presbyterian Churches the following year make very interesting reading. Statistics show remarkable increases at communion and other services in places such as Dundrod with around one hundred more at communion; Donaghcloney with fifty more; Dromore with one hundred more. Many congregations added additional comments to their statistical returns, describing wonderful blessing such as many conversions or describing the co-operation of other denominations or of dramatic changes in society. But Moira reported that there were ten new communicants and made no comment.[250]

At the same time, in Lurgan and Magheralin, God was moving mightily. Queen Street Methodist Church in Lurgan saw one thousand people converted in 1859. The Rector of Lurgan, Rev. Thomas Knox, said in 1860:

> Congregations in church and in cottage lectures, greatly increased. The increase is composed in a great measure, of young men and women who were formerly indifferent to spiritual matters …. We require

___

[249] Moira – a historical handbook Rev. Canon C R J Rudd.
[250] The year of grace by Rev. William Gibson. Publ. 1860.

> accommodation for five hundred more, at least, in the church which I hope will be ready for them in about eighteen months.

The Rector of Magheralin wrote on 16th April 1860,

> There is a hungering and thirsting after the Word of God, as is clearly evidenced by the full attendance on every means of grace. My church was built to accommodate five hundred.[251] Yesterday morning there were five hundred and thirty-one ….. Before this awakening (about three years ago) I commenced an evening service in the village; but after some time I discontinued it because I could get no attendance. Now, had I a service every evening in the week, I could command a meeting. Beside all this, morality, in every sense of the word, is the order of the day. The change indeed is a mighty one.[252]

For reasons known only to the secret, sovereign purposes of God, Moira sat in much spiritual darkness for many years. Great preachers moved among us; great blessing fell in communities around us; yet Moira appears to have had lengthy periods when it was largely untouched by the Spirit of God. But God builds His church and over the years faithful preachers have served the Lord here in the churches of our village.

The message of Wesley and others, calling men to "know God and Jesus Christ whom He has sent" is still resounding in this community. And I count it a privilege to have ministered with them here in this generation when, I think it is fair to say, the Gospel is more widely and more faithfully preached in the

---

[251] The church had been built only fifteen years earlier.
[252] The year of Grace: A history of the Ulster Revival of 1859 by William Gibson.

village and community than in any previous generation.

Their footprints and ours

What a significant place Moira would be if only the Castle and demesne had survived like other grand houses in the National Trust collection. How delightful it would be, if after a long day in the city, you could drive through Moira without traffic jams. Of if when you got home you could eat a leisurely tea in a long quiet back garden surrounded only by fruit trees and the quiet hum of the honey bees.

Today the gardens and meadows are filled with mortgaged houses and apartments, the street is jammed with stressed commuters and life is so very hectic.

It is tempting to look in the rear-view mirror of life to see days long gone and think of how much better those days appear. Yet were we to retrace those footprints to a simpler life, we would not want to spend too long there.

Thankfully, while the demesne is only a shadow of its former glory, two centuries after the castle was demolished it is a place to unwind and tread on footprints of the past. More recent improvements to the demesne have greatly enhanced the experience of locals and visitors. With over forty acres of parkland including beautiful walkways, award-winning rose beds, picnic sites, play areas and sport facilities, it is a space for all ages to enjoy the great outdoors.

The canal is no longer navigable but the towpath is another haven from a hectic lifestyle, attracting walkers, cyclists, bird-watchers and photographers. As you walk where labourers sweated to dig channels and where heavy horses hauled barges you can float away from the pressures of life for a while.

To enter some village restaurants and coffee shops, inns and older church buildings is to step back in time. Next time take a moment to think of those who lived there, worked there, worshipped there and who have left their footprints over Moira. Even with the requirements of twenty first century commerce and infrastructure, the careful blending of the contemporary with the historic should ensure Moira continues to be a desirable place to live, work or visit for generations to come.

Hopefully, having learned about places we walk past so often, we will enjoy Moira a little more. And having looked back at fading footprints, let us be careful how we tread, for perhaps a hundred years from now someone will write a history of Moira. What will they write about us in this generation? What footprints are we leaving?

Footprints Found

As the first edition of this book was about to go to print in the summer of 2018, something amazing happened. After weeks of unusually dry weather, the yellowing footprint of the foundations of Moira Castle began to appear in the well-kept lawns of the demesne.

For perhaps the first time in almost two hundred years we could see where so much history has been buried. This has sparked a whole new interest in investigating the site and in May 2019 initial archaeological excavations revealed evidence of some footprints left by our illustrious founders. Maybe hoofprints would be a better description, for the dig uncovered the floor of an eighteenth century stable with cobbled surface and waste gullies. There is also evidence of an earlier phase of human settlement so we await with anticipation further revelations in the future and hope to bring those to you in later editions or on the website.

And who knows, we might one day even solve the mystery of the tunnel!

Appendix 1.

Was the Battle of Moira at Moira?

There is an argument propounded that this battle was not fought at Moira at all but near Newry. For further investigation see The Battle of "Magh Rath:" Its True Site Determined by J.W. Hanna, Ulster Journal of Archaeology, First Series, Vol. 4 (1856), pp. 53-61, Published by: Ulster Archaeological Society Stable URL:
http://www.jstor.org/stable/20608792 page count: 9.
Hanna did not believe there was a church near Moira named after Ronan Finn.

However The Right Rev. Monsignor James O'Laverty M.R.I.A. writing in the Ulster Journal of Archaeology Volume XI. Publ. 1905 says that Moira was uniformly accepted as the scene of the Battle until J.W. Hanna published his paper saying the Battle was fought at Crown Rath near Newry.

O'Laverty continues, "One of (Hanna's) principal arguments was that there was not a church of St. Ronan Finn in the district of Moira, though that church is mentioned in the ancient tale. The identification of the site in Kilminiogue and even the name of that townland dispose of that argument."

Further evidence is an entry in the Book of Lecan, a medieval Irish manuscript written between 1397 and 1418, which reads, "Lann Ronain Finn, in Corco Ruishen in Magh Rath."[253]

---

[253] Quoted in Ecclesiastical antiquities of Down, Connor and Dromore by the Rev. William Reeves M.B. M.R.I.A. p.378. Publ. 1847.

Appendix 2.

Full text of the letter by John Wesley to Lady Elizabeth Rawdon. Liverpool 18th March 1760.

Wesley was writing in the context of Lady Moira's mother suffering greatly at the news that Elizabeth's cousin, Earl Ferrers, had murdered his land steward on 18th January 1760. He would be hanged on 5th May, a matter of weeks after this letter was written. Wesley visited Moira Castle was on 1st May and he returned on 12th May. Is it possible he returned, not only to preach one more time in a hard place, but to give spiritual comfort and exhortation to Lady Moira? I am inclined to agree with Faith Cook who suggests that Wesley's letter and the family circumstances, "could well have been the means of turning Elizabeth's heart back once more to the truths she had once professed." [254] However the letter to her husband on 18th May would indicate that at that point Wesley had no assurance that Elizabeth had yet come back to Christ.

> MY LADY,
> It was impossible to see the distress into which your Ladyship was thrown by the late unhappy affair without bearing a part of it, without sympathizing with you. But may we not see God therein? May we not both hear and understand His voice? We must allow it is generally "small and still"; yet He speaks sometimes in the whirlwind. Permit me to speak to your Ladyship with all

---

[254] Selina, Countess of Huntingdon by Faith Cook. The Banner of Truth Trust. Publ. 2001.

freedom; not as to a person of quality, but as to a creature whom the Almighty made for Himself, and one that is in a few days to appear before Him.

You were not only a nominal but a real Christian. You tasted of the powers of the world to come. You knew God the Father had accepted you through His eternal Son, and God the Spirit bore witness with your spirit that you were a child of God. But you fell among thieves, and such as were peculiarly qualified to rob you of your God. Two of these in particular were sensible, learned, well-bred, well-natured, moral men. These did not assault you in a rough, abrupt, offensive manner. No; you would then have armed yourself against them, and have repelled all their attacks. But by soft, delicate, unobserved touches, by pleasing strokes of raillery, by insinuations rather than surly arguments, they by little and little sapped the foundation of your faith - perhaps not only of your living faith, your "evidence of things not seen," but even of your notional. It is well if they left you so much as an assent to the Bible or a belief that Christ is God over all. And what was the consequence of this? Did not your love of God grow cold? Did not you measure back your steps to earth again? Did not your love of the world revive? Even of those poor, low trifles, which in your very childhood you utterly despised?

Where are you now? full of faith? looking into the holiest, and seeing Him that is invisible? Does your heart now glow with love to Him who is daily pouring His benefits upon you? Do you now even desire it? Do you now say (as you did almost twenty years ago)? –
Keep me dead to all below,

Only Christ resolved to know;
Firm, and disengaged, and free,
Seeking all my bliss in Thee?

Is your taste now for heavenly things? Are not you a lover of pleasure more than a lover of God? And oh what pleasure! What is the pleasure of visiting? Of modern conversation? Is there any more reason than religion in it? I wonder what rational appetite does it gratify. Setting religion quite out of the question, I cannot conceive how a woman of sense can relish, should I say? No, but suffer so insipid an entertainment. Oh that the time past may suffice! Is it now not high time that you should awake out of sleep? Now God calls aloud! My dear Lady, now hear the voice of the Son of God, and live! The trouble in which your tender parent is now involved may restore all that reverence for her which could not but be a little impaired while you supposed she was "righteous over-much." Oh how admirably does God lay hold of and "strengthen the things that remain" in you! - your gratitude, your humane temper, your generosity, your filial tenderness! And why is this but to improve every right temper; to free you from all that is irrational or unholy; to make you all that you were - yea, all that you should be; to restore you to the whole image of God?

I am, my Lady,
Yours,
John Wesley.

Printed in Great Britain
by Amazon

Innovations in Teaching History

'The skills imparted by an undergraduate history degree are both timeless and constantly changing. This volume brings together seven innovative examples of how historians of the 18th century are changing pedagogy to meet the challenge of teaching with objects and texts – real, digital and sensational – online and in person. It is essential reading for anyone who thinks seriously about history and how we teach it.'

—Tim Hitchcock, Professor Emeritus of Digital History, University of Sussex, UK

Innovations in Teaching History

Eighteenth-Century Studies in Higher Education

Edited by Ruth Larsen, Alice Marples and Matthew McCormack

UNIVERSITY OF LONDON PRESS

Available to purchase in print or download for free at https://uolpress.co.uk

First published 2024 by
University of London Press
Senate House, Malet St, London WC1E 7HU

© the Authors 2024

The right of the authors to be identified as authors of this Work has been asserted by them in accordance with sections 77 and 78 of the Copyright, Designs and Patents Act 1988.

This book is published under a Creative Commons Attribution-NonCommercial-NoDerivatives 4.0 International (CC BY-NC-ND 4.0) license.

Please note that third-party material reproduced here may not be published under the same license as the rest of this book. If you would like to reuse any third-party material not covered by the book's Creative Commons license, you will need to obtain permission from the copyright holder.

A CIP catalogue record for this book is available from the British Library.

ISBN 978-1-908590-61-9 (hardback)
ISBN 978-1-908590-60-2 (paperback)
ISBN 978-1-908590-62-6 (.epub)
ISBN 978-1-908590-63-3 (.pdf)
ISBN 978-1-914477-69-0 (.html)

DOI https://doi.org/10.14296/yypo7070

Cover image: Scholars at a lecture [graphic], 1736. William Hogarth. Courtesy of the Lewis Walpole Library, Yale University.

Cover design for the University of London Press by Hayley Warnham.
Book design by Nigel French.
Text set by Westchester Publishing Services UK in Source Sans Pro, designed by Paul D. Hunt.

In memory of Arthur Burns (1963–2023)

Contents

List of figures	ix
List of tables	x
Notes on contributors	xi
Acknowledgements	xiv
Introduction Ruth Larsen, Alice Marples and Matthew McCormack	1

Part I Digital history

1. Letting students loose in the archive: reflections on teaching 'At the Court of King George: Exploring the Royal Archives' at King's College London   19
   Arthur Burns and Oliver C. Walton

2. Introducing Australian students to British history and research methods via digital sources   37
   Simon Burrows and Rebekah Ward

Part II History in the classroom

3. Sensational pedagogy: teaching the sensory eighteenth century   67
   William Tullett

4. Let's talk about sex: 'BAD' approaches to teaching the histories of gender and sexualities   87
   Ruth Larsen

5. Engaging students with political history: citizenship in the (very) long eighteenth century   109
   Matthew McCormack

Part III Material culture and museum collections

6. Beyond 'great white men': teaching histories of science, empire and heritage through collections   127
   Alice Marples

7. Teaching eighteenth-century classical reception through university museum collections   151
   Lenia Kouneni

   Index   177

List of figures

Figure 1.1: The contents of the Georgian Papers at Windsor. 23

Figure 6.1: Fold-out from Charles White, *An Account of the Regular Gradation in Man, and in Different Animals and Vegetables* (London: Dilly, 1799). Wellcome Collection, Public Domain Mark. 134

Figure 6.2: Photograph of Manchester Museum Collections encounter. Image credit: Alice Marples. 138

Figure 7.1: Upper College Hall, North Street, St Andrews, looking east, c. 1910. Courtesy of the University of St Andrews Libraries and Museums, ID: StAU-BPMus-1. 153

Figure 7.2: Upper College Hall, North Street, St Andrews, looking west, c. 1910. Courtesy of the University of St Andrews Libraries and Museums, ID: StAU-BPMus-2. 154

Figure 7.3: Room and desk arrangement. Image credit: Lenia Kouneni. 157

Figure 7.4: Students looking at impronte (plaster cameos). Image credit: Lenia Kouneni. 159

Figure 7.5: James Tassie, medallion portrait of Lieutenant General Robert Melville, vitreous paste, 1791. Courtesy of the University of St Andrews Libraries and Museums, ID: HC982. 161

Figure 7.6: Screenshot of Exhibit (https://exhibit.so/exhibits/6YwhPoBWivhGsLXyO2Dw) featuring Thomas Moody, 'Journal of a tour through Switzerland and Italy in 1822', with twenty-four watercolour illustrations by Joseph Axe Sleap. Courtesy of the University of St Andrews Libraries and Museums, ID: msD919.M7E22 (ms229). 165

List of tables

Table 2.1: List of research method podcasts. 40

Table 2.2: Assessment grid for project proposal exercise. 44

Table 2.3: Weekly reminder, week 9. 46

Table 2.4: Student enrolments and completion rates. 52

Table 2.5: Grades in 'Britain in the Age of Botany Bay, 1760–1815' (BABB) compared with 'Enlightenment and Revolution', 2013/15. 52

Table 2.6: Student Feedback on Unit returns for 'Britain in the Age of Botany Bay, 1760–1815' (BABB) in 2014 and 2016 compared with average returns for Western Sydney University (WSU) and School of Humanities and Communication Arts (SHCA). 55

Notes on contributors

Arthur Burns was Professor of Modern British History at King's College London and Academic Director of the Georgian Papers programme. He was Literary Director and Vice President of the Royal Historical Society and Honorary Fellow of the Historical Association. He led three major digital history projects and published widely on Hanoverian and Victorian religious history.

Simon Burrows is Professor in History and Digital Humanities at Western Sydney University, Australia and previously worked at the universities of Waikato (New Zealand) and Leeds (United Kingdom). A digital innovator in research and teaching, he has since 2007 led the award-winning 'French Book Trade in Enlightenment Europe' database project. Simon has convened a series of events which have contributed to the development of digital humanities locally and internationally, including the first 'Digitizing Enlightenment' symposium (2016) and the global online 'Building Digital Humanities' symposium (2022). He has led the Western Sydney's Digital Humanities Research Group since 2016. Simon's most recent book is *Digitizing Enlightenment: Digital Humanities and the Transformation of Eighteenth-Century Studies* (2020), which he co-edited with Glenn Roe.

Lenia Kouneni is Lecturer at the School of Art History, University of St Andrews, where she offers modules on classical reception and Byzantine art. Her primary research interests are centred on classical reception, women travellers and the history of archaeology. She has published various articles on late medieval transcultural contacts in the Mediterranean and edited a collection of essays on *The Legacy of Antiquity: New Perspectives in the Reception of the Classical World* (2013). She is currently working on a project to uncover and contextualise the excavation of the palace of Byzantine emperors in Istanbul during 1930–50.

Ruth Larsen is Programme Leader for undergraduate history programmes at the University of Derby, where she teaches on a number of different modules that explore eighteenth-century history, gender history, the history of the body and material culture studies. She has published a number of articles and chapters on the history of the country house, aristocratic women and the history of letter writing. She is on the steering committee of the East Midlands Centre for History Teaching and Learning.

Alice Marples is Research and Postgraduate Development Manager at the British Library and a historian of science and medicine in Britain and its colonial networks, c. 1650–1850. Her work focuses on the collection and management of manuscript, material and human resources across institutions and international networks. She is interested in the connections between science, state and commerce and how these can be used to disrupt traditional histories of scientific practice, knowledge creation and public culture from the early modern period to the present day. Her first book, *The Transactioneer: Hans Sloane and the Rise of Public Natural History in Eighteenth-Century Britain*, is forthcoming with Johns Hopkins University Press.

Matthew McCormack is Professor of History and Head of the Graduate School at the University of Northampton. He has published widely on British history, his most recent book being *Citizenship and Gender in Britain, 1688–1928* (Routledge, 2019). He has taught a range of modules on British history and also on historical methods, research skills and historiography. He is currently President of the British Society for Eighteenth-Century Studies.

William Tullett is Lecturer in Early Modern History at the University of York. He is a sensory historian who has published widely on smell and sound in eighteenth-century Britain, including his first monograph, *Smell in Eighteenth-Century England: A Social Sense* (Oxford University Press, 2019), and his second book, *Smell and the Past: Noses, Archives, Narratives* (Bloomsbury, 2023). His other pedagogical publications include a recent collaboration with Odeuropa colleagues on an online module, 'Knowing by Sensing: How to Teach the History of Smell', for the *American Historical Review*. His chapter refers to his time teaching at Anglia Ruskin University, Cambridge.

Oliver C. Walton taught 'At the Court of King George' with Arthur Burns in his capacity as George III Project Coordinator and Curator, Historical Manuscripts at the Royal Archives, Windsor Castle. He has extensive experience in teaching with manuscript sources both in relation to this project and also his role as Researcher for the Prince Albert Society and the German Historical Institute project: 'Common Heritage: The Collections of Windsor and Coburg'. His primary research interest lies in British naval history.

Rebekah Ward is a sessional academic at Western Sydney University. Her research focuses on the history of print culture, particularly the twentieth-century book trade. Rebekah's doctorate, which blended traditional archival research with digital humanities approaches, explored how Angus & Robertson (the largest Australian publishing house) used book reviews as a promotional tool. She has published in *Australian Literary Studies*, *Publishing Studies* and *History* and presents widely on publishing history, book reviewing and the digital humanities.

Acknowledgements

This is a book about teaching history, but the process of it coming into being has a history of its own. It partly arose from a panel at the 2019 International Society for Eighteenth-Century Congress in Edinburgh on 'Innovations in Teaching the Long Eighteenth Century', featuring Alice alongside Sally Holloway and Peter D'Sena. Matthew was in the audience, and he and Ruth wanted to run an event on teaching the eighteenth century under the aegis of the East Midlands Centre for History Teaching and Learning (EMC), which at the time was hosted by Ruth's department at the University of Derby. They therefore joined forces with Alice to organise a workshop in June 2020: the EMC agreed to fund it, for which we are grateful. The COVID-19 pandemic meant that the conference had to move online, and we had interesting discussions about online teaching, which many of us were grappling with for the first time. Two years later we finally managed to have an in-person event at the University of Northampton, where the authors and other colleagues gathered for a workshop discussing the chapter drafts.

We would like to thank the authors for their excellent chapters and everyone who participated in the workshops for their contributions. As we were preparing the final manuscript in October 2023 we received the sad news that Arthur Burns had passed away. Arthur had always been upfront about his illness and nevertheless participated in the workshops and the writing process with his characteristic generosity, insight and good humour. He was a big part of this project, and cared very deeply about the teaching of history, so we would like to dedicate the volume to his memory.

—Ruth Larsen, Alice Marples and Matthew McCormack

Introduction

Ruth Larsen, Alice Marples and Matthew McCormack

In recent years, the eighteenth century has been a notable growth area in historical studies and related disciplines. This has not always been the case. A generation or two ago, its study was rather neglected, as it was sandwiched between two centuries that dominated scholarly attention because of their constitutional and social upheavals. Historians of the period therefore tended to work with scholars from other disciplines under the banner of 'eighteenth-century studies'. This led to the creation of a rich field that was often interdisciplinary and theoretically informed. The field today is thriving, and scholars working on the eighteenth century engage with very current topics such as colonialism, material culture, emotions, sexualities and ecology, among many others.[1] In particular, there is now more focus on the global aspects of the century, which are essential to understanding the period and its legacies. Given that the eighteenth century is often regarded as a foundational one for the modern world, much of this research has an overt contemporary relevance.

The eighteenth century is now widely taught in university history departments, but it also presents challenges. Students will typically not have encountered it as part of their school curriculum and they may have preconceptions that are off-putting.[2] The source material can appear long-winded or, in manuscript form, illegible. Much of this source material is now online, so students require digital skills to evaluate it, which they may not already have. The theoretical nature of some of the critical writings can make it challenging to teach, especially at undergraduate level. And undergraduates schooled in a single discipline (such as they typically are in the UK) can find the interdisciplinary nature of this literature difficult to engage with. Academics who work on the period are keen to convey that this is a fascinating and important period to study, but it can be a tough sell. Eighteenth-century modules have to compete for enrolments with fare that is more familiar from school, such as the Tudors or the Nazis in the English 'A' Level curriculum in England. In marketised higher education, where the viability of optional modules relies on students picking them, this can dictate whether a topic survives on the curriculum.

This collection of chapters will therefore reflect on how we teach the history of the long eighteenth century, focusing on pedagogical innovation and current developments in the discipline. Sometimes it can be a challenge to innovate in one's teaching. Once the considerable effort has been expended on creating a new course, the temptation is to roll it out again in successive years, and pressures on academics' time often prevent us from reflecting on and enhancing our teaching practice. Doing something new and creative can also face institutional obstacles, since university frameworks and quality assurance mechanisms often require teaching and/or assessment to be delivered in a particular way. Such work is highly necessary, however, so this book has two linked objectives. On the one hand, we want to offer a critical exploration of how eighteenth-century history is taught at university, with reference to developments in the field of learning and teaching. On the other, we want to give some practical examples of innovations in the teaching of history, focusing on particular modules and courses where this has been put into practice. This is intended to provide a guide for educators and to offer some exciting ideas to add to their toolkits. In this aim, it is hoped that this volume will be of interest not only to scholars teaching the eighteenth century but also to those who teach the study of the past more generally. As Alan Booth and Paul Hyland argued in their classic collection *The Practice of University History Teaching* (2000), there is a value to bringing colleagues together 'to review, research and innovate in history teaching' since it helps 'not only to promote the realisation of good practices and their testing under various conditions, but also to ensure that findings are more widely disseminated and embedded in the work of whole departments and the traditions of the discipline'.[3]

While research on the eighteenth century is a booming area for academic publication, there are relatively few published works that focus on teaching it at university level. Most pedagogical studies focus on literature[4] and tend to be within the US higher education context.[5] History at university level has its own distinctive pedagogies and disciplinary characteristics, so it requires dedicated treatment. But here too, relatively little has been published in comparison with the large literature focusing on the teaching of history in secondary education.[6] In UK higher education, much of this activity has been under the auspices of the Higher Education Academy and History UK, formerly the History at University Defence Group. This body was instrumental in the development of the subject benchmark for history in 2000, alongside other university disciplines. The history subject benchmark outlined the typical features of a history degree and the skills a student should cultivate while studying it. With periodic updates, the benchmark remains current to this day.

The current benchmark statement lists seventeen 'generic skills' that a student should have on completing a history degree.[7] Most of these are common to other subjects too, although this particular combination is characteristic of history. Much of the political discourse around history in British higher education concerns skills. This is also the case in other national academes such as Australia, although in the US there is more of an emphasis on maintaining a healthy democracy. Non-vocational subjects like the humanities are under pressure to demonstrate that they teach 'transferable skills' that prepare students for employment, countering charges that they are 'low value' in economic terms. John Tosh argues that it would be more effective to argue that disciplines like history teach skills 'whose value lies precisely in the fact that they are *not* generic, while still being relevant and useful'.[8]

This raises the question of how far history is a distinctive discipline, and the extent to which it has things in common with its disciplinary neighbours. History acquired a strong self-identity as a discipline relatively late: it was not until the mid-nineteenth century that it became institutionalised as a university subject, with its own epistemology and way of operating. In the eighteenth century, the people who wrote 'histories' would not necessarily have seen themselves as historians. They tended to be men of letters (and some notable women) who were recognised for their contributions to other fields, such as literature or philosophy. History was an imaginative activity and was regarded as a branch of the arts, rather than the science that it would try to become in the following century. This is arguably closer to the situation today, where cultural history is the dominant mode within the discipline. History has always been a magpie discipline, so the interdisciplinary world of eighteenth-century studies is a comfortable home for historians, and a good reflection of the century they study. Indeed, cultural history is fast becoming the dominant mode within eighteenth-century studies itself – which only a decade ago was dominated by literary studies – and has become the meeting place for other subjects across the arts and humanities.[9]

On the other hand, history does have distinctive features as a discipline. As well as listing generic skills, the history benchmark statement does a good job of outlining the cluster of attributes associated with studying the subject. For example, it argues that on completing a history degree, a graduate should be able to:

- understand the problems inherent in the historical record itself
- appreciate complexity and diversity of situations, events and mentalities in the past and, by extension, present
- understand how people have existed, acted and thought in the always-different context of the past
- marshal an argument in pursuit of meaningful questions about the past and, by implication, the present and future.[10]

Thinking about what is distinctive about historical study is instructive, not least because many of the assumptions students have about their identity as 'historians' can be problematic. Some of these are inherited from their experience at school, which is much more focused on gathering 'facts' and deploying them for assessment. One of the challenges of teaching first-year undergraduates is getting them to move beyond these assumptions, which can be deeply held. Students often dismiss 'bias' in primary sources, whereas perspective can be their most important feature. Students often assume that they should reject presentism, whereas historical writing is inevitably informed by the circumstances of its writing, and should arguably be activist. And students often seek to demonstrate empathy, which can be valuable but also tends to highlight the sameness of the past rather than its radical differences.

Fundamentally, it is important that students are aware of the nature of the discipline they are studying. History – as it is practised in twenty-first-century universities – is not a natural thing to do, and is the product of centuries of development and debate. Arguably students studying joint honours have a more critical perspective on this than their single-honours colleagues in the English higher education system, since they have to step outside of that way of studying to engage with their other subjects. History degrees typically have a component that covers the history and philosophy of the discipline, but students are less confident talking about methodology than in other disciplines where it is more explicit: indeed, historians often self-identify as having a 'common-sense' approach, so students can find it uncomfortable to critique this.[11] The eighteenth century often features prominently in these courses, since it was a key phase in the development of the discipline, which in its modern form rests upon Enlightenment forms of knowledge. It is perhaps not surprising that there has also, in recent years, been an increased focus on eighteenth-century research, teaching and learning practices and skills acquisition, both inside and outside universities, across a number of areas.[12]

It is vital to understand this since, as David Pace notes, 'all academic learning is discipline specific'. Learning takes place within disciplines and 'a discipline such as history represents a unique epistemological and methodological community'.[13] Not only should students understand the nature of their discipline but teachers' efforts to enhance learning should be cognisant of it as well. Pace and his colleagues have argued that it is important to 'decode' the disciplines. Tutors should start by identifying 'bottlenecks' in a course that prevent students from learning. These often arise from unspoken assumptions about the nature of the discipline, so making these explicit can help students to learn about the discipline they are studying while also removing obstacles to learning. They argue that this process can help with student motivation and fosters deeper understanding.[14] While not necessarily following the 'decoding the disciplines' model, the chapters in this collection agree that it is vital for students to understand their discipline, both for its own sake and for the benefit of their wider learning.

It is with this in mind that this volume is structured around three key themes. The first of these is digital; one of the great benefits of studying the eighteenth century is the richness of digital materials that can be used by both researchers and students. The availability of resources such as Eighteenth-Century Collections Online (ECCO) means that research tasks that previously would have taken many days and miles of travel can be undertaken within a classroom setting. As the chapter by Burrows and Ward shows, however, students need to be guided in using these materials in a way that not only helps them with the immediate project but also enables them to develop transferable skills they can use when working with data in both research and business environments in the workplace. These skills are both qualitative and quantitative. Numeracy skills tend to be neglected in history degree programmes, but they are essential when handling 'big data'. While sources can easily be retrieved from large datasets and analysed qualitatively, this can lead to cherry-picking, whereas to get a sense of their representativeness and significance it is important to think about them quantitatively as well. Therefore, engaging with digital materials can require students to develop new skills.

Students' technical skills can also be employed to widen access to archival materials that have been digitised. There are growing numbers of projects looking for volunteers to transcribe archival materials so they can be used by the wider public, such as the 'Voices through Time: The Story of Care' programme, which is helping the Coram Foundation to digitise parts of the Foundling Hospital Archive.[15] There is a growing trend for students to undertake research projects commissioned by external organisations, in the form of live briefs, as part of their programme of study. This can include digital projects or producing archival guides for future researchers, reflecting the growing emphasis on 'authentic assessment' within higher education curricula.[16] The chapter by Burns and Walton shows how important it is to create a community of researchers among our students, and how this can have a positive impact on the wider network of researchers, as it has done with the Georgian Papers programme. This type of project develops both the subject-specific and transferable skills that are required of graduates in the twenty-first century.

These types of projects became especially important in 2020–21 when, because of restrictions following the outbreak of the COVID-19 pandemic, there was a shift towards remote learning. Although history is a popular subject among those providing massive open online courses (MOOCs), within the UK there is very little provision of online BA History programmes.[17] While there has been some pedagogic work on teaching the eighteenth century online, the shift to digital teaching and learning meant a significant change in practice for many academics.[18] This led to a period of swift innovation in teaching and History UK captured some of this best practice in their 'Pandemic Pedagogy Handbook'.[19] This process has meant that academic staff are now incorporating some of the new approaches to teaching that they developed during this period, so thinking critically about both digital learning and digital skills is important in the development of new provision.

Advances in digital learning and teaching has not meant that there has been an abandonment of the classroom, however. It is important to remember that just because an approach is 'traditional' in its delivery style, it does not mean that it cannot be innovative. The vast majority of students' tutor-led learning, as opposed to independent study, is based within a seminar room or lecture theatre. We therefore need to consider both what and how we teach within these settings. Being 'student centred' is a key theme that appears throughout this volume as a whole, and is a particular focus of the second part of the collection on learning in the classroom. A student-centred approach can include engaging the students' senses, whether using smell, sight or their ability to listen and engage, as discussed in the chapters by Tullett and Larsen. Encouraging active learning can help to move students away from being passive recipients of their education and towards becoming co-creators in their educational journey. The concept of the 'flipped classroom' has been fashionable in recent years – whereby students prepare beforehand, apply these insights in class in a supported way, then explore further afterwards – but seminar teaching in the humanities has long employed variations of this model. Larsen's chapter explores how we as educators can best focus on what happens before, after and during the class.

Active learning can also be an important way of encouraging students to recognise their own responsibilities in the classroom, and outside of it. The theme of citizenship is picked up in the chapter by McCormack, both as a historical topic and as a way of thinking about oneself as a member of a society. This can include discussing complex subjects such as race or engaging in activities, such as singing, which can make students feel a degree of discomfort. As the chapters in this part show, this should not be avoided; rather, strategies should be employed to help students face things they find difficult or awkward. As Cohen has argued, by avoiding the 'uncomfortable', scholars can further marginalise historians and ideas that challenge received models of understanding.[20] This can be especially important in the discussions relating to the complex histories of the global majority, whose experiences are often ignored or simplified by many traditional narratives of the history of the eighteenth century. Therefore, engaging with the unfamiliar should be a central part of university education, and so providing a space where they can be safely 'uncomfortable' is a key consideration when thinking about module and programme design.

One of these uncomfortable but safe places can be the museum. The third theme of this volume is material culture and collections, which considers the ways in which using collections can enable students to develop interdisciplinary methodologies that can help them to explore the past. In recent years there has been a shift towards the 'material turn' among historians, and many of those writing about the use of objects in learning and teaching have been eighteenth-century scholars.[21] As Henry Glassie notes, an artefact-centred approach to the past can help scholars to explore the 'wordless experience of all people, rich and poor, near or far'.[22] Using objects with students can provide an engaging learning experience, and an enjoyably different one if they are accustomed to learning with texts. An encounter with a historical object can take you radically out of the present and provide a sense of connection with the past, which in turn can lead to reflection about what 'the past' – and the nature of our 'connection' with it – actually is. This again highlights the importance of engaging the senses and the emotions in learning, and of thinking about them historically.

Marples explores how, through the examination of collections, considering both the items and their object biographies, students can reflect on the intellectual, economic and social structures which meant that some things, and not others, came to form part of individual and national museums. The importance of collections for teaching has long been recognised, with many universities forming museums or special collections to support their students' education in a range of different disciplines.[23] As Kouneni's chapter considers, thinking about how these collections can be utilised effectively can benefit not only those staff working within institutions that have access to this form of collection but everyone who teaches with objects. Both of these chapters highlight how these collections can also enable students to encounter directly the colonial histories of the eighteenth century, and to think about the associated histories of the institutions and how they are displayed. In this, they speak to broader bodies of critical scholarship and activist practice working to decolonise higher education at every level of operation, highlight and address historical and contemporary links between the histories of education and histories of structural inequality, and advocate for more open dialogues between research, education, creativity and praxis.[24] This drive towards decolonised teaching practices exists alongside a strong backlash in the form of an actively hostile journalistic and social media climate that promotes the right-wing notion of a 'culture war'. Many higher education institutions display extreme operational inconsistency in this context: publicly championing increased diversity when it is advantageous but remaining silent when there is any perceived reputational risk. They also generally fail to address entrenched problems in racist, sexist, ableist and classist hiring and promotional practices, or adequately supporting or protecting those who do the hard, frontline work of improving teaching and research centred on individuals with protected characteristics.

Of course, there are other inequalities in the structures of academic research and teaching. In the UK, despite a proclaimed desire for 'research-led teaching', there is a tendency to separate universities into those with 'Teaching Excellence' and those with 'Research Excellence', according to the governmental frameworks which allocate funding depending on performance. Within departments, too, there can be a large divide between staff who are actively engaged in teaching (often younger scholars who are keen to embed inclusive teaching and service practices but are not necessarily established enough to be able to do so) and those who prioritise funding capture to pursue their own research (often from positions of privileged security with little demand for 'upskilling'). Other pressures include loss of permanent job status through large-scale departmental closures; difficulties in retaining talent in academic institutions due to precarity and blocked pipelines; and the excessive burdens involved in producing research and teaching materials, whether in addition to doctoral studies or within a particular area of work – for example, the demands often made on scholars of colour for additional research or forms of academic service in support of greater equality, diversity and inclusion, however real or tokenistic that may be. Reflections on teaching innovations can therefore open up further critical examinations of higher education.

The chapters by Marples and Kouneni reflect on the disparities in terms of the types of collections that are available to students at different types of university, since archival and museum collections tend only to be available in older and less accessible institutions. In recent years, though, there has been a growing focus on digital access to collections, which can make objects open to a wider range of learners. This has meant that students can now access objects from home, whether they are from their own institution's collections or those from museums on the other side of the world.[25] However, the importance of sensory engagement with individual objects can be lost when access to them is mediated either through a digital screen or a glass cabinet in a museum setting. Similarly, much early discussion of digitisation among academics and curators centred on the need to preserve and communicate the important material clues for understanding eighteenth-century manuscripts that might otherwise be missed, and this is demonstrated in various ways across different digital archives. This reflects a common theme throughout many of the chapters in this volume that reflexive learning along with gaining a deeper knowledge of the practices of historical research can support students to develop their own understandings of the past.

Throughout the volume, there is a strong focus on student-centred learning, an approach which can be applied to learning beyond modules focused on eighteenth-century history. By encouraging students to engage with their learning, whether it is through objects, in the classroom or digitally, they can be made aware of the endless complexities of the period without being overloaded. In many of these chapters, students are encouraged to think about 'lived experiences' – their own and those of the people they come across in the study of history. This means that they are aware of the wide diversity of experiences and peoples in the past, which can help them to 'foster empathy, and respect for difference', one of the characteristics associated with history graduates.[26] Considering students' own positionality and processes of learning allows for more responsive teaching. Innovative teaching is often shaped by holistic approaches that meet the students where *they* are and in terms of their priorities, motivations and personal epistemologies. However, it can also remind them that their 'place in the world' is not, and was not, shared by everyone, encouraging them to think about and reflect on the histories and impacts of difference. By giving them the tools to research the past, and to develop their own voices as historians, a history degree can foster the life-long skills that are crucial in a quickly changing world.

As well as being focused on student-centred learning, these chapters also consider the experiences of those teaching the students. All of the chapters share examples of teaching practice, including practical strategies for engaging students, drawn from a range of historians: from early career researchers to senior academics, and including researchers working both within and outside of universities, in the UK and Australia. The chapters demonstrate the value of investing in staff and subjects and embedding connected programmes of learning and development within university departments instead of the current reactive model that often relies on the exploitation of early career scholars on short-term, unstable contracts. In many cases, the examples of practice here seek to overcome or at least mitigate the obstacles created by the increased marketisation of higher education. The diversity of experiences presented here also draw attention to the structures of teaching and learning in the hopes of promoting further conversation and critical examination. The absences also speak volumes. We would have liked to have included a chapter that directly engaged with global histories and/or the histories of race, empire and colonialism, as these are increasingly central to our understandings of the eighteenth century. However, it is pleasing to see how these issues have been explored by a number of the authors in their chapters, showing how they are topics which are increasingly integrated into the teaching of this period.

We therefore hope that this volume encourages readers to consider the positionality of their own practice. Although explicitly focused on teaching the eighteenth century, the ideas presented within these chapters can also be utilised by those teaching other time periods or other related disciplines. While distinctive in its own histories (as all time periods are), there is nothing unique to the age which means that it requires its own exclusive approach. Many of the concerns of the age, such as the mediation of knowledge, constructions of self-identity and the relationship between the individual and the state, can be related to other centuries. Likewise, the focus on digital learning, classroom-based settings and the use of collections can also be applied to a wide range of modules. In bringing these chapters together, we hope to inspire others in developing their own innovative practices.

Notes

1 Penelope Corfield, 'The Exploding Galaxy: Historical Studies of Eighteenth-Century Britain', *Journal for Eighteenth-Century Studies*, 34:4 (2011), 517–26.

2 As noted by Katherine Burn, 'Making Sense of the Eighteenth Century', *Teaching History*, 154 (2014), 18–27.

3 Alan Booth and Paul Hyland (eds), *The Practice of University History Teaching* (Manchester: Manchester University Press, 2000), pp. 9–10.

4 Mary Ann Rooks (ed.), *Teaching the Eighteenth Century* (Newcastle: Cambridge Scholars, 2009); Kevin Binfield and William J. Christmas (eds), *Teaching Laboring-Class British Literature of the Eighteenth and Nineteenth Centuries* (New York: Modern Language Association, 2018); Jennifer Frangos and Cristobal Silva (eds), *Teaching the Transatlantic Eighteenth Century* (Newcastle: Cambridge Scholars, 2020). See also the essays in Bonnie Gunzenhauser and Wolfram Schmidgen (eds), 'Special Focus Section: New Approaches to the 18th Century', *College Literature*, 31:3 (2004), 93–205.

5 For example, Katherine Lubey, 'Teaching Eighteenth-Century Black Lives', *Studies in Eighteenth-Century Culture*, 49 (2020), 145–9.

6 As noted by David Pace: 'The Amateur in the Operating Room: History and the Scholarship of Teaching and Learning', *American Historical Review*, 109:4 (2004), 1171–92.

7 Quality Assurance Agency, 'Subject Benchmark: History' (2022), www.qaa.ac.uk/the-quality-code/subject-benchmark-statements/history (accessed 20 January 2023), p. 16.

8 John Tosh, *Why History Matters* (Houndmills: Palgrave, 2008), p. 128.

9 For example, contrast contributions to the *Journal for Eighteenth-Century Studies* in the 2000s with today.

10 Quality Assurance Agency, 'Subject Benchmark', p. 4.

11 John Tosh, *The Pursuit of History: Aims, Methods and New Directions in the Study of History* (Abingdon: Routledge, 2021), p. 124.

12 Malcolm McKinnon Dick and Ruth Watts, 'Eighteenth-Century Education: Discourses and Informal Agencies', *Journal of the History of Education Society*, 37:4 (2008), 509–12; N. A. Hans, *New Trends in Education in the Eighteenth Century* (London: Routledge, 2013).

13 Pace, 'Amateur in the Operating Room', p. 1173.

14 David Pace and Joan Middendorf (eds), 'Decoding the Disciplines: Helping Students Learn Disciplinary Ways of Thinking', special issue of *New Directions in Teaching and Learning*, 98 (2004).

15 'The Foundling Hospital Archive', Coram Story, https://coramstory.org.uk/the-foundling-hospital-archive (accessed 12 April 2023).

16 Zahra Sokhanvar, Keyvan Salehi and Fatemeh Sokhanvar, 'Advantages of Authentic Assessment for Improving the Learning Experience and Employability

Skills of Higher Education Students: A Systematic Literature Review', *Studies in Educational Evaluation*, 70 (2021). doi: 10.1016/j.stueduc.2021.101030.

17 Although there are a number of both Foundation and Master's-level programmes that are taught exclusively online, very few UK universities offer a full undergraduate history degree that can be studied remotely, with the Open University and the University of the Highlands and Islands being among the notable exceptions.

18 Timothy Jenks, 'Spatial Identities, Online Strategies, and the Teaching of Britain's "Long Eighteenth Century"', *The History Teacher*, 51:4 (2018), 597–610.

19 Katie Cooper et al., 'The Pandemic Pedagogy Handbook', *History UK*, www.history-uk.ac.uk/the-pandemic-pedagogy-handbook (accessed 12 April 2023).

20 Michèle Cohen, 'Is the Eighteenth Century a Foreign Country Too Far?', *Gender and Education*, 27 (2015), 947–56.

21 See, for example, the essays in Karen Harvey (ed.), *History and Material Culture: A Student's Guide to Approaching Alternative Sources* (London: Routledge, 2009) and Serena Dyer, 'State of the Field: Material Culture', *History*, 106:370 (2021), 282–92.

22 Henry Glassie, *Material Culture* (Bloomington, IN: Indiana University Press 1999), p.44.

23 For example, see Umberto Veronesi and Marcos Martinón-Torres, 'The Old Ashmolean Museum and Oxford's Seventeenth-Century Chymical Community: A Material Culture Approach to Laboratory Experiments', *Ambix*, 69:1 (2022), 19–33.

24 Jason Arday and Heidi Safia Mirza (eds), *Dismantling Race in Higher Education: Racism, Whiteness and Decolonising the Academy* (London: Palgrave Macmillan, 2018); Gurminder K. Bhambra, Dalia Gebrial and Kerem Nişancıoğlu (eds), *Decolonising the University* (London: Pluto Press, 2018); Paulette Williams et al., *The Broken Pipeline: Barriers to Black PhD Students Accessing Research Council Funding* (Leading Routes report, 2019); Amanda Behm et al., 'Decolonising History: Enquiry and Practice', *History Workshop Journal*, 89 (2020), 169–91; Björn Lundberg, 'Exploring Histories of Knowledge and Education: An Introduction', *Nordic Journal of Educational History*, 9:2 (2022), 1–11; Darren Chetty, Angelique Golding and Nicola Rollock, 'Reimagining Education: Where Do We Go from Here?', *Wasafiri*, 37:4 (2022), 1–3.

25 For a discussion about the virtual field trip, see Ruth Larsen, 'Pandemic Pedagogy 2.0. Oh, the Places We Will Go! Running Virtual Field Trips', *History UK*, www.history-uk.ac.uk/2021/02/10/pandemic-pedagogy-2-0-ruth-larsen-oh-the-places-we-will-go-running-virtual-field-trips (accessed 12 April 2023).

26 Quality Assurance Agency, 'Subject Benchmark', p.4.

References

Arday, Jason and Mirza, Heidi Safia (eds), *Dismantling Race in Higher Education: Racism, Whiteness and Decolonising the Academy* (London: Palgrave Macmillan, 2018).

Behm, Amanda et al., 'Decolonising History: Enquiry and Practice', *History Workshop Journal*, 89 (2020), 169–91.

Bhambra, Gurminder K., Gebrial, Dalia and Nişancıoğlu, Kerem (eds), *Decolonising the University* (London: Pluto Press, 2018).

Binfield, Kevin and Christmas, William J. (eds), *Teaching Laboring-Class British Literature of the Eighteenth and Nineteenth Centuries* (New York: Modern Language Association, 2018).

Booth, Alan and Hyland, Paul (eds), *The Practice of University History Teaching* (Manchester: Manchester University Press, 2000).

Burn, Katherine, 'Making Sense of the Eighteenth Century', *Teaching History*, 154 (2014), 18–27.

Chetty, Darren, Golding, Angelique and Rollock, Nicola, 'Reimagining Education: Where Do We Go from Here?', *Wasafiri*, 37:4 (2022), 1–3.

Cohen, Michèle, 'Is the Eighteenth Century a Foreign Country Too Far?', *Gender and Education*, 27 (2015), 947–56.

Cooper, Katie et al., 'The Pandemic Pedagogy Handbook', *History UK*, www.history-uk.ac.uk/the-pandemic-pedagogy-handbook (accessed 12 April 2023).

Corfield, Penelope, 'The Exploding Galaxy: Historical Studies of Eighteenth-Century Britain', *Journal for Eighteenth-Century Studies*, 34:4 (2011), 517–26.

Dyer, Serena, 'State of the Field: Material Culture', *History*, 106:370 (2021), 282–92.

'The Foundling Hospital Archive', *Coram Story*, https://coramstory.org.uk/the-foundling-hospital-archive (accessed 12 April 2023).

Frangos, Jennifer and Silva, Cristobal (eds), *Teaching the Transatlantic Eighteenth Century* (Newcastle: Cambridge Scholars, 2020).

Glassie, Henry, *Material Culture* (Bloomington, IN: Indiana University Press, 1999).

Gunzenhauser, Bonnie and Schmidgen, Wolfram (eds), 'Special Focus Section: New Approaches to the 18th Century', *College Literature*, 31:3 (2004), 93–205.

Hans, N. A., *New Trends in Education in the Eighteenth Century* (London: Routledge, 2013).

Harvey, Karen (ed.), *History and Material Culture: A Student's Guide to Approaching Alternative Sources* (London: Routledge, 2009).

Jenks, Timothy, 'Spatial Identities, Online Strategies, and the Teaching of Britain's "Long Eighteenth Century"', *The History Teacher*, 51:4 (2018), 597–610.

Larsen, Ruth, 'Pandemic Pedagogy 2.0. Oh, the Places We Will Go! Running Virtual Field trips', *History UK*, www.history-uk.ac.uk/2021/02/10/pandemic-pedagogy-2-0-ruth-larsen-oh-the-places-we-will-go-running-virtual-field-trips (accessed 12 April 2023).

Lubey, Katherine, 'Teaching Eighteenth-Century Black Lives', *Studies in Eighteenth-Century Culture*, 49 (2020), 145–9.

Lundberg, Björn, 'Exploring Histories of Knowledge and Education: An Introduction', *Nordic Journal of Educational History*, 9:2 (2022), 1–11.

McKinnon Dick, Malcolm and Watts, Ruth, 'Eighteenth-Century Education: Discourses and Informal Agencies', *Journal of the History of Education Society*, 37:4 (2008), 509–12.

Pace, David, 'The Amateur in the Operating Room: History and the Scholarship of Teaching and Learning', *American Historical Review*, 109:4 (2004), 1171–92.

Pace, David and Middendorf, Joan (eds), 'Decoding the Disciplines: Helping Students Learn Disciplinary Ways of Thinking', special issue of *New Directions in Teaching and Learning*, 98 (2004).

Quality Assurance Agency, 'Subject Benchmark: History' (2022), www.qaa.ac.uk/the-quality-code/subject-benchmark-statements/history (accessed 20 January 2023).

Rooks, Mary Ann (ed.), *Teaching the Eighteenth Century* (Newcastle: Cambridge Scholars, 2009).

Sokhanvar, Zahra, Salehi, Keyvan and Sokhanvar, Fatemeh, 'Advantages of Authentic Assessment for Improving the Learning Experience and Employability Skills of Higher Education Students: A Systematic Literature Review', *Studies in Educational Evaluation*, 70 (2021). doi: 10.1016/j.stueduc.2021.101030.

Tosh, John, *Why History Matters* (Houndmills: Palgrave, 2008).

Tosh, John, *The Pursuit of History: Aims, Methods and New Directions in the Study of History*, 7th edition (Abingdon: Routledge, 2021).

Veronesi, Umberto and Martinón-Torres, Marcos, 'The Old Ashmolean Museum and Oxford's Seventeenth-Century Chymical Community: A Material Culture Approach to Laboratory Experiments', *Ambix*, 69:1 (2022), 19–33.

Williams, Paulette et al., *The Broken Pipeline: Barriers to Black PhD Students Accessing Research Council Funding* (Leading Routes report, 2019).

Part I
DIGITAL HISTORY

Chapter 1

Letting students loose in the archive: reflections on teaching 'At the Court of King George: Exploring the Royal Archives' at King's College London

Arthur Burns and Oliver C. Walton

One of the great pleasures and advantages of researching the history of Britain in the eighteenth century over the past thirty years or more has been the vibrant international, interdisciplinary and methodologically diverse community of scholarship. This provides a setting and support for both individual and collaborative research projects, manifest in the flourishing British Society for Eighteenth-Century Studies, a number of active research centres in British universities and well-attended seminars such as that for British History in the Long Eighteenth Century convened at the Institute of Historical Research (IHR) in London. The century has also been at the heart of a number of the most important initiatives in digital humanities based in the UK, in many cases with a strong commitment to serving a wider historical public beyond the academy.[1] When in 2019 the IHR seminar convened a well-attended symposium on the theme of 'Eighteenth Century Now: The Current State of British History', as much as the themes of growing contemporary relevance and the diversity of approaches on display, it was the sense of a shared project developed over time and warm collegiality across sub-disciplinary divides and generations that was a key takeaway for many of the participants.

Almost all history degrees in British universities seek to develop students' skill as historical researchers and to expose them to the challenge of a variety of types of archive, commonly through the inclusion in the final year of a degree programme of a dissertation project. This certainly provides a good opportunity to develop the core subject skills that might eventually lead to the production of academic articles or monographs in traditional 'lone-scholar' mode. History degrees also increasingly include provision for group work, and modules which focus on public history and the forms of delivery most appropriate to it.[2] Nevertheless, group work can be a source of anxiety for students who are concerned that it places their assessment scores at the mercy of the weakest member of the group;[3] elsewhere in assessment collaboration may be explicitly discouraged; and decisions about the audience for projects are usually predetermined in the module specifications. In modules where there is a substantial body of historical knowledge to be delivered, there can also often be little time available to work on the skill-sets needed to translate these either into good academic prose or more public-facing forms – especially where online forms of publication are involved, for the functional digital native remains an elusive presence among the undergraduate population.

In all these formats the undergraduate experience cannot capture the serendipitous manner in which academically rigorous research and public engagement often come together in historians' research lives. Nor do they reproduce the experience of a supportive community, not just among student peers but also with senior and junior scholars and archivists, that characterises the most enjoyable research projects, especially those which are based on collaboration rather than conducted in lone-scholar mode. Such projects enjoy a growing significance in the humanities. In this essay, we discuss a module which was designed to capture these aspects of the research culture in British eighteenth-century studies by drawing on the resources of a specific research project, the Georgian Papers programme, and reflecting on both the experience of teaching it and the student response.[4]

'At the Court of King George' and the Georgian Papers programme

'At the Court of King George: Exploring the Royal Archives'[5] (henceforth CKG) was created in 2017 as one of a suite of so-called 'opportunity modules' to be delivered in the Arts and Humanities faculty at King's College London. The modules were required to be interdisciplinary and sit outside department teaching offers, to accommodate experimentation in teaching and assessment, to reflect key themes in the scholarly life of the College and explicitly to promise students who selected them an expansion of their skill-set. This gave Arthur Burns a long-desired opportunity to create a module which would aim to bring students into the exciting world of collaborative humanities research, which had been an unusually strong feature of his own career. Ideally such a module should also help them to understand the way knowledge was produced out of an archive, and would emphasise the centrality of public history to any proper understanding of the historian's craft. Furthermore, the module would give students the opportunity to explore and experience the power of the digital in changing the way historians work. Thus it was important to use not cutting-edge but fairly basic – and thus accessible and inclusive – digital tools to develop critical approaches towards using archival catalogues, online presentation and website design, which would allow students to advance the research agenda and create knowledge through computation and visualisation, and to be creative in communicating their ideas electronically, liberated from the constraints of text on sequential pages but having to consider new issues such as usability.[6]

Arthur identified the perfect foundation for this module in the Georgian Papers programme (henceforth GPP).[7] This project, launched by Queen Elizabeth II at Windsor in 2015, was a unique collaboration between King's College London and the Royal Collection Trust, joined by primary US partners the Omohundro Institute of Early American History and Culture and William & Mary, with additional contributions from the Library of Congress, Mount Vernon and the Sons of the American Revolution. Its aim was to digitise, conserve, catalogue, transcribe, interpret and disseminate some 425,000 pages (65,000 items) in the Royal Archives and Royal Library relating to the period 1714–1837. In 2017 Arthur had become one of two academic directors of the programme, alongside Karin Wulf, then-executive director of the Omohundro Institute, taking responsibility for both the academic and public programming for the project in collaboration with Oliver Walton, a historian based in the Royal Archives as GPP Coordinator. All three were working with colleagues at the Royal Archives, William & Mary and King's Digital Laboratory on scholarly support for the digitisation and transcription programme under the oversight of Royal Archives Manager Bill Stockting and Patricia Methven, the former archivist of King's College London.[8]

The programme owed its origins in part to the Royal Collection Trust's recognition that the Georgian Papers in the Round Tower at Windsor were an underused resource. This was partly because there was no proper catalogue, but also reflected the fact that their nature was widely misunderstood. Although some 15 per cent had previously been published, the editions mainly focused on a narrow, predominantly political, subset of the whole collection. In seeking to make the whole collection accessible, the GPP helped transform understanding of it. Alongside – and in some cases to make possible – the cataloguing of the collection, the project partners sponsored an extensive and sustained programme of scholarly investigation of the archive through active research, leading to the creation of a network of over sixty GPP fellows who have each pursued their own highly varied projects in the Windsor archives, reporting back to the archivists on their findings and approaches, as well as sharing insights with each other and the project team at a series of workshops and public events.[9]

The Georgian Papers at Windsor are extensive, rich and diverse. While the largest single sections are those for the reigns of George III and George IV, the papers' chronological span extends from 1714 through to 1837. Monarchs loom large throughout, but there are papers relating to many other members of the royal family, notably royal women. They offer important materials on eighteenth-century medicine (including the reports, correspondence and other papers of the doctors who treated George III during his 'madness'), education, politics, cultural life and foreign affairs. There are courtiers' papers, financial papers and documents relating to the court, royal residences and household administration. The cast list is extensive. The contents are roughly classified in Figure 1.1; it should be remembered that with over 400,000 pages, even small slices of this pie chart can represent large numbers of documents.

The GPP therefore offered an ideal platform for a module of the kind envisaged. Although strongly associated with the court, this single archive offered a very wide range of documents and objects (from books to bundles of hair) which could support research into widely differing aspects of eighteenth-century history; it had a strong international research community already associated with it drawn from a variety of disciplines and sub-disciplines; and it had a community of archivists, librarians and cataloguers with considerable familiarity with the collection as a whole, which the wider project team was also gradually acquiring. Finally, it had

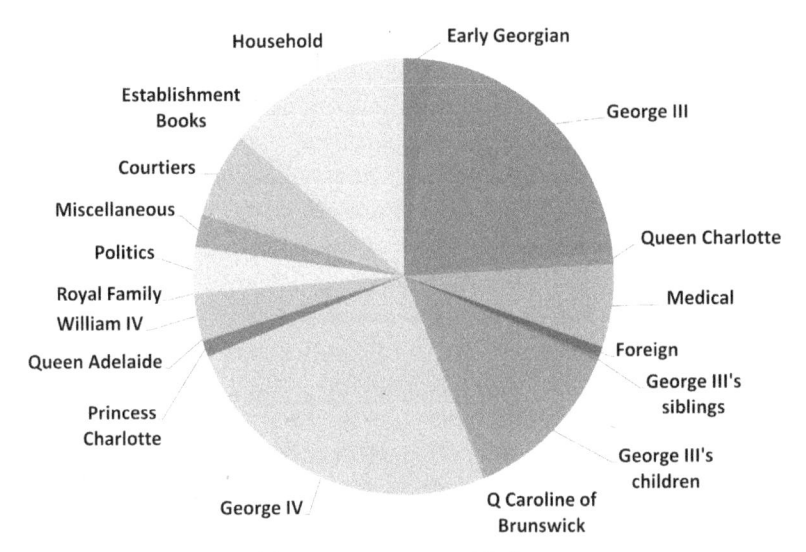

Figure 1.1: The contents of the Georgian Papers at Windsor.

a strong and varied outreach and impact agenda, with regular coverage in the press (even featuring at one point in *Hello* magazine), work with the Royal Mint and the Library of Congress, two major TV documentaries, and collaborations with two important stage productions during the course of the project: the West End production of *Hamilton: An American Musical* and the Nottingham Playhouse production of *The Madness of George III*, which was then selected by the National Theatre (NT) for an NT Live showing, recycled as part of NT at Home during the COVID-19 pandemic. These collaborations could not only excite students who saw evidence of the impact of the project with which they were associated beyond the university but also help them to think imaginatively about how historical research could make its way from an academic project into the wider public realm, and how their own work could find expression in ways that might also have potential in this regard.

Design principles

In conversations with Oliver and other colleagues, Arthur now sought to design a module that would reflect both the archive on which it was based and the learning objectives that had been established. Since the module had to be made available to students on different disciplinary programmes, it was likely that it would set a demanding challenge to students, especially those who were not historians: in one sense we would need to find a way to make them *all* historians, capable of researching content for a historical project, not least the 'facts' that underpinned it, even if their own discipline's skills could also be deployed.

It was decided that we should start with the documents in the archive. We should aim to introduce students to the full range of skills involved in presenting such documents to a variety of audiences. Central to this should be preparing some form of edition of a particular document or set of documents; indeed, we both believe editing has a rather undervalued place in historical training, not least because it demands both precision and rigour. The final choice of the document could be left in the student's hands but with the support of the module tutor(s): part of the challenge and also part of the excitement of the module would be getting students to select documents from among those digitised by the GPP that suited their own interests and skills, making it more likely that they would have the necessary enthusiasm to complete the project. It would also be the student's decision as to what sort of audience they wanted to work towards: we would encourage everything from a serious academic treatment to projects aimed at a wider public or school audience. The only common factor was that at the heart would be a digital and accurate presentation of the document(s) or object, accompanied by a transcription. Given the parallels between this and the GPP's own activity, this would be part of a wider aim of making students feel they were actively part of the project, rather than simply watching it from the sidelines, or indeed having things handed to them on a plate. Finally, again, very importantly to Arthur because of his long involvement in promoting history as a discipline of key importance in schools and universities as a source of highly desirable life and work skills, there should be opportunities in the module for the students to recognise the transferability beyond the academy of the skills they were acquiring and deploying in the course of the module.[10]

Delivering CKG

As eventually implemented, CKG became a final-year undergraduate module delivered over ten weeks, with a series of two-hour seminars capped off by a three-hour workshop in which each student presented their work in progress. For a number of the seminars the module lead tutor was joined by colleagues with appropriate expertise, thus modelling the collaborative spirit underpinning the module.[11] Oliver led sessions introducing the archive and training students in how to navigate and describe archival resources, as well as workshopping academic issues later in the module and co-assessing student work; for two sessions, concentrating on the digital skills involved in mounting the edition (on which more below), we were joined by a technology specialist from the faculty.[12] (In 2021 circumstances forced a role-reversal, with Oliver leading the module and Arthur making cameo appearances.) The edition constituted 90 per cent of the module's assessment, the other 10 per cent being derived from a group presentation at the halfway point in the module.

The module is supported by a very extensive virtual learning environment, which came into its own when the module had to be delivered online in pandemic conditions. As well as resources for each class, there is a huge range of resources which can be employed in the final editions, such as digitised maps and timelines on which events can be plotted, links to other internet resources relevant to the period (such as the public databases mentioned above) and other collections of digitised sources, major library and archival catalogues, recorded interviews with a number of scholars associated with the programme (concerning, for example, the monarchy's Hanoverian possessions, the court at the royal palaces, George III and his daughters), and an online archive of TV documentaries (including but not confined to those involving the GPP), films and plays which might inform and support the students' learning. Most importantly, there is also a bibliography of more than 400 items selected from the Royal Historical Society Bibliography of British and Irish History, accompanied by a set of short biographies of the key contributors to the historiography.

The delivery of the module had several distinctive features. Perhaps most strikingly, given the differences in prior exposure to history of the students taking the module, there was no direct teaching at all of the history of the Georgian monarchy or period aside from short introductions to both at the start of the very first seminar. Instead, in the first two sessions students were asked to tell the module tutors what *they* knew about George III, and to suggest the kind of topics that they might find interesting in the Georgian period more generally through delivering short presentations to the class about objects or images which encapsulated those themes (with the tutors also taking part in the exercise to emphasise that all were embarking on a journey of discovery together).

The teaching over the first half of the module focused on techniques and approaches. After an exploration of the GPP website's own resources, and the catalogue of the Georgian Papers maintained on the Royal Collection Trust website through which the digitised images are accessed,[13] there followed detailed introductions and exercises in exploring, interrogating and retrieving items from an archive, whether physical or digital; a discussion of the key objectives in creating editions for different types of audience; an introduction to palaeography and the tricks of the trade in reading eighteenth-century hands; and a discussion of how to research material effectively for contextualisation or annotation of a document or object. In the age of Google, students are often blithely unaware that search results retrieved in this manner are ripped asunder from their context. But for historical scholarship, of course, context is everything. We therefore invested time in teaching the students how to bridge the imaginative and intellectual gap between the digital surrogates they were working with and the archival and material realities of the original documents. In week five of the module students discussed with the tutor(s) their initial thoughts on document selection, receiving guidance on whether or not the document(s)/object(s) would present particular challenges, how to explore the themes that seemed most appropriate to the edition and the type of edition they hoped to produce. At this point the tutors assured themselves that the project was not either over- or under-ambitious, suggesting ways to refine the choice of document(s) as required.

All of these skills were initially put to use in the group projects. For these the students were divided up, on the basis of the interests they had declared in the initial sessions, to work together on a class presentation of a document selected by the tutors to reflect those interests. The groups then remained in place for the remainder of the course as peer-support groups for the individual editions. More generally, the students were encouraged to take note of fellow students' strengths, and to seek help from each other on issues such as palaeography and translation, as well as identifying contexts: thus modern-language students assisted others with short passages in foreign languages in documents for those without the relevant languages, while music, English literature and philosophy students often assisted historians in return for guidance on unfamiliar historiographies.

It is through such interactions that a research community is built and the lone-scholar model of humanities research challenged; building what has been called a 'community of inquiry' in pedagogical literature for history.[14]

The group presentations gave the students the opportunity not only to test the skills they had acquired in a low-stakes assessed exercise but also to apprehend the module tutors' expectations of the quality of work for the module. They were also able to see and learn from how others did things better (or worse!), whether in contextualising, text analysis, creativity or overall approach – something they could discuss in a short reflective exercise worth half the marks for the group project assessment, in which they offered an account of the successes and failures of their group and their own part in these, often with disarming honesty!

Just before the students selected their individual project, we introduced them to the platform for their digital editions. This was the open-source software Xerte, initially developed at the University of Nottingham[15] to help academics and other educators build viable virtual learning environments without requiring programming or coding skills. It is equally adaptable for the presentation of materials by students. It provides users with a considerable library of webpage templates on which they can mount documents or images and accompany them with hotspots, zoom functions, tables, timelines, film inserts or quizzes. It is thus in effect an entire toolkit for building a suite of webpages with very little prior technical knowledge, but which is not so elaborate as to completely solve every design issue at the click of a button. In places, workarounds sometimes become necessary, and ingenuity may be required. If a student is familiar with coding, they have been able to personalise their project further. Xerte has enabled each student to design, build and implement a suite of webpages to support an edition at the heart of which sits a digital image of an original document or object accompanied by a transcription (and sometimes translation) of the text where appropriate, alongside pages of contextualisation, interpretation, annotation, argument and other apparatus. The content, arrangement, balance and navigation of these pages were part of what was ultimately assessed: for example, was the Xerte object designed to support the user in the way most appropriate to the type of edition the student had opted to produce? Students presented an advanced plan for the webpages in an extended final class, in which the whole group was encouraged to query decisions and offer suggestions for further improvements, before the students worked further on the edition after teaching had ended.

Two further key decisions were taken about the approach to the assessment challenge which both differentiated the task from those for other modules at King's. First, no word limit was set for the edition. This reflected our view that, depending on what type of edition students wanted to do, very different approaches might be appropriate in terms of the balance of text and image, or between detailed textual commentary/annotation and discursive introduction/contextualisation. Rather than becoming unduly exercised over hitting a target length, we wanted students to think about the amount of effort a project would involve, and then support their decisions once an appropriate scale had been decided upon. This certainly felt risky, and it led on occasion to some quite substantial projects where a student's enthusiasm had been especially engaged. However, it did not result in students feeling overburdened, and they generally got the point that longer was not necessarily better. With sufficient consultation with the tutors we believe students have been good at setting appropriate goals for themselves, and it has removed one potential source of stress.

One thing that may have facilitated this was our wider approach to assessment criteria. We took the decision that these would not be made available until the halfway point in the module when the students had both been introduced to the techniques involved in producing a good edition and done some work on applying these in their group projects. Moreover, not least as a means of consolidating the learning from this section of the module, a classroom session saw the students themselves review the generic faculty assessment criteria, and then discuss in their groups how these could be 'translated' into edition-related specifics, the resulting lists being collected at the end of the class and then consolidated along with any additional criteria the teachers deemed essential into the 'official' assessment criteria for the module published on the virtual learning environment. We hoped that this would allow students to take some ownership over the module's approach, and to internalise the criteria and how they can be applied to the very diverse range of editions that could be attempted. We did not hand over assessment itself to the student body, however, as this would have required knowledge of the historical context for other students' editions, which would not necessarily have been available to other members of the class. As we noted above, class teaching focused on editorial and research methods and interpretation of results, leaving students to learn individually about the historical context relevant to their document(s); nevertheless, this historical context remained essential for the assessment of the content of the edition and its rigour.[16]

During the second half of the module, teaching moved into a workshop model as the students began work on designing and researching their individual projects. During these sessions, as already indicated, the groups formed in the first half of the course provided an immediate support circle for each student, while the tutors moved between groups to offer guidance and establish the needs, if any, of each student for more focused support. In two of these workshops the focus was squarely on academic questions relating to the historical content of the edition, giving students a surgery to which they could bring specific challenges or requests for guidance. In advance of the session, students were asked to compile a short 'who's who?' with short biographies of individuals who would be named in their edition, ensuring that they had commenced any relevant biographical research beforehand, not least in order to highlight persons whose identity remained uncertain. A third workshop focused on the design and presentation of the Xerte object, along with discussion of transcriptions and annotation in digital editions, a session attended by the technology specialist. The final session, in which the students presented their plans, managed to combine a celebratory mood with a last opportunity for students to test out their ideas and raise any nagging doubts they might have before heading off to complete work on their editions.

Outcomes and reflections

After several years of teaching CKG, we judge the module to have achieved or surpassed most of the aims we had in creating it. It has also achieved a degree of recognition for offering a new model for research-led teaching. Presentations about CKG at international conferences on pedagogy have attracted a lot of interest, and in 2020 the module was awarded the Teaching Prize of the British Society for Eighteenth-Century Studies.

So what would we identify as the successes of this module? First, we have been delighted with the extent to which the module has managed to generate a 'research community' encompassing the students in ways that echo the wider community of eighteenth-century researchers. This has been partly within the context of the student cohort itself, where interdisciplinarity has been key. Students enjoyed learning from each other as they acted as 'subject specialists' in their various disciplines. During the group projects in particular they learnt to appreciate the different perspectives on a single document of the linguist, literature student, historian and philosopher, and this raised the level of their work. At the same time, we were particularly pleased with the way CKG generated connections between the students and the many academics who have been working on the GPP as fellows. In many cases the students were conducting detailed investigations of particular documents which could be of considerable assistance to academics with limited time in the archive, or without the time to look for references to their research outside the core archives for the theme in question. We were struck by the willingness and indeed enthusiasm with which senior researchers welcomed exchanges with students which might in other circumstances have felt burdensome. One explanation is that such contact took place at a point when the student had built up some intellectual capital of their own in relation to the document; another that such dialogue had been a strong feature of the GPP community more generally, with its workshops and sense of collective endeavour; a third that such contacts had been brokered by the module leads who themselves were part of that community.

Second, the editions have indeed ranged from the most traditional forms of scholarly edition, heavily annotated with careful identifications of events, persons and quotations in the text serving in some cases as the basis for redating or redescribing the document being considered, to public-facing introductions to documents designed to stimulate interest or engagement. Perhaps the most extreme example of the latter was an edition of the Anglo-Portuguese treaty of 1807 presented as a series of online games (involving, for example, transcription or identifying British property on a map of Lisbon) contextualised by a Brazilian mother filmed in Rio de Janeiro explaining Brazilian history to her child. Others have included tracing the subsequent history of diamonds identified in Queen Charlotte's inventories and presenting a first-hand account of Queen Caroline of Ansbach's death in the context of an explanation of the nature of her malady, with an actor voicing the testimony to give it greater immediacy (the soundtracks provided for many of the editions have been remarkable, with in one case readings of letters in the original French against a background of specially composed music).

In some cases the opening up of a document has involved extensive work on the part of the student to make it accessible. Two good examples of this involved documents written in archaic German scripts setting a palaeographic and a linguistic challenge. In both cases native German-speaking students were able to concentrate their energies on the former, and even allowed some playfulness, with at one stage of the navigation of one edition a set of options appearing to ask the reader whether they wished to skip a section on the technicalities of decoding the archaic script. One of the editions produced a translation and analysis of a large document detailing the contents of the Hanover Treasury for which the student received assistance from interested scholars in Germany, producing as far as we know the first transcription and translation of this document.

A number of editions have made research discoveries of their own. Several have helped identify the sources on which members of the royal family or court drew in their essays or commonplacing: one student did this for a meticulous edition and analysis of an essay by George III on Iceland; another (a mathematician) for his geometrical notes; another looked at Mary Hamilton's commonplacing, which revealed Mary Wollstonecraft among her readings. An early example which gave an indication of what was to come was a student who managed to make sense of the curious letter codes Queen Charlotte deployed in her jottings on early French kings as representing the dates of their accession, for which we have so far found no other example from the period. Soon after, another analysed the Prince of Wales's spending habits in the West End, identifying and mapping the shops he patronised, as well as suggesting that he was not quite as incorrigible a spendthrift as his reputation suggests.

Finally, a number of editions have shown great imagination and exploited the full potential of Xerte in interpreting a document. For example, despite the pandemic conditions, one visiting student used an inventory of George II's paintings at Kensington both to analyse the artistic traditions represented in his collection and to recreate the hang on a room-by-room basis. The resulting edition and transcription of a seventy-page manuscript went on to win a prize for the best undergraduate research conducted by a student overseas at the student's home university.

These latter projects have already been of great use to a number of researchers and the project team in their cataloguing of the collection. We hope before too long to mount the results of the best of them on the GPP website, along with many of the high-quality transcriptions the students have produced. This is a terrific testimony to the students and their engagement, and indicates that the idea of involving them actively in the bigger research project has not just been rhetoric, something that is not lost on students who have followed in their footsteps.

The module was a joy to teach, and the tutors learnt much from the students along the way. Student reactions to the module have also been overwhelmingly positive. They show not only that they genuinely felt that they were part of the GPP but also that they identified ways in which it provided opportunities to advance their historical skills which they had not enjoyed elsewhere. Rather than bemoaning the lack of lectures conveying the basic historical information, they often relished being given responsibility for their own research and information retrieval. We have also been delighted that for a number of students it has clearly been a significant factor in shaping their future plans; and even for those for whom this is not the case, they have left the module with a set of webpages which they had built and populated with immense imagination that they could share with potential employers.

To conclude, let us share some of the comments we have received from students who have taken CKG:

> This module was easily my favourite . . . It was very engaging all ten weeks and aroused my interest not only in the Georgian era but generally in research on historical topics . . . It was really a refreshing module as it is less academic and more of an interactive research based one . . . The atmosphere of the sessions were always great because of the kind manner of tutors and the active participation that was required from the students.

> It has been fantastic to feel part of an international historical project as it develops. I hope we can observe its development further after we finish as I now feel very engaged and invested in it. I have been very excited to feel I am putting my skills as a historian to new use, and it has been fantastic to engage in new methods of carrying out and presenting historical research beyond essay writing. It's been useful to think about these new ways of offering history to different audiences, and it is definitely something I plan to take further in my career.

> It has been a while since I took Court of King George III, but I just wanted to say . . . I had such a great time in your classes and it really has had a big influence on me. I spent the last few months

volunteering for a . . . Museum [and] had the opportunity to create part of their website. The experience working on a digital edition in your class gave me the confidence to attempt this project. The course also made me realize that it is my passion to work on digital editions and in the digital humanities field. In April I started a MA [and] have chosen to make Digital History the main focus of my degree . . . I hope to continue gaining experience in this field as I seek to pursue digital edition-related internships in the future. I just wanted to say thank you. It was you . . . who introduced me to this field in the first place, which I now know that I would love to pursue as a career.

I'm currently in the process of compiling my applications to history PhD programs in the US and I've been thinking a lot about how my research with you really impacted my academic career and research interests. Everyone I've spoken to about the project, or just the course in general, has been very interested, and I find myself talking about it for very long with anyone who will listen!

I can genuinely say this was one of the most unique and exciting courses I have ever been a part of! I would love to keep receiving updates on the Georgian Papers Programme!

Notes

1 Among others, the Bentham Project, the Clergy of the Church of England Database, the Legacies of British Slavery Encyclopedia of British Slave Ownership, London Lives 1690–1800, the Old Bailey Online and (behind a paywall) Eighteenth-Century Collections Online.

2 Both approaches are embedded within the subject benchmarking document maintained by the UK Quality Assurance Agency for Higher Education (QAA). See the March 2022 iteration at www.qaa.ac.uk/quality-code/subject-benchmark-statements/history (accessed 28 March 2023).

3 For a summary account, see Center for MH in Schools & Student/Learning Supports, 'Group Work in Education: Addressing Student Concerns', 2021, https://smhp.psych.ucla.edu/groupwork.pdf (accessed 28 March 2023).

4 The genesis of this module was very much the outcome of the authors' practical experience in the classroom. In this chapter we make only sparing reference to pedagogical literature in part to underline how little this shaped the module, although many (though not all) features of it align closely with themes prominent in that literature. The specific context of the creation of the opportunity modules allowed us to overcome our frustration with the limitations of other formats for 'research-led' teaching by 'breaking the rules' of discipline-specific programme regulations. The case was made on the basis of the unique opportunity presented by the GPP, and we were enormously grateful to the external examiners and programme boards more generally who approached the module in such a supportive manner, judging it in terms of results rather than conformity to existing practice.

5 6AAHCF01 in the King's College London module catalogue.

6 There is a wealth of publications on user experience (UX), but a good starting point is the collection of resources provided by the Neilsen Norman Group, for example Jakob Nielsen, 'How Users Read on the Web' (1997), www.nngroup.com/articles/how-users-read-on-the-web (accessed 28 March 2023). Our thinking about non-linear communication is in part inspired by debates in museology, for example Helen Gaynor, 'Non-Linear Documentary and Museum Exhibition Design: Interdisciplinary Inspirations', *International Journal of Creative Media Research*, 3 (2020); Nina Simon, 'Museum 2.0: Should Museum Exhibitions Be More Linear? Exploring the Power of the Forced March in Digital and Physical Environments', *Museum 2.0* (9 January 2013), http://museumtwo.blogspot.com/2013/01/should-museum-exhibitions-be-more-linear.html (accessed 28 March 2023).

7 For the GPP, see the project website: https://georgianpapers.com (accessed 28 March 2023).

8 Other key members of the team were Julie Crocker, Sarah Davis, Laura Hobbs, Rachel Krier (Royal Archives), James Smithies, Sam Callaghan, Paul Caton (King's Digital Lab), Angel Luke O'Donnell (King's College London), Deborah Cornell (William & Mary) and Shawn Holl (Omohundro Institute). The full team is listed on the GPP website: https://georgianpapers.com/about/the-team (accessed 28 March 2023).

9 See the GPP website, in particular the list of fellows (https://georgianpapers. com/get-involved/full_list_fellows), the record of scholarly publications flowing from the fellowships (https://georgianpapers.com/2022/04/26/the-impact-of-the-georgian-papers-programme-on-scholarly-research) and the events page (https://georgianpapers.com/get-involved/events) (all accessed 28 March 2023).

10 This focus on 'learning by doing' and developing historical scholarship as a set of skills and practices is grounded in similar concerns to inquiry-based learning, on which there is a substantial literature. For a good introduction see Patrick Blessinger and John M. Carfora (eds), *Inquiry-Based Learning for the Arts, Humanities, and Social Sciences: A Conceptual and Practical Resource for Educators. Vol. 2. Innovations in Higher Education Teaching and Learning* (Bingley: Emerald Group Publishing Limited, 2014), https://doi.org/10.1108/S2055-364120142 (accessed 28 March 2023).

11 In its first iterations there was also a teaching assistant to help cope with large numbers, Miranda Reading, herself a GPP research fellow.

12 In recent years David Reid Matthews.

13 Georgian Papers Online website: https://gpp.rct.uk/default.aspx (accessed 28 March 2023).

14 See Peter Seixas, 'The Community of Inquiry as a Basis for Knowledge and Learning: The Case of History', *American Educational Research Journal*, 30:2 (June 1993), 305–24; Adrian Jones, 'Teaching History at University through Communities of Inquiry', *Australian Historical Studies*, 42:2 (June 2011), 168–93.

15 We are very grateful to Professor Jamie Wood of the University of Lincoln who first introduced Arthur to the possibilities of this software. For more information, see https://xerte.org.uk; for the range of page templates on offer, see www.nottingham.ac.uk/toolkits/play_8203 (both accessed 28 March 2023). For further discussion of the ways Xerte can assist in achieving assessment objectives, see Maria Kutar, Marie Griffiths and Jamie Wood, 'Ecstasi Project: Using Technology to Encourage Creativity in the Assessment Process' (2015), *UK Academy for Information Systems Conference Proceedings 2015*, http://aisel.aisnet.org/ukais2015/32. Wood's blog, 'Making Digital History' at https://makingdigitalhistory.co.uk (accessed 28 March 2023), platforms several relevant posts.

16 There is of course a considerable literature on student engagement in assessment, but for an example which explicitly engages with such engagement in the context of assessment remaining in the hands of the teachers, see Rosario Hernández, 'Students' Engagement in the Development of Criteria to Assess Written Tasks', *REAP International Online Conference on Assessment Design for Learner Responsibility, 29th–31st May, 2007*, www.reap.ac.uk/reap/reap07/Portals/2/CSL/t2%20-%20great%20designs%20for%20assessment/students%20deciding%20assessment%20criteria/Students_engagement_in_development_of_assessment_criteria.pdf (accessed 28 March 2023).

References

Blessinger, Patrick and Carfora, John M. (eds), *Inquiry-Based Learning for the Arts, Humanities, and Social Sciences: A Conceptual and Practical Resource for Educators. Vol. 2. Innovations in Higher Education Teaching and Learning* (Bingley: Emerald Group Publishing Limited, 2014).

Center for MH in Schools & Student/Learning Supports, 'Group Work in Education: Addressing Student Concerns' (2021), https://smhp.psych.ucla.edu/groupwork.pdf (accessed 28 March 2023).

Gaynor, Helen, 'Non-Linear Documentary and Museum Exhibition Design: Interdisciplinary Inspirations', *International Journal of Creative Media Research*, 3 (2020).

Hernández, Rosario, 'Students' Engagement in the Development of Criteria to Assess Written Tasks', *REAP International Online Conference on Assessment Design for Learner Responsibility, 29th–31st May, 2007*, www.reap.ac.uk/reap/reap07/Portals/2/CSL/t2%20-%20great%20designs%20for%20assessment/students%20deciding%20assessment%20criteria/Students_engagement_in_development_of_assessment_criteria.pdf (accessed 28 March 2023).

Jones, Adrian, 'Teaching History at University through Communities of Inquiry', *Australian Historical Studies*, 42:2 (June 2011), 168–93.

Kutar, Maria, Griffiths, Marie and Wood, Jamie, 'Ecstasi Project: Using Technology to Encourage Creativity in the Assessment Process', *UK Academy for Information Systems Conference Proceedings 2015* (2015), http://aisel.aisnet.org/ukais2015/32.

Nielsen, Jakob, 'How Users Read on the Web' (1997), www.nngroup.com/articles/how-users-read-on-the-web (accessed 28 March 2023).

Quality Assurance Agency, 'History' (2022), www.qaa.ac.uk/quality-code/subject-benchmark-statements/history (accessed 28 March 2023).

Seixas, Peter, 'The Community of Inquiry as a Basis for Knowledge and Learning: The Case of History', *American Educational Research Journal*, 30:2 (June 1993), 305–24.

Simon, Nina, 'Museum 2.0: Should Museum Exhibitions Be More Linear? Exploring the Power of the Forced March in Digital and Physical Environments', *Museum 2.0* (9 January 2013), http://museumtwo.blogspot.com/2013/01/should-museum-exhibitions-be-more.html (accessed 28 March 2023).

Chapter 2

Introducing Australian students to British history and research methods via digital sources

Simon Burrows and Rebekah Ward

This chapter explores a pedagogical experiment: the development and impact of a unit on 'Britain in the Age of Botany Bay, 1760–1815' (BABB), taught at Western Sydney University (WSU) in Australia, from the perspective of the instructor and a former student. The unit, a third-year BA class in the History and Political Thought (HPT) specialism, taught in 2014 and 2016, attempted to capitalise on the ready availability of digital resources for studying eighteenth- and early nineteenth-century history. Its key assessment outcome was a 3,500–4,000-word extended essay based on original research using online primary sources. The unit operated across a fifteen-week semester, comprising thirteen teaching weeks, a one-week mid-term break and a study week. This presented various teaching, learning and assessment challenges for students and staff. The ways in which we addressed these challenges, and lessons arising from their mixed success, have wider applicability for teaching digital history and the provision of practical primary research to undergraduate students.

Contexts and challenges

WSU is a large regional/metropolitan university spread across eleven campuses in Richmond, Bankstown, Penrith, Campbelltown and Parramatta.[1]

This area, covering half of Sydney's population, is the motor of New South Wales's economic growth and home to a socially diverse community, including many recent migrants and traditionally working-class or deprived areas. Uniquely among Australian universities, WSU has a regional focus and mission written into its founding charter. This has given the university a mandate for socially focused research, a stance which contributed to its first-in-world position in the *Times Higher* Impact Rankings 2022 and again in 2023.[2]

By enrolments, WSU is Australia's second largest university, with around 50,000 students who speak almost 200 birth languages. Disproportionately large numbers of WSU students are first-in-family to attend university. In addition, a significant number of BA students are teacher trainees, so the HPT specialism needs to cater for their needs. This includes ensuring accreditation as modern history teachers by the New South Wales Board of Studies, Teaching & Educational Standards and, since 1 January 2017, its replacement, the New South Wales Education Standards Authority.

The HPT specialism arises from the Australian custom of having combined history and politics departments, though by 2014 the programme's emphasis was on modern history and the history of political thought. At the time that BABB was taught, the HPT major contained four compulsory units, including first-year survey units on 'Modern European History and Politics' and 'Global History'; a second-year thematic unit on the secularisation of political thought; and a third-year unit on 'Theories and Methods in History'. Nowhere in the HPT major was there a requirement to produce a sustained piece of primary source research. This is standard for Australian BA History programmes, though it has not always been the case. Research opportunities at WSU were reserved for an optional fourth-year honours dissertation. However, by the mid-2010s honours was being phased out in favour of a two-year Master of Research, based on the Bologna model. BABB was designed precisely to fill this gap: to allow students a taste of research and an opportunity to develop transferable, higher-level skills. Motives for this were intellectual, pragmatic and personal.

On an intellectual level, the unit's instructor Simon was convinced that WSU history graduates, particularly those who intended to pursue a teaching career, needed hands-on experience to understand the generation of historical knowledge. This would also align with official expectations – set out in the Australian History Threshold Learning Outcomes – that history graduates should be able to 'interpret a wide range of . . . primary materials' and 'examine historical issues by undertaking research according to the methodological and ethical conventions of the discipline', as well as more explicit statements around primary source-based research in comparable international benchmark statements.[3]

On a more practical level, the unit aspired to give WSU graduates an edge in a competitive employment market. Higher-level skills associated with historical study are highly valued by employers. These skills include formulating a research question; designing a systematic inquiry; gathering, recording and processing large amounts of information; data analysis; and presentation of findings. Indeed, the local business lobby has since recognised the critical importance and scarcity of humanities-trained graduates.[4] For these reasons, the BABB unit focused on helping students become aware of and able to articulate the transferable skills they were honing or acquiring. This is an area where the historical profession traditionally has a poor track record. In 2008–9, a survey of 1,445 first- and third-year history students at eleven Australian universities found few students associated historical thinking with skills and primary evidence, but instead emphasised research via books and articles.[5]

Finally, on a personal level BABB would allow the instructor to continue supervising undergraduate research projects. This had been a particularly rewarding aspect of his previous time at the University of Leeds (UK) where undergraduates in single honours history were required to undertake a 12,000-word dissertation, usually aligning it with their two-paper third-year 'Special Subject'. Having worked intensively with around a dozen third-year dissertation students annually between 2000 and 2012, Simon was excited at the possibilities for developing a scaled-down version for Australian students. It was also hoped such a unit would help recruit students into higher-degree study. As WSU does not offer European languages, prospects for recruiting students via his flagship 'Enlightenment and [French] Revolution' unit were poor.

The pedagogical philosophy of BABB was based on research suggesting that students engage better with historical methodology and research skills when 'embedded in the curriculum'.[6] This approach involves 'learning by doing' rather than attempting to teach skills in a more abstract manner, which many students find harder to understand. BABB included a set of skills podcasts, each recommended for watching at the appropriate week, to offer students targeted support with planning, research, analysis and writing processes (see Table 2.1). This ensured students had asynchronous

Table 2.1: List of research method podcasts

Week	Topic title	Week	Topic title
1	The Research Process	8	Planning Your Essay
2	Choosing a Topic	9	(Intersession break - no set pod)
3	Choosing Sources	10	Writing up the Literature
4	Interrogating Sources	11	Writing up Your Methods
5	Preparing a Bibliography	12	Findings, Intro and Conclusion
6	Starting Research	13	Reference
7	Work in Progress Report	14	Reviewing a Draft

access to training materials and, it was envisaged, would enable an experimental online-only delivery option. For technical reasons, online-only delivery was abandoned in favour of face-to-face classes (see below), but the podcasts were retained.

While BABB was therefore designed to allow students to engage with primary source materials, there was a simultaneous effort to expose students to (some of) the impressive digitised historical resources that are now available. Simon believed that an awareness of these resources and capacity to use them effectively were vital skills for both the future historians and history teachers who were undertaking the unit.

This ambition was well suited to the unit's thematic focus. As Simon Burrows and Glenn Roe observed in 2020, the eighteenth century has been perhaps uniquely well served among historical eras for richness and comprehensiveness of digital materials.[7] BABB capitalised on this by drawing particularly on three resources available to WSU students: Old Bailey Online and two remarkable research collections published by Gale, Eighteenth-Century Collections Online (ECCO) and the Seventeenth- and Eighteenth-Century Burney Collection of Newspapers (henceforth the 'Burney Collection').[8] These sources gave students access to several centuries of records from London's central criminal court, the majority of books and pamphlets published in Britain or the English-speaking world across the eighteenth century, and a large sample of mostly London newspapers covering 150 years of British history.

It was not compulsory to use these digital resources but almost all students did so, particularly since accessing non-digital materials was impractical. Some students exploited other digital collections, too, including the Reading Experience Database (RED) or, for early Australian connections and newspapers, the Trove repository (a national database of Australiana holding over 6 billion digital objects), as well as holdings in the WSU Library, which aspires to host the best digital collections of any Australian university.[9] Particularly useful given BABB's focus on the long eighteenth century were ProQuest's British Periodicals and Gale's Nineteenth-Century British Newspapers.[10]

Interrogating digitised primary source materials requires specific skill-sets. There is, of course, significant overlap with traditional archival practices (such as critical treatment of sources, ability to synthesise and evaluate information, awareness of preservation processes and discussion of the impact of historical context) but other tasks require quite different competencies. For example, the relevance and scale of results within digital resources depends heavily on effective search techniques, and the comparatively easy access to huge swathes of information changes decisions around scope and sampling. BABB therefore needed to be designed in a way that addressed both types of skills. The development of these research skills – particularly in the context of the previous experience of students upon enrolment in BABB – is addressed in the following sections.

The specific collections featured in BABB – ECCO, the Burney Collection and Old Bailey Online – built on Simon's extensive experience using them in teaching and research. His Leeds honours dissertation students had been expected to choose topics related to his French Revolution Special Subject, but few felt confident with French-language sources. He therefore guided most students to research topics for which ECCO housed English-language translations of key sources, or to explore British reactions to the Revolution, particularly in the newspaper press via the Burney Collection.

As a specialist press historian, this played to Simon's strengths.[11] In particular, he could advise students how to sample and analyse complex eighteenth-century newspaper sources, and on the application of theoretical models for understanding newspaper materials. For example, some of his Leeds students found Habermas's conception of the 'public sphere' heuristically useful and empowering.[12] Others adapted Herman and Chomsky's model of filters in *Manufacturing Consent* to understand what appeared on the printed page, or devised thematic tables and symbological approaches to represent and analyse key themes and trends in a body of texts, drawing on Rolf Reinhardt and Hans-Jürgen Lüsebrink's work on the Bastille.[13] These competencies were employed again in BABB.

Also significant for developing the unit was Simon's experience of co-developing online research training and support materials at Leeds. These materials took MA and honours students through the various stages of their research process and served as a model and inspiration for the research pods in BABB. Monitoring the resource websites revealed each Leeds cohort, comprising around 220 undergraduates per year, viewed the dissertation support pages over 1,000 times. This proved an important way of supplementing the two hours of one-to-one supervision each student was entitled to receive. External examiners also praised these resources, linking them to discernible improvements in the quality and rigour of both undergraduate and MA dissertations and conference presentations. Several even recommended the Leeds model as best practice to their own institutions. The online training resources may also have contributed to an exponential growth in the Leeds MA history programmes, which grew in a single decade from eleven to sixty enrolments. Nevertheless, the big question remained: could these approaches and materials be adapted effectively to support an Australian undergraduate cohort in a more limited research exercise?

It was clear this adaptation would involve significant challenges. The most obvious was a lack of content knowledge among Australian students, most of whom had not studied British history before. It would thus be necessary to provide them with a crash course on the period at the very moment that they were being asked to choose a research topic. Nor were students likely to come to the unit with the same level of prior historical study that British undergraduates brought to their first experience of sustained research. The Australian education system follows a Scottish model, with students taking a diverse range of subjects at high school and in university humanities degrees. WSU students only need eight papers to complete an HPT major in a twenty-four-paper degree.

Further, what methodology or research skills students might have acquired at university were unevenly spread. The best prepared would have completed the HPT compulsory third-year unit on 'Theories and Methods in History', but some had not yet taken it and others were studying the units in parallel. Further, lower-level compulsory units were not built around skills acquisition. Instead, students would have taken a range of specialist historical units, including possible cross-listings from other specialisations, notably International Relations and Asian Studies or Cultural and Social Analysis. Many students also had no experience writing extended essays over 2,000 words or working with historical primary sources. Among those who had, some had only encountered primary sources at high school. However, Higher School Certificate history was not a prerequisite for enrolling in HPT.

Unit design and delivery

Simon was aware of the challenges that his BABB unit would present. During his first year in Australia he therefore consulted widely with colleagues, especially distinguished Australian colonial historian Carol Liston, a foundation member of the HPT team at WSU and an innovative teacher. Together they devised a strategy for supporting students through the research process, to try to ensure no-one was left behind or felt too daunted by the expectations of the unit. Fundamental to these attempts was an assessment philosophy that sought to reward engagement with process, and a week-by-week mapping of activities including face-to-face meetings, online support materials, lectures, tutorials, methods podcasts and assessments. Formal marks would be awarded in the planning stage for a project proposal, in the research phase for a work-in-progress video and during the writing-up stage for preparing source lists, glossaries and appendices, collectively amounting to 50 per cent of their grade. The main text of the extended essay was worth the remaining 50 per cent.

The project proposal was a formulaic planning document. It required students to provide an essay title (approved in advance by the tutor); a short description outlining the topic, its significance and how students would go about the research; a list of three to five questions they intended to ask of their sources; and an annotated list of primary and secondary sources. Detailed instructions were provided in the Unit Learning Guide (Course Outline) and students were provided with a worked example. A detailed assessment grid set out the expectations for each part of the document (see Table 2.2). This tick-box approach proved a double-edged sword. Despite a high level of guidance and support, some students struggled to score points against the rubric. For an exercise that was intended to reward student engagement with academic research processes, some students achieved grades significantly below the pass mark.

Table 2.2: Assessment grid for project proposal exercise

Criteria	1 mark	2 marks	3 marks	4 marks	5 marks
Title	Offers a viable, appropriate and approved title	Not applicable. Only one mark is available under this criterion.			
Project Description (PD)	Describes a historical project, but in current form it is poorly conceived or unrealisable due to issues of scope, scale, originality or sources	Offers a viable essay topic in theory, but approach, methods and/or sources are ill-suited to the task	Describes a viable essay topic based on valid sources, but approach method, and/or historical significance need further elucidation	Describes a strong, original and viable topic based on valid sources but may require fine-tuning to realise full potential of topic	Fluently outlines strong, coherent and original project based on appropriate sources and addressing a valid historical problem
Key questions	Some questions could be answered from selected primary sources, but most are poorly focused or badly worded	Questions generally are answerable from chosen sources but wording or conception needs to be fine-tuned to produce a strong essay	Questions are generally well-worded and can be answered from sources, but do not fully address topic or all its angles	Questions are well-worded, appropriate to sources, and likely to give a rounded to questions in PD answer, but may be unrealistic or insufficient in scope	Questions are well worded, appropriate to sources, realistic in scope and likely to elicit a comprehensive answer to questions raised in PD
Primary and secondary sources	Identifies some useful primary sources and secondary literature	Identifies and differentiates between appropriate primary sources and some key secondary literature	Identifies appropriate quantity and quality of primary sources and helpfully prioritises key secondary literature	Identifies best available primary sources for task and systematically identifies and prioritises key secondary literature	Not applicable. Only four marks are available under this criterion.

To track student progress, offer variety in assessment and provide preliminary feedback on methods and findings, the second assignment was a work-in-progress video. The aim of this exercise was to show the topic was viable from available primary materials and worthy of study, and to give students feedback on their approaches and ideas. The resultant videos (mostly filmed on mobile phones) were a highlight of the unit and played to local student strengths. Most WSU students are verbally articulate and confident at presenting when compared with British peers. This is partly because of the prevalence of teacher trainees among the WSU student cohort, but also because public speaking has a more central role in Australian schooling. Students also reported the ability to record themselves made this less daunting than a traditional presentation. Recordings were also more equitable, since they could be reviewed more than once.

Finally, to further build student confidence and certainty, source lists, glossaries and appendices could be submitted in advance of the essay and awarded a provisional baseline mark. Students could make improvements to those materials before they submitted their final essay in order to raise their grade. As marks were awarded against relatively objective criteria, students who had engaged effectively with process could approach the essay secure in the knowledge that they would probably pass the unit even if they underachieved in the written component.

Using the activity map, Simon devised a timeline for activities with corresponding reminders (see Table 2.3). This was important because students only had a notional 150 study hours. By way of comparison, Leeds honours dissertation students had a notional 800 hours, comprising 400 hours of study in the 'Special Subject' and a further 400 hours to research and write their dissertations. Weekly reminders advised BABB students of impending deadlines, classes and opportunities to meet with him. Generally, the reminders suggested students run activities over several weeks. In the first week they might be told to 'start' or 'plan' an activity, in the second and third weeks to 'continue', and in the fourth week to 'finish'. This allowed students to track progress against key tasks but also allowed leeway for slippage.

The activity map also helped Simon to plot instalments of the unit's most distinctive feature: the fable of 'Lazy Toad and Stressed Bunny'. The protagonists in this allegorical tale are BABB students. Stressed Bunny, like many WSU students, is a hard-working, time-poor single mum who aspires to good grades. Lazy Toad is a carefree, slightly sleazy, chilled-out dude,

Table 2.3: Weekly reminder, week 9

- This week is the mid-term break so there are no online classes, methods podcasts or formal clinic hours. Students can email me to arrange an appointment at Kingswood on Tuesday or Parramatta on Wednesday
- Use this time wisely (Uncle Simon's Avuncular Tip: taking a few days away to freshen your mind away from uni work counts as a wise use of time)
- This is the best week to prepare your Work-in-Progress video presentation (due week 10). See the Unit Outline for more information.
  Remember this task has to be uploaded to YouTube – this takes time and requires a Gmail account – so allow time to organise the submission. Be prepared for technical hitches. You have plenty of time so technology failure is not an excuse for late submission
- We're still in the research phase. Keep plugging away at those primary sources
- While conducting your research, don't forget to collect unfamiliar C18 terms and submit them to the Unit Glossary on vUWS by week 13. You need to have done this to qualify for the Glossary Marks.

who believes, in local parlance, that 'P's ["Pass" grades] make degrees'. He uses every trick in the book to minimise workload.

Week by week, Bunny and Toad confront the twin challenges of life and study. They compare notes and tips, highlight the tutor's key messages and verbally spar as Bunny graciously knocks back Toad's invitations to chill by his pool. Prominent in their banter, however, are ways for students to work more efficiently, save time and hone research. Pride of place goes to Toad's triumphal realisation he can get by with sampling newspaper stories on his topic, London coffee-houses. Whereas Bunny sees sampling as a way to maximise the representative chronological coverage of her essay, Toad sees it as a means to cut his workload by 80 per cent. Nevertheless, the results of Toad's efforts surprise him. His methodological rigour in sampling earns him a distinction, but the thinness of his material prevents him from achieving his first ever high distinction. Thus the fable of Bunny and Toad addressed student anxieties in a light-hearted way, sharing study tips and reinforcing the messaging in the weekly reminders.

A key challenge of the unit was to ensure students got face-to-face supervision time. This had been an issue in the Leeds dissertation model, where, as noted above, staff supervision was rationed. In the context of WSU's thirteen-week teaching semesters, there was no way to give each student two hours of individual time. However, the structure of teaching at WSU provided useful ways to maximise supervision for students who attended regularly. Australian universities have relatively high drop-out rates from individual units, as students can re-sit or take alternative units. Class attendance is not compulsory, and work, assignments and family considerations, as well as, with increasing frequency, environmental factors (especially bushfires and floods), impact attendance. So, although twenty-five students could theoretically be accommodated in each hour-long tutorial, weekly classes averaged eight to ten students, allowing for more individualised supervision. Students were also encouraged to seek out the instructor during his weekly office hours.

Once they had chosen a topic, students were divided into groups of three to six students organised around their chosen subjects or sources. For example, in 2016, at the Bankstown campus, there were groups on 'Crime', 'Social Life' and 'Politics and the Press'. Each group was asked to attend a session each fortnight instead of a weekly class. These sessions combined intensive supervision with peer-to-peer discussion of ideas, challenges, approaches and use of digital resources. Across the unit, students who attended these sessions received greater supervisor assistance, and more peer support, when compared to individual students at Leeds.

Most WSU students had no prior knowledge of British history or the eighteenth century. A well-structured 'crash course' was thus essential. It comprised twelve hours of short lecture podcasts grouped into thematic clusters. These were posted online and could be accessed throughout the semester. Students could thus dip into topics that interested them, and if necessary (following Toad's example) ignore those that looked peripheral to their research. Tying the lecture podcasts together was an overview podcast and a 'case study' orientation podcast which sought to relate the material to students' local knowledge. It focused on a historical figure of local renown, the Reverend Samuel Marsden.

Marsden (1765–1838) was the second Anglican clergyman to arrive in colonial New South Wales.[14] Marsden's presence is ubiquitous across western Sydney but is also found in Leeds and New Zealand. To pique student curiosity, Simon stressed how Marsden's life and his own were mostly lived in the same places. Born in Farsley (Leeds), Marsden initially worked in his father's blacksmith's shop in Horsforth, where Simon lived from 2006 to 2012.[15] Via a youthful flirtation with Methodism, Marsden attracted attention from Anglican evangelicals, notably William Wilberforce, who paid for him to attend school in Hull and the University of Cambridge (Simon's hometown), before securing him a position in New South Wales.

In Australia, Marsden is notorious as 'the flogging parson' due to his reputation for handing out stiff court sentences to recidivist convicts. Across 'the Ditch', he is celebrated for having brought Christianity to Aotearoa-New Zealand. On Christmas Day 1814, he preached the first Christian sermon to Māori. A Christmas carol, *Te Harinui*, commemorates him and the event. Naturally, Simon sang a few lines and recalled performing it at a carol concert while working at the University of Waikato.

Marsden had a residence at Parramatta, the colony's one-time seat of government and site of multiple WSU campuses. A major street there carries his name. More than 20 kilometres away, on a 2,000-acre estate, Marsden built a homestead, Mamre House. An arterial road and a local Anglican school are named after it. All three are a short distance from WSU's Kingswood campus and Simon's first home in Australia. The charitable trust that runs Mamre House kindly allowed him to film his lecture podcast on Marsden there. Students saw for themselves the pasture where Marsden introduced merino sheep gifted to him by George III to help improve Australian wool yields. Marsden sent his wool back to be milled in Leeds.

Reflecting on Marsden's life story, Simon was able to link places and stories familiar to WSU students to major themes of British eighteenth-century social, economic, political, cultural and colonial history. The narrative covered religion, crime and justice, agricultural, industrial, and commercial revolutions, imperial expansion, global trade, monarchy, and, via Wilberforce, patronage, the slave trade, abolitionism and party politics. Ideas about race, class and the first peoples of Australia and New Zealand were also interwoven. Finally, the timing of Marsden's departure from Britain (July 1793) and arrival in Australia (March 1794) provided a jumping-off point to discuss the French Revolutionary Terror, the British patriotic response, and the Revolutionary and Napoleonic Wars.

The most pressing challenge for students commencing BABB was to identify a research topic by the end of the third week. This was a new exercise for most students. Teaching materials gave them multiple forms of assistance. The Learning Guide included guidance on viable topics and contained a list of five potential thematic areas – consumer goods; fame, celebrity and the media; crime; sports and popular pastimes; and family, sex and marriage – with suggested topics for each. Every content podcast concluded by suggesting four or five potential topics for investigation, and the week 2 research method podcast addressed choosing a topic and preparing a project proposal. With this guidance, almost every student succeeded in submitting a topic for their essay assignment on schedule, or, failing that, a theme, which could then be honed into a topic through consultation with the instructor.

Having chosen a topic, students were supported and their progress monitored by regular small assessments items. The project proposal described above was due in week 6 of the semester; and the work-in-progress video provided an indication of how students were tracking in week 10. Glossary entries were due by week 13, though early submission was encouraged. There were also options for handing in a non-assessed essay plan and to bring bibliographies and appendices for 'pre-marking' in face-to-face meetings. The research essay itself was due at the end of week 15 (study week). This model had the disadvantage of imposing a significant number of deadlines but allowed tracking and interventions. Simon's relatively high research and administration loadings, which allowed him to teach into only one unit per semester, were helpful here. These factors allowed him to concentrate on BABB, facilitating fast feedback turnarounds and support to students.

Outcomes

Despite the time pressure, students came up with innovative topic choices. While some submissions, such as 'Sport and Leisure in the Georgian Era, 1760–1815' or 'Causes of the American War of Independence', read like undergraduate essay titles and required scaling back and refocusing, others showed ingenuity, imagination and a clear grasp of what might be feasible. The more novel and manageable topics included 'Marketing of Tobacco' and a study of 'Aldersgate General Dispensary and the Politics of Pharmaceuticals'. A significant number of students were inspired to study crime by the availability of Old Bailey Online and newspaper sources, and for some this linked to the convict origins of New South Wales, as in a project on women's transportation. One particularly imaginative student looked at the treatment and outcomes for Irish defendants at the Old Bailey.

The gender dimensions of crime and punishment were popular choices, with essay topics including 'Factory Women and Crime'. On the Kingswood campus, there was sufficient interest in gender issues to justify an entire 'topic group' of six students working on everything from domestic spaces to Hannah Snell's cross-dressing or the depiction of vice in *Harris's List of Covent Garden Ladies*. There were also groups at both Kingswood and Bankstown focused on politics and/or the press, including studies of newspaper coverage of Methodism and of the 1794 Polish rising. Another group looked at 'reading, culture and intellectual life', reflecting Simon's own interest in book history and student engagement with another WSU unit on 'Cultural History of Books and Reading'. The co-author of this chapter, Rebekah, was one of the students in this group. Here is how she describes the evolution of her project:

> I undertook BABB in 2016 in the third year of my BA. At the outset, the unit sounded simultaneously daunting and fascinating. I was eager to engage with historical methodologies, particularly to use primary sources to study a topic of my choosing. The idea that my entire grade rested upon a single project was unfamiliar, and thus intimidating, but the scaffolding outlined by the instructor was reassuring.
>
> Inspired by a content pod[cast] about the novel in the eighteenth century and a tutorial about the Burney Collection, I wanted to research newspaper coverage of books. This turned out to be an apt choice given Simon's speciality. Through consultation, I eventually decided to explore the initial reception of Jane Austen's novels. I had read (and enjoyed) the novels but did not want this to be a literary study.
>
> Secondary research, mostly in journal articles and monographs held in the WSU Library, revealed there was little consensus about Austen's immediate reception. Studies seemed to reach one of three (contradictory) conclusions: that Austen was initially a critic's novelist; her novels were not subject to critical commentary until the 1900s; or Austen was scarcely known before 1870. It became clear such contradictions had methodological foundations. Traditional reception studies relied on critical reviews (typically written by men), while other studies (often feminist ones) focused on the so-called forgotten voices of predominately female readers. I hypothesised analysis of the digital collections featured in BABB proposed a solution. These collections, I thought, would make it feasible to

simultaneously address various types of reception and thus, hopefully, resolve such contradictions.

My project focused on the years 1811–21, so rather than ECCO or the Burney Collection, I relied on other digital collections. After some initial training (involving watching the pre-recorded pods, alongside specialised assistance from the instructor), I was able – without leaving my remote home on the outskirts of western Sydney – to research what had been written about Austen in Britain some 200 years earlier. I located and examined literary reviews (via British periodicals), everyday reader responses (transcribed in RED), newspaper advertisements for the novels (in Nineteenth-Century British Newspapers), and library holdings and print run information (Cardiff University's 'British Fiction, 1800–1829'). Using materials across these various collections allowed me to conclude Austen's novels were well known and well received by both the British press and general public in the first ten years after publication, revising dominant narratives about one of the world's most famous novelists.

Not all students could be expected to relish the novelty as much as Rebekah. One enduring concern was that, daunted by the challenges, students might drop out of the unit. At WSU, drop-out rates are measured against enrolments on 'census day', which is several weeks into the semester. In the mid-2010s, drop-out rates tended to exceed 10 per cent. Rates of 20 per cent, not uncommon, were considered cause for concern.[16] The first time the unit ran, in 2014, one-third of students (n=17) enrolled at census day did not complete the unit. Of these, six did not submit any work and eleven only submitted the early assignments (see Table 2.4). Some of these students may have withdrawn due to their marks, but six were on passing grades when they withdrew. The high attrition rate was probably partly linked to the perceived challenge. As a result, in 2016 Simon focused on explaining what might reasonably be expected for each exercise. To build confidence, he informed students that there had been a near 100 per cent pass rate for students who completed the unit in 2014.[17] This expectation management seems to have had the desired result. In 2016 the drop-out rate more than halved (15 per cent, n=7).

Measured in terms of grades achieved, student outcomes in BABB were similar to those in the instructor's other third-year unit, 'Enlightenment and Revolution', which ran in 2013 and 2015, and had a drop-out rate between those of BABB in 2014 and 2016 (see Table 2.5).[18] This provides the most appropriate comparator because at undergraduate level in Australia there is no systematic double-marking or moderation via external examiners. Instead, internal exam boards keep a watchful eye on grade distributions to ensure general comparability.

At the top of the grade scale, the project provided an opportunity for students to shine: the rate of high distinctions in BABB was double than that in 'Enlightenment and Revolution'. The rate of distinctions was comparable. The fail rate among completing students was marginally lower in 'Enlightenment and Revolution', but not to a statistically significant degree. The main discrepancy in grades was at the pass/credit level. A relatively higher number of students in BABB scored passes and commensurately fewer scored credits, but this seemed to be due to demographic factors.[19] Thus, in terms of grade outcomes, BABB appears to have been no more challenging than comparable units. Further, despite only having 150 hours to learn the subject background and find and research a topic, with due allowance made for scale, the best essays in BABB compared favourably with good first-class honours dissertations at Leeds. This was an extraordinary finding.

Table 2.4: Student enrolments and completion rates

Year	Full enrolment (census day)	Passive: no submissions	Active: did not complete	Active: completed
2014	46	6	11	29
2016	45	2	5	38

Table 2.5: Grades in 'Britain in the Age of Botany Bay, 1760–1815' (BABB) compared with 'Enlightenment and Revolution', 2013/15

Grade band	Comparable unit	BABB 2014	BABB 2016	BABB (all)
Fail	6 (5.8%)	1 (3.4%)	4 (10.5%)	5 (7.5%)
Pass (50–64)	30 (29.1%)	9 (31%)	18 (47.4%)	27 (40.3%)
Credit (65–74)	41 (39.8%)	8 (27.6%)	8 (21.1%)	16 (23.9%)
Distinction (75–84)	22 (21.4%)	8 (27.6%)	6 (15.8%)	14 (20.9%)
High Distinction (85–100)	4 (3.9%)	3 (10.3%)	2 (5.3%)	5 (7.5%)

So what did students think of this experiment? Student evaluation at WSU takes two forms, a questionnaire on teaching and another on the unit. This division can be helpful in drawing distinctions between teaching quality and issues such as workload, administrational issues and teaching spaces. This proved the case with BABB. It should, however, be borne in mind that return rates for the surveys were low due to logistical issues involved in administering them.[20] In addition, Student Feedback on Teaching (SFT) results for 2016 never materialised. The results should therefore be treated with caution. They nevertheless remain some of our best evidence available.

The 2014 SFT survey was unusually positive. On a ten-point scale, and across all categories, BABB averaged 0.7 and 1.1 points above the university average.[21] These categories spanned Learning/Academic Value; Staff Enthusiasm; Organisation/Clarity; Group Interaction; Individual Rapport; Breadth of Coverage; Examinations/Grading; Assignments/Readings; and Overall Rating.

Given this blanket approval, qualitative responses give a clearer guide as to what the students appreciated. Most mentioned instructor enthusiasm, but quality of feedback and the time spent with students were also commended. One student commented: 'lecture pod[cast]s are full of valuable and precise information. Great feedback on assignments'. The same student praised 'one-on-one time spent teaching me ways of finding sources and improving my understanding'. More unusually, another student applauded the way BABB prepared them for further study: 'Teacher is very enthusiastic and this really made the subject great. It was sufficiently challenging for a 3rd level unit and I would recommend it as a prerequisite for honours or any other postgraduate [course].'

The main negative criticism in the SFT pointed to technical problems experienced in the online-only classes. Strange as it sounds after the experience of COVID-19 lockdowns, in 2014 the technology used at WSU for online classes proved unreliable, and even with a technician sitting with the instructor, students experienced issues of access and participation. After one session, the online classes were abandoned as impracticable. The only other suggestion for improvement in the student surveys was 'demonstrating the ways in which to use the resources within a class'. Thus in 2016 greater efforts were made to target support and offer resource demonstrations in class time.

In contrast, the 2014 Student Feedback on Unit (SFU) surveys identified some issues for attention (see Table 2.6). In particular, two students 'strongly disagreed' with the statement that the workload was reasonable. One student clarified they felt the 'professional academic standards required' were unrealistic, and another added 'not everyone has the time or the wits to research, come up with and answer a unique question that they feel meets the marker's requirements'. However, of the six other respondents, four agreed the workload was 'reasonable' and the remaining two were neutral. Thus the majority of students, perhaps surprisingly, did not experience the workload as being out of kilter with other units. This conclusion was reaffirmed two years later when, of eight respondents, four students strongly agreed the workload was reasonable, two disagreed (but not strongly) and two were neutral. These improved results, if statistically meaningful, might reflect the expectation management measures described above and consequent reduction in student anxiety the second time the unit ran.

Across the 2014 SFU, scores for most questions were pulled down by two negative replies.[22] This may reflect the responses of two students at a moment when they felt challenged and insecure about the essay. But some answers hinted at identifiable issues, even paradoxical ones. Two students disagreed with the statement: 'There were clear guidelines for all assessment tasks in this unit'. This perhaps indicates that an abundance of support materials can overwhelm. A member of the 2016 cohort explained: 'different assessments were slightly confusing even though they were explained several times'. However, the comment may also have resulted from a specific difficulty some students had distinguishing between 'historic' and unfamiliar uses when deciding which words to include in their glossary. The glossary instructions were clarified in 2016.

The most positive SFU feedback validated the development of support materials. In 2014 no students disagreed with the propositions that 'The learning resources provided for this unit helped me to engage in learning' and 'This unit helped me develop my skills in critical thinking, analysing, problem solving and communicating'. These were the areas into which Simon had put most work and emphasis. Two years later, the SFU recorded improved scores in both these areas, and across the board.[23] In these areas SFU scores now exceeded WSU norms, indicating the unit was achieving its core aims. Moreover, taken as a whole, the SFU scores were at or above

Table 2.6: Student Feedback on Unit returns for 'Britain in the Age of Botany Bay, 1760–1815' (BABB) in 2014 and 2016 compared with average returns for Western Sydney University (WSU) and School of Humanities and Communication Arts (SHCA)

Question	2014 WSU	2014 SHCA	2014 BABB	2016 WSU	2016 SHCA	2016 BABB
Coverage matched learning guide	4.2	4.3	3.8	4.3	4.3	4.3
I saw relevance to my studies	4.2	4.0	3.9	4.2	4.1	4.1
Learning activities helped my learning	4.0	4.0	3.6	4.1	4.1	4.3
Assessments helped me learn	4.0	4.0	3.4	4.0	4.1	4.1
I was able to learn from feedback	3.9	3.9	3.6	3.9	4.0	4.4
Clear guidelines for assessment tasks	4.0	4.0	3.4	4.0	4.0	4.3
Learning resources aided engagement	4.0	4.0	4.0	4.0	4.1	4.3
Unit provided flexibility for study	4.0	4.0	3.5	4.1	4.1	4.1
Learning spaces were adequate	4.1	4.1	3.8	4.1	4.2	4.0
Workload was reasonable	4.0	4.0	3.0	4.1	4.1	3.9
People treated each other with respect	4.3	4.3	4.5	4.3	4.4	4.1
Developed skills in critical thinking, analysing, problem solving, communication	4.0	4.0	3.9	4.1	4.1	4.3
Overall experience satisfactory	4.0	4.0	3.8	4.1	4.1	4.1

the university average for most questions. Aside from the workload question, student 'disagreement' – and hence negativity – had disappeared almost entirely. Among those studying in BABB in 2016 was Rebekah, who describes her experience thus:

Upon enrolment, it was immediately evident that this unit would be different to anything I had previously done in my undergraduate studies. BABB called for a new skill-set: selecting a topic; navigating unfamiliar digital collections; analysing primary sources; and writing a long-form essay. This amounted to a steep learning curve. Yet the curve and workload – which originally seemed unattainable in bald terms – were both manageable if you kept up with the schedule set out by the instructor. In my experience, the early weeks were particularly vital: you had to watch the pods and learn what sources were available as quickly as possible in order to select a viable research question. As Toad reflects in the 'Guide', being organised from the start was essential. After that, methods pods explained how specific collections might be used to find relevant materials (if any existed at all) as well as how to meaningfully navigate the immensity of various digital resources and how to critically interrogate primary sources such as, for my project, newspapers, letters and diary entries. Having access to the pods throughout the semester meant it was possible to rewatch them as needed.

This general content was supported by specialised assistance from the instructor during 'topic group' sessions, including advice for improving searches in the digital collections and analysing primary source materials. We also discussed the use of quantitative analysis in history, including the potential limitations, the effectiveness of sampling techniques and the importance of clearly explaining your methodology.

Challenges aside, the research process was remarkable. I was astonished by the ready availability of primary sources in the digital collections, particularly my capacity to access materials created 200 years ago on the other side of the world. And I was enthralled by the stories that could be told using those sources, particularly by drawing together records from distinct, but related, collections. Ultimately, the unit was the catalyst for me to undertake postgraduate historical research at WSU, first in a Master of Research and currently in a PhD, with the BABB instructor as my primary supervisor. Both projects have incorporated the analysis of book reviews (in this case from the archives of an Australian publisher) and have relied on skills I developed in BABB relating to dual digital-archival methodologies.[24]

Conclusions

Rebekah's experience, Simon's observations and available SFT and SFU evidence all concur that on many levels the BABB experiment was successful. Despite the time pressure and lack of familiarity with background material, historical methods and, in some cases, primary source materials, most students rose to the challenge of conceiving, planning, researching and writing a research essay within the space of a 150-hour unit. In the process, they extended and documented their transferrable skills and, in a few cases, produced studies of near publishable standard. Even the less successful students, by a series of carefully scaffolded exercises building up to the final essay, could demonstrate awareness of basic research skills and an ability to apply them. There were thus benefits to all students in a very mixed-ability teaching environment.

The experiment's success depended on careful planning, a well-conceived learning and assessment strategy, prior experience in teaching research methodologies, the ready availability of digital resources, and a support strategy that was generous with the instructor's time. He also found it necessary to review communication strategies around what was expected of students to build their confidence and reduce drop-out rates.

Worries remain that some students found the essay too daunting, perceived or experienced the workload as too high or considered the unit's demands too incessant. Some found the requirement to choose their own topic challenging, particularly as they were unfamiliar with British history and the period. Equally, student feedback suggests the unit's success depended heavily on the instructor's experience, engagement and teaching skills. In other words, personal factors may be important to the success of the pedagogical model described.

These observations point to ways to develop the model. Although a huge amount of thought went into planning the unit, from a student experience point of view an even tighter structure would have been helpful. The research essay could, for example, be further reimagined as a portfolio of assignments, in which students progressively write up research background, methods and findings, as well as appendices and source lists, particularly if topic and source choice were to be constricted. Giving students a more narrowly circumscribed set of topics and a 'paint-by-numbers' walkthrough of resources could streamline their experience and help reduce student anxiety. It would also enhance the utility of the 'topic group'.

Finally, WSU students might benefit from introducing changes to the HPT programme, notably by introducing a compulsory second-year unit addressing methodologies and sources. In combination, these developments point us towards relaunching and rebranding the unit under the more generic umbrella of 'digital history'. This would open up new opportunities for other WSU colleagues to teach into the unit on topics with which they are familiar across a broader spectrum of time periods, branches of history, digital resources and theoretical/methodological approaches. Equally, the co-authors of this chapter could leverage their own growing familiarity with digital resources for Australian history, notably Trove (particularly the newspaper collections) and the Digital Panopticon project (which brings together Old Bailey Online records with Australian convict archives). If these proposals can be navigated imaginatively, the original vision of a capstone research-focused unit might be achieved without leaving any student behind.

Notes

1 Information on WSU can be found on the university website at www.western-sydney.edu.au. Since 2016 the university has added new vertical campuses in Parramatta, Liverpool and Bankstown.

2 See www.timeshighereducation.com/impactrankings#! (accessed 1 August 2023).

3 Australian Threshold Learning Outcomes in History are laid out in Ian Hay et al., *Learning and Teaching Academic Standards Project: Arts, Social Sciences and Humanities – History. Learning and Teaching Academic Standards Statement* (Sydney: Australian Learning and Teaching Council, December 2010). This document offers comparisons to the British Quality Assurance Agency for Higher Education (QAA) History Benchmark Statement, available at www.qaa.ac.uk/quality-code/subject-benchmark-statements/history and the Tuning History-Specific Competencies for Europe and Latin America. For comparative evaluation of the various Tuning History-Specific Competencies, see György Nováky, 'The Same History for All? Tuning History' in *Enriching History Teaching and Learning: Challenges, Possibilities, Practice – Proceedings of the Linköping Conference on History Teaching and Learning in Higher Education*, ed. David Ludvigsson and Alan Booth (Linköping: Linköping University Press, 2015), pp. 101–19.

4 'Business Doubts on Jobs after Uni Move,' *The Australian*, 2020. This article describes the response of the Australian Industry Group and the Australian Chamber of Commerce and Industry to the Morrison government's university fees reform. Both expressed concerns about the fee structures and particularly charging premium prices for humanities degrees, a move some commentators saw as an ideologically driven continuation of Australia's 'culture wars'.

5 Marnie Hughes-Warrington, Jill Roe, Adele Nye et al. *Historical Thinking in Higher Education: An ALTC Discipline-Based Initiative* (Sydney: Australian Learning and Teaching Council, 2009).

6 Hannah Barker, Monica McLean and Mark Roseman, 'Re-Thinking the History Curriculum: Enhancing Students' Communication and Group-Work Skills' in *The Practice of University History Teaching*, ed. Alan Booth and Paul Hyland (Manchester: Manchester University Press, 1999), pp. 60–69.

7 Simon Burrows and Glenn Roe, 'Introduction' in *Digitizing Enlightenment: Digital Humanities and the Transformation of Eighteenth-Century Studies*, ed. Simon Burrows and Glen Roe (Liverpool: Oxford University Studies in the Enlightenment, 2020), pp. 1–24.

8 For the Old Bailey Online, see www.oldbaileyonline.org (accessed 15 June 2022). ECCO and the Burney Collection are accessed from subscribing libraries' online catalogues worldwide.

9 See www.open.ac.uk/Arts/RED/index.html and https://trove.nla.gov.au (both accessed 15 June 2022).

10 These resources are accessed from subscribing libraries' online catalogues worldwide.

11 For his most sustained treatment of the press, see Simon Burrows, *French Exile Journalism and European Politics, 1792–1814* (Woodbridge: Royal Historical Society, 2000).

12 Jürgen Habermas, *The Structural Transformation of the Public Sphere: An Inquiry into a Category of Bourgeois Society*, trans. Thomas Burger (Cambridge, MA: MIT Press, 1989).

13 Edward S. Herman and Noam Chomsky, *Manufacturing Consent: The Political Economy of the Mass Media* (New York: Pantheon Books, 1988), chapter 1; Rolf Reinhardt and Hans-Jürgen Lüsebrink, *The Bastille: A History of a Symbol of Despotism and Freedom* (Durham, NC: Duke University Press, 1997). Tables produced by Reinhardt and Lüsebrink cross-reference date-stamped printed works or addresses with key themes, using page ranges (p. 8) or a range of symbols to depict how themes are portrayed (p. 50).

14 There are a number of studies of Marsden. For a summary outline, see A. T. Yarwood, 'Marsden, Samuel (1765–1838)', *Australian Dictionary of Biography*, https://adb.anu.edu.au/biography/marsden-samuel-2433 (accessed 17 October 2023).

15 Marsden's place of birth and his father's workshop are commemorated by a plaque in Farsley and a discreet brick cross in the ground and notice at the top of Horsforth high street. Marsden is, however, almost entirely unknown in his hometown.

16 Since 2014–16, emphasis on retention has increased at WSU, partly driven by falling enrolments, but especially by the 2020 fee changes mentioned above, which exacerbate the cost of students failing to pass.

17 In 2014, twenty-eight out of twenty-nine students who completed the final essay received clear pass grades and the other was borderline.

18 Twenty-eight out of 131 (21.4 per cent) students enrolled in 'Enlightenment and Revolution' on census day did not complete the unit, of whom almost two-thirds handed in at least one piece of work. This was a significantly lower drop-out rate than for BABB in 2014, but higher than in 2016.

19 Specifically, the BABB student cohort in 2016, which was the cause of the discrepancy, drew more of its students from Bankstown campus, which recruits from a relatively socially deprived and ethnically mixed area where English is frequently not the birth language, and other history staff at WSU report students are more likely to find essay writing challenging. 'Enlightenment and Revolution' was never taught at Bankstown campus, and BABB was not offered there in 2014.

20 There were only ten responses to the 2014 SFT and eight for the 2014 and 2016 SFUs. In 2016, although the forms were submitted, the results were never returned to the instructor.

21 Aggregate scores for these categories across WSU in 2014 averaged between 7.3 and 7.9.

22 Across the thirteen categories in the 2014 SFU, eight had two negative answers, one had three and one had one. There were no negative responses to the three other questions.

23 Across all thirteen questions in the 2016 SFU, on a five-point scale, BABB scored on average 0.1 points above the university average.

24 Rebekah Ward, 'Publishing for Children: Angus & Robertson and the Development of Australian Children's Publishing, 1897–1933' (Master's thesis, WSU, 2018), http://hdl.handle.net/1959.7/uws:51862 (accessed 17 October 2023). The doctorate is titled 'Creatively Curating Culture: Angus & Robertson's Mass Reviewing Strategy, 1895–1949'.

References

Barker, Hannah, McLean, Monica and Roseman, Mark, 'Re-Thinking the History Curriculum: Enhancing Students' Communication and Group-Work Skills' in *The Practice of University History Teaching*, ed. Alan Booth and Paul Hyland (Manchester: Manchester University Press, 1999), pp. 60–9.

Burrows, Simon, *French Exile Journalism and European Politics, 1792–1814* (Woodbridge: Royal Historical Society, 2000).

Burrows, Simon and Roe, Glenn, 'Introduction' in *Digitizing Enlightenment: Digital Humanities and the Transformation of Eighteenth-Century Studies*, ed. Simon Burrows and Glen Roe (Liverpool: Oxford University Studies in the Enlightenment, 2020), pp. 1–24.

'Business Doubts on Jobs after Uni Move,' *The Australian*, 2020.

Habermas, Jürgen, *The Structural Transformation of the Public Sphere: An Inquiry into a Category of Bourgeois Society*, trans. Thomas Burger (Cambridge, MA: MIT Press, 1989).

Hay, Ian et al., *Learning and Teaching Academic Standards Project: Arts, Social Sciences and Humanities – History. Learning and Teaching Academic Standards Statement* (Sydney: Australian Learning and Teaching Council, December 2010).

Herman, Edward S. and Chomsky, Noam, *Manufacturing Consent: The Political Economy of the Mass Media* (New York: Pantheon Books, 1988).

Hughes-Warrington, Marnie, Roe, Jill, Nye, Adele et al. *Historical Thinking in Higher Education: An ALTC Discipline-Based Initiative* (Sydney: Australian Learning and Teaching Council, 2009).

Nováky, György, 'The Same History for All? Tuning History' in *Enriching History Teaching and Learning: Challenges, Possibilities, Practice – Proceedings of the Linköping Conference on History Teaching and Learning in Higher Education*, ed. David Ludvigsson and Alan Booth (Linköping: Linköping University Press, 2015), pp. 101–19.

Reinhardt, Rolf and Lüsebrink, Hans-Jürgen, *The Bastille: A History of a Symbol of Despotism and Freedom* (Durham, NC: Duke University Press, 1997).

Ward, Rebekah, 'Publishing for Children: Angus & Robertson and the Development of Australian Children's Publishing, 1897–1933'

(Master's thesis, WSU, 2018), http://hdl.handle.net/1959.7/uws:51862 (accessed 17 October 2023).

Yarwood, A. T., 'Marsden, Samuel (1765–1838)', *Australian Dictionary of Biography*, https://adb.anu.edu.au/biography/marsden-samuel-2433 (accessed 17 October 2023).

Part II
HISTORY IN THE CLASSROOM

Chapter 3

Sensational pedagogy: teaching the sensory eighteenth century

William Tullett

In his 1710 book *The Sensorium*, Matthew Beare informed his readers 'all the Senses may be reduc'd to the Touch alone; since 'tis by this, that all the others receive the Impression of Objects, striking on the external Organs'.[1] The idea of a sensational subject, who learnt about the world as it forced itself upon the senses, was central to how eighteenth-century writers (including educators) thought about the world.[2] This chapter asks how taking a sensational approach to pedagogy today can help teachers and students to understand eighteenth-century society and culture.

One of the recent turns in historical research has been towards the study of the senses, emotions and embodiment. A historiography of the senses has emerged that, influenced by work in sensory studies from anthropologists and sociologists, stresses the culturally constructed nature of sensory perception. This work traces the social relationships mediated by particular hierarchies of the senses and managed by techniques of sensorial power. It has also begun to unpick the types of sensory skill and habit that patterned past modes of perception.[3]

This chapter seeks to ask how we teach sensory – embodied – history in the classroom effectively and what implications this might have for teaching *eighteenth-century* history specifically. It focuses on how we might go beyond texts and images that are read or closely examined with curious eyes towards enlivening the senses of our students. This chapter focuses on a series of examples from the author's teaching that range across multiple senses but which chiefly concern themselves with smell, taste and sound.

The examples derive from modules investigating the history of food in early modern England and the history of sound, environments and technology since the sixteenth century.

It is worth highlighting that, as the above suggests, most of the modules in which I use the senses or discuss sensory history are not purely focused on the eighteenth century. They frequently cover the period 1500–1800 and often longer periods such as 1500–1980. I often find myself offering modules with wider chronologies. There are a number of reasons for this. There is a general tendency at many institutions in the UK for students to prefer modern history. A bit of nineteenth- or twentieth-century history sugars the eighteenth-century pill, a piece of disguise to trick the senses that the eighteenth century knew well.[4]

However, there are further practical and pedagogical reasons. I formerly worked at an institution with a very small number of staff who, due to lower numbers of students, teach a BA History degree with a limited number of optional modules. My chief reason for prefacing my chapter with this observation is that I think there is an interesting conversation to be had here about how we teach the eighteenth century as part of chronologically broader modules or in its own right (and whether those differ). There is also a conversation to be had about where eighteenth-century history sits in the context of curricula that are being hemmed in by various institutional pressures that result in smaller numbers of modules on BA History degrees.

However, there are also intellectual reasons for situating the eighteenth century in the context of broader sensory-historical modules. One of the strengths of sensory history is – or at least should be – its potential to rewrite our chronologies and to help us think outside of the chronological box set by centuries (whether long, short or average in length) or terms such as medieval, early modern and modern. As will be seen below, one of my goals in teaching sensory history is to enable students to expand their sense of chronological possibility in ways that are already being modelled in sensory scholarship. This might involve connecting contemporary tastes to a longer history that stretches back in time. For example, to understand the taste for contemporary street food sold in the City of London's square mile, we can trace shifting gustatory preferences that have origins in the sixteenth century.[5] Or, it might involve exploring the long-term continuities or submergence and resurfacing of particular relationships between the senses and society. For example, our own desires to regulate noise in order to promote privacy and nurture intellectual work find echoes in similar complaints ranging from the nineteenth century, through the Renaissance, to antiquity.[6]

Before I turn to some examples of how we might draw on such insights in teaching the eighteenth century, I want to briefly set out the pedagogic and historiographical context from which this chapter has developed.

The scholarly context: turning towards the material and the sensory

Over the last thirty years or so an increasing amount of historical work has focused on the senses and the emotions, mirroring a general turn towards the senses across the arts, humanities and social sciences.[7] In history this trend has emerged – largely but not exclusively – from a concern with the linguistic turn's focus on discourse.[8] Instead of a world full of texts, historians have begun to argue for a return to 'lived experience' – a tendency apparent not just in histories of feeling but in studies of material culture.[9]

This shift is mirrored in our pedagogic practice as well. In particular, material culture of all sorts has become increasingly integral to the way many of us teach, whether through direct engagement with material stuff or through the more mediated access to objects provided by the museum display or the photographic image. The popularity of resources such as Eighteenth-Century Collections Online, the Old Bailey Online and the digitised Burney Newspapers has put increased pressure on eighteenth-century-ists to also give access to – or at least emphasise the importance of – the *material* text when discussing primary material with students.

In recent years we have also seen the emphasis on the consumption, materiality and production of stuff in eighteenth-century history grow stronger than ever. We have far more knowledge of how shopping was negotiated than when a 'consumer revolution' was first identified in the 1980s. How things were made, how processes of production contributed to the meanings of things and how bodies, spaces and objects acted on each other have all been the focus of work in the last twenty years. So, in this context, it should make sense to integrate materiality further into our teaching and, in doing so, make room for the senses through which the material world was mediated.

There are, of course, other reasons for us to interrogate and deploy the senses in our learning that go beyond shifts in historical practice, teaching and scholarship. Increasing criticism has been mounted against scholarship that separates the senses into discrete learning styles.[10] Using the sense of smell in a teaching and museums context has been shown to aid the retention of memories and experience, diversify access and promote the well-being of learners.[11] We are only just beginning to get to grips with how the senses might be deployed critically in the classroom. But the work that does exist suggests that there are additional benefits to be derived from a multi-sensory pedagogic practice.

However, here we have to recognise that there is an ongoing debate within sensory history about how we – as teachers and researchers – should use our senses (or not, as the case may be). On the one hand, we have scholars who believe that we can, with varying degrees of accuracy, conjure precisely what it was like to hear, smell or taste the past.[12] On the other hand, we have individuals who are profoundly sceptical of any attempt to recreate the feelings of other periods or peoples.[13] According to this latter perspective, the very idea that the senses are historical militates against any attempt for us to engage sensorially with the past in the present. Both our own sensory habits, built up through twentieth- and twenty-first-century forms of education and experience, and the changed sense-scapes in which we exist mean that we can never come close to recapturing what it was like to experience the sensory past.

There are scholars who have walked the valley between these two opposing hills. One set contains those interested in physical space: for example, trying to figure out how far George Whitefield's preaching voice might have reached in a crowded street.[14] Rather than claiming to reconstruct how the past felt, these are attempts to reconstruct the affordances for smells and sounds offered by material environments. But another, middling, tendency has been to pay closer attention to sensing as a learnt, acquired, practice that is developed over time. The best recent work on the senses in eighteenth-century studies has done this.[15] From texts and material culture we can attempt to read back to these sensory practices.

Crucially, this work does not necessarily claim that we can reconstruct how the past 'felt'.[16] In fact, by attending to habits acquired over time, this scholarship highlights a roadblock on the path to 'feeling' the past – our own learned sensory habits as teachers and those of our students.[17] Our inability to unlearn the sensory baggage we have acquired in our own lives means that the type of embodiment thus produced will never be in complete sensorial simpatico with the past.[18] But this is not just a lament. We can turn this awareness of complexity to our advantage. What the senses can do in the classroom is teach us about how people in the past *learnt* to perceive their worlds. Many of the fields of knowledge that historians are interested in, from medicine and food to engineering and knitting, have relied on forms of sensory education and continue to do so in the present.[19] In doing so we can explore both the distancing differences and intimate similarities between our own sensory worlds and those of the past.

Sensing in practice

So let us consider some examples of how this might work in practice. Several examples I will now discuss come from a module for final-year undergraduate students on 'Food in Early Modern Society', which examined food – principally in Britain – from 1500 to 1800. The second seminar, after an introductory week on methodology and interdisciplinary approaches to food, took the students on a journey through understandings of food and taste in medicine across the period covered by the module. It centred principally on dietetics – first the humoralism dominant in the sixteenth and seventeenth centuries – and indeed still apparent long into the eighteenth century – and secondly the rise of iatromechanical dietetics associated with figures such as William Cheyne in the eighteenth century.[20] In preparation students were asked to read some extracts from a range of works on regimen and some letters from doctors to their eighteenth-century patients.

After a lecture in which we introduced the key changes in the relationship between medicine and food, the seminar aimed to do two things. Firstly, I wanted students to understand how early modern individuals used their senses to understand the potential effects of foods on their bodies. I wanted students to get how heat, cold, moisture and dryness could be detected in foods; how links were formed between sensory impressions and qualities. I wanted them to understand the kind of broader analogical reasoning that could be found in eighteenth-century culture; the idea that roast beef makes one stubborn, strong, bloody and blunt.[21] Secondly, I wanted them to understand what it meant to be 'your own' doctor in the early modern period – and how this related to the more diffuse distribution of expertise about the body – including diet – that we find in the era before medical 'professionalisation' and the clinic.[22] At the end of the seminar students needed to go away with a feeling for how the senses were trained to recognise what was good or bad for you. They also needed to understand how, for fashionable eighteenth-century physicians, the exertion of authority over a patient's diet was often a matter of trying to educate them in and out of their senses. More broadly, I wanted students to understand how this might be similar – or different – to our current sensorial relationship with food.

To do this, the seminar focused around tasting a range of foods and drinks. Cheese, bread, cold meats, fresh herbs, spices, vegetables, fruits, milk, wine and some other food and drinks were set out on a table. Students were given some descriptions of different constitutions – largely based around humoral ones taken from seventeenth- and eighteenth-century sources. They were encouraged to identify how they would describe their own constitution by reference to these. Once they had done this, they were asked to fill a plate with items they felt would be 'good' for them and explain why – particularly referring to the smell, taste, appearance and feel of the foods.

The students were then encouraged to make a second plate. This time they were given an early eighteenth-century 'identity'. These identities contained a number of things – occupations, the place where they lived, gender, nationality and so on. The students then had to explain – based on their reading, the lecture and discussion thus far in the seminar – why they had put together the second plate and how it matched up to their given identities. Finally, the students were asked how these plates might have differed if their doctor was William Cheyne and he was applying his own principles of regimen to them. Students were paired up – one had to take on the role of the patient, the other had to embody Cheyne. The Cheynes were then tasked with making their iatromechanical theories seem common sense by reference to the qualities of the food arrayed on the table.

This series of tasks offered students the opportunity to effectively put seventeenth- and eighteenth-century medical thought into practice. Firstly, it denaturalised their own senses by getting them to approach their own relationship to food through a different perceptual schema. As experiments with contemporary sensory panels have shown, we might describe the same material that was used by early modern medical practitioners in very different ways today – drawing on a rich vocabulary of sensory comparison that invokes other scents or tastes that would have been unfamiliar to a seventeenth- or eighteenth-century individual.[23] The session gave students the opportunity to explore that experiential gap.

Secondly, in learning how to sense like an early modern gentleman, gentlewoman or physician, students were exploring how connections could be created between regimen texts, doctors' advice and the evidence of the senses, and how they could then articulate those connections. In other words, they were learning about how people learnt to sense – rather than directly re-enacting past experiences or re-embodying the feelings of past actors. Finally, by developing an eighteenth-century sensory identity for the second plate, only to be confronted with Cheyne's prescriptions for the final plate of the seminar, students were introduced to a key problematic in eighteenth-century dietetics – in a world where the patient's senses and embodied instincts were taken seriously, how did physicians make claims to medical authority and how could they use the exterior qualities of foods to make claims about their interior bodily effects?[24] To do this effectively, students had to work from the perspective of eighteenth-century sensory dispositions – patients of different types as well as physicians.

Perhaps the most pleasing part of this was that the students closed the circle I was creating in the seminar before I had to – they began to reflect on the distinctions between early modern ideas about food and the body and our contemporary fascination with invisible chemical constituents such as calories – they were interrogating contemporary notions that they might otherwise accept as 'common sense'.[25] By inhabiting a different sensory perspective, the students learnt something about their own day-to-day sensory practices. They thereby learn about the distance that separated their own senses from those of past subjects.

These activities also opened a conversation about the role of race, colonialism and imperialism in the maintenance of eighteenth-century sensory practices. Western academic traditions of knowledge production have, since the seventeenth century, 'conceived of the senses as necessary evils, indispensable but treacherous vehicles to be sorted out or unmasked'.[26] The same period that saw the emergence of new fields of knowledge and, latterly, academic disciplines in the West also saw attempts to match hierarchies of the senses to racial and cultural hierarchies. From Aristotle to the present, philosophers, medics and cultural critics have placed the senses into hierarchies – ordering them in terms of their utility, objectivity and stability. In the era of European expansion and settler colonialism these were mapped onto racialised hierarchies. This dismissal of certain ways of knowing the world – especially those beyond hearing and seeing – has been described as a form of 'epistemicide'. As Andrew Kettler's work has shown, Europeans in North America consistently emphasised the sagacious sensitivity possessed by indigenous noses. On the peripheries of empire, French Jesuits and Anglo-American naturalists both used their noses and the olfactory knowledge of Native Americans to seek out sustenance and saleable commodities. Yet in the European metropole this olfactory knowledge was de-emphasised in visual tabulations of botanical knowledge or treated with a degree of suspicion.[27]

Teaching through the senses offers an opportunity re-engage with the sensory habits that have been lost to practices of epistemicide or self-congratulatory histories of European 'improvement' of indigenous practices. One of the sample foods we smelled in our class was therefore chocolate. As historians have shown, the idea that Europeans adapted the scent and taste of chocolate to their own sensibilities, replacing spices with sugar, is largely untrue. Europeans in fact sought to recreate the indigenous experience of chocolate consumption, along with vanilla, pepper and foamy froth.[28] Students drew out the contemporary smell and taste profile of the average bar of milk chocolate consumed in contemporary Europe, with its soft, milky, rich and slightly cloying scent. This was then compared with a reproduction of early modern drinking chocolate, which included the spices that Europeans had in fact eagerly added in a recreation of the original indigenous drink. This led to an exploration of how Europeans often co-opted indigenous olfactory and culinary practices, altering their own palates to reflect the new consumables that they were importing. Rather than presumptions about how Europeans 'improved' the smell and taste of chocolate, students left the class with a sense of the hidden archives of indigenous sensing embedded in early modernity's new consumables.

Learning about how we learn to perceive – stepping outside our senses – is a crucial, perhaps radical, pedagogical tool. Early innovators in sensory studies often taught their students *how to feel* – for example, Raymond Murray Schafer, inventor of the term 'soundscape', who taught his students through a regime of 'ear cleaning' that privileged the sounds of nature over modern noise.[29] However, we want to teach students to sense critically, picking apart such normative sensory claims, rather than sense correctly according to a pre-ordained standard of 'good' or 'natural' sensory stimuli. Instead of teaching students how to feel, or how the past felt, we can teach them how people *learnt* to feel. This resonates with eighteenth-century pedagogic practice, which placed great emphasis on the senses.[30] In museums and collections knowledge was often consumed (quite literally in the case of specimens in the Royal Society and Ashmolean) through the senses.[31]

But these teaching methods also develop the capacity of students to lend a far more critical eye, ear, nose, tongue and touch to the world around them today. They are not discovering how people *learnt* to feel but they are developing their own ability to critique and understand their own subjectivities. They are learning about how they have learnt to feel and what they have learnt to feel. Drawing on Bruno Latour's discussion of Geneviève Teil's ethnography of perfumery trainees, we might describe this as a process of 'articulation'. In the course of training with kits of scents, perfumers are said to 'gain' or 'become' a nose. In the same way, encouraging our students to learn about the past through scent causes them to gain access to the senses of the past and greater understanding of their own senses. As Latour goes on to suggest, 'the more contrasts you add, the more differences and mediations you become sensible to'.[32]

We can see this process of articulation – in which both students' own sensory habits and those of past actors emerge into view – in a second example from the module on early modern histories of food. Trying to get students to understand the different conditions in which food was bought and sold in the eighteenth century, I gave my students a guide to sensory ethnography. This equipped them with a guide on observation as an ethnographic method for understanding both sensory atmospheres and the modes of sensing that occur within them.[33] I then provided my students with a range of source materials that were also to be read in preparation for that week's seminar. These sources were a set of excerpts on shopping from eighteenth-century housekeeping manuals, which often focused on ways of assessing quality and freshness.[34] When it came to the seminar, we spent the first half performing a sensory ethnography of Anglia Ruskin University's canteen. We then discussed the key aspects of the canteen that the students had noticed: the way the food was displayed; how people were expected to interact with the space; the acoustics of the room; and even the relationship between the smellscape and soundscape of the canteen and rooms around it.

I then asked the students to apply the same ethnographic methods that they had read about to the historical texts they had been asked to read. In particular, I asked them to consider how useful these sources were as a guide to the sensory experience of shopping in the eighteenth century. In discussing this question, the students explored what these sources might have missed and what other materials we might need to fill in the gaps in our knowledge about the sensory experience of buying and consuming.

But this also opened out into a far more interesting and important discussion about what sensory information does or does not make its way into our historical sources. We asked: how does sensing get converted into text – and how might that have differed in the eighteenth century? By moving from contemporary ethnography using their own senses to the eighteenth-century source material, the students were better equipped to think through these questions and about how sensory dispositions and habits might filter what does or does not make it into texts. But we also discussed the way in which these books were themselves used as tools for articulating eighteenth-century servants' or housewives' relationship to the sense-scape of shopping.

This led to a discussion about the kinds of tacit knowledge that could not be written down but only acquired through practical, hands-on experience. One of the great benefits of deploying sensory pedagogy is that by enlivening sources and putting them into action, we acquire a better knowledge of the gaps in knowledge or technique that had to be filled in by the user of a text. Recipe books and household manuals are a great eighteenth-century case study, but the same applies to more modern audio-visual sources. For example, in a course on modern American media at Stanford, Kristen Haring asked her students to watch Julia Child's highly popular 1960s and 1970s cookery show *The French Chef* before asking them to recreate the recipes in a kitchen using their notes. In doing so, the students were able to understand the ways in which Child and the televisual medium made cooking accessible for 1960s Americans.[35]

A final example of how this articulation might work in practice comes from my module on sound and technology in the West from the 1500s to the present. One session focused on the relationship between time and sound. A wide-ranging historiography has examined the shifting relationship between the senses and time-telling. While noting that this was undoubtedly a halting and uneven process, even the most revisionist work admits that a shift in time-telling emerged in the course of the eighteenth and nineteenth centuries as domestic, public and personal timepieces proliferated. An older regime of time in which sound had been absolutely central – with the twinkling bells and clock-born chimes – was slowly joined by an emphasis on the visual elements of time-keeping introduced by clocks and their hands.[36]

I wanted students to critically engage with the debate over this transformation in time-telling. Was there really a shift from acoustic to visual ways of marking time in the course of the eighteenth and nineteenth centuries and to what extent is that shift still with us today? In order to broach that question, I encouraged my students, once again, to pursue a form of ethnography. I required each student to produce a sound diary, noting down the sounds around them during the course of a normal day. In putting together this diary I wanted my students to explore the extent to which their daily rhythms were indexed against sounds. After a lecture, which examined the relationship between time and sound in the seventeenth and eighteenth centuries, we then compared their diaries with what they had learnt about the early modern period. While the key point I wanted the students to understand was that there was a limit to the sense in which vision 'replaced' sound as a mode of time-telling, the ensuing discussion actually brought out a series of other themes: students contrasted the private modes of time-telling embedded in contemporary phones, computers or clocks with the very public or civic time sounded by chimes or bells; they noted the contemporary proliferation of devices that told time such as microwaves, radios and TVs and this opened out into a discussion of other eighteenth-century time-telling tools aside from watches or clocks that included candles or the time it took to say a paternoster. In other words, the diary had helped students to articulate both past and contemporary relationships to time and had encouraged them to recognise the multiple times embedded in different visual, acoustic and material cues.

Conclusion

Using examples in which I deployed smell, taste and sound in the classroom, this chapter has argued that encouraging students to use their senses performs three interlinked roles. Firstly, it denaturalises the senses of students, forcing them to recognise that their own ways of perceiving are the product of both their particular social and cultural contexts and a series of historical changes that have taken place since the eighteenth century. Secondly, students are encouraged to sense differently – to try and understand the particular ways of sensing unique to the eighteenth-century subjects they are reading about and thereby adding material context to texts. Thirdly, and finally, students develop a more critical appreciation of their own sensory subjectivities. The process of learning through the senses, rather than just about the senses, is a route by which students learn to articulate their sensory subject position in relation to both contemporary and past worlds.

This sensory self-awareness should extend to how we treat pedagogical spaces. Sensory history has recently begun to make its influence felt in the history of education, where scholars have paid attention to the sensescapes of schooling.[37] Our classrooms are not the only spaces that both we and students use where specific sensory habits have been encouraged. The relative hush and absence of odours in libraries has a history. Rules about the proper *habitus* expected of patrons have often been used to exclude people from library spaces.[38] The same can be said of museums and galleries. Despite a renaissance of interest in multi-sensory curation, many of the museums that we use in teaching still expect students to embody a nineteenth-century 'look and don't touch' engagement with their spaces rather than a seventeenth-century sensory economy in which all the senses (including eating) were deployed.[39] We do not learn in a sensory vacuum and we ought to engage our students more with the sensory history of the spaces in which they learn.

As humanities scholars, our role is not just to provide content or skills but also to create individuals who are able to critically engage with the worlds around them. Art history and visual culture have, for the past few decades, noted the importance of training students to look, notice, attend and judge through the eye. One of the oft-noted justifications for this mission is that most people living in the UK, Europe and North America live in a highly mediatised world in which we interact with and consume visual media almost constantly. However, taste, smell and hearing are no less important. The vast amounts of sensory labour and design that go into our daily lives, from the smell of petrol and the taste of food to the sound of phones or the feel of the fabrics we wear, deserve critical attention. As in the case of visual culture, a humanities (and eighteenth-century studies) that engages all the senses of students will help students to avoid merely skimming the sensory surface in their future lives and careers. It will help to create graduates attuned to the complexity of the sensory world that surrounds and enfolds us, but which we frequently take for granted due to 'common-sense' habituation.

Notes

1 Matthew Beare, *The Sensorium* (Exeter: Sam Farley, 1710), p. 10.

2 See, for example, the introduction and special issue, Manushag N. Powell and Rivka Swenson, 'Subject Theory and the Sensational Subject', *The Eighteenth Century*, 54 no. 2 (2013), 147–51.

3 For a recent overview, see William Tullett, 'State of the Field: Sensory History', *History*, 106 no. 373 (2021), 804–20; for an attempt to plot the future of the field, see Mark Smith, *A Sensory History Manifesto* (University Park, PA: Penn State University Press, 2021).

4 For example, in the form of syrup, see William Buchan, *Domestic Medicine* (London: A. Strahan and & T. Cadell, 1790), p. 694.

5 Alex Rhys-Taylor, *Food and Multiculture: A Sensory Ethnography of East London* (London: Routledge, 2017), pp. 41–56.

6 Niall Atkinson, 'Thinking through Noise, Building toward Silence: Creating a Sound Mind and Sound Architecture in the Premodern City', *Grey Room*, 60 (2015), 10–35.

7 Although claims of a 'sensual' or sensory 'revolution' seem overdone, it is a notable outpouring of work. See Michael Bull et al., 'Introducing Sensory Studies', *The Senses and Society*, 1 no. 1 (2006), 5–7.

8 Carolyn Birdsall et al., 'Forum: The Senses', *German History*, 32 no. 2 (2014), 256–73.

9 See the telling references to experience in Sasha Handley, Rohan McWilliam and Lucy Noakes (eds), *New Directions in Social and Cultural History* (London: Bloomsbury, 2018).

10 C. Morris, 'Making Sense of Education: Sensory Ethnography and Visual Impairment', *Ethnography and Education*, 12 no. 1 (2016), 1–16; F. Coffield et al., *Learning Styles and Pedagogy in Post-16 Learning: A Systematic and Critical Review* (London: Learning and Research Skills Council, 2004).

11 On memory, see J. P. Aggleton and L. Waskett, 'The Ability of Odours to Serve as State-Dependent Cues for Real-World Memories: Can Viking Smells Aid the Recall of Viking Experiences?', *British Journal of Psychology*, 90 no. 1 (1999), 1–7; on access, see 'Pilchards Pits and Postcards' Heritage Lottery Fund, 2015, www.sensorytrust.org.uk/projects/pilchards-pits-postcards.html (accessed 17 April 2023); on well-being, see Helen Chatterjee and Guy Noble, *Museums, Health and Well-Being* (Farnham: Ashgate, 2013), pp. 84, 86.

12 Peter Charles Hoffer, *Sensory Worlds in Early America* (Baltimore, MD: Johns Hopkins University Press, 2005), pp. 12–13.

13 Mark Smith, 'Producing Sense, Consuming Sense, Making Sense: Perils and Prospects for Sensory History', *Journal of Social History*, 40 no. 4 (2007), 841–58.

14 Braxton Boren, 'Whitfield's Voice' in *George Whitefield: Life, Context and Legacy*, ed. D. Jones and G. Hammond (Oxford: Oxford University Press, 2016), pp. 167–89.

15 For example, see Serena Dyer, 'Shopping and the Senses: Retail, Browsing and Consumption in Eighteenth-Century England', *History Compass*, 12 no. 9 (2014), 694–703; Mark Jenner, 'Tasting Lichfield, Touching China: Sir John Floyer's Senses', *The Historical Journal*, 53 no. 3 (2010), 647–70.

16 For other ways in which researchers and students can use their senses, see William Tullett, *Smell and the Past: Noses, Archives, Narratives* (London: Bloomsbury, 2023).

17 The fact that when are in a classroom we are bodies in a physical space seems to have escaped the literature on history pedagogy (outside of work on object-based learning).

18 Mark Smith, *The Smell of Battle, the Taste of Siege: A Sensory History of the Civil War* (Oxford: Oxford University Press, 2014), pp. 2–4; Holly Dugan, *The Ephemeral History of Perfume: Scent and Sense in Early Modern England* (Baltimore, MD: Johns Hopkins University Press, 2011), p. 10.

19 For examples, see Anna Harris, *A Sensory Education* (London: Routledge, 2020); Karin Bjisterveld, *Sonic Skills: Listening for Knowledge in Science, Medicine and Engineering (1920s–Present)* (Basingstoke: Palgrave Macmillan, 2018).

20 The core content was the sort of material discussed in the first three chapters of David Gentilcore, *Food and Health in Early Modern Europe: Diet, Medicine, and Society, 1450–1800* (London: Bloomsbury, 2015).

21 For the longer history of these ideas, see Ken Albala, *Eating Right in the Renaissance* (Berkeley, CA: University of California Press, 2002).

22 See the essays in Roy Porter (ed.), *Patients and Practitioners: Lay Perceptions of Medicine in Pre-Industrial Society* (Cambridge: Cambridge University Press, 2003).

23 Nils-Otto Ahnfelt, Hjalmar Fors and Karin Wendin, 'Historical Continuity or Different Sensory Worlds? What We Can Learn about the Sensory Characteristics of Early Modern Pharmaceuticals by Taking Them to a Trained Sensory Panel', *Berichte zur Wissenschafts-Geschichte*, 43 no. 3 (2020), 412–29.

24 For example, see Steven Shapin, 'Trusting George Cheyne: Scientific Expertise, Common Sense, and Moral Authority in Early Eighteenth-Century Dietetic Medicine', *Bulletin of the History of Medicine*, 77 no. 2 (2003), 263–397.

25 A transition described in Steven Shapin, '"You Are What You Eat": Historical Changes in Ideas about Food and Identity', *Historical Research*, 87 no. 237 (2014), 390–91.

26 Boaventura de Sousa Santos, *The End of the Cognitive Empire: The Coming of Age of Epistemologies of the South* (Durham, NC: Duke University Press, 2018), p. 166.

27 Andrew Kettler, '"Ravishing Odors of Paradise": Jesuits, Olfaction, and Seventeenth-century North America', *Journal of American Studies*, 50 no. 4 (2016), 827–52; Andrew Kettler, 'Delightful a Fragrance: Native American Olfactory Aesthetics within the Eighteenth-Century Anglo American Botanical Community' in *Empire of the Senses: Sensory Practices of Colonialism in*

Early America, ed. Daniela Hacke and Paul Musselwhite (Leiden: Brill, 2018), pp. 223–54.

28 Marcy Norton, 'Tasting Empire: Chocolate and the European Internalization of Mesoamerican Aesthetics', *The American Historical Review*, 111 no. 3 (2006), 660–91.

29 Raymond Murray Schafer, *Ear Cleaning: Notes for an Experimental Music Course* (London: Clark & Cruickshank, 1989); for a critique of Schafer's 'aesthetic moralism', see Marie Thompson, *Beyond Unwanted Sound: Noise, Affect, and Aesthetic Moralism* (London: Bloomsbury, 2017).

30 Susan C. Lawrence, 'Educating the Senses: Students, Teachers and Medical Rhetoric in Eighteenth-Century London' in *Medicine and the Five Senses*, ed. W. F. Bynum and Roy Porter (Cambridge: Cambridge University Press, 1993), pp. 153–78; Silvy Chakkalakal, 'The Child of the Senses: Education and the Concept of Experience in the Eighteenth Century', *The Senses and Society*, 41 no. 2 (2019), 148–72.

31 Constance Classen, 'Museum Manners: The Sensory Life of the Early Museum', *Journal of Social History*, 40 no. 4 (2007), 896–914.

32 Bruno Latour, 'How to Talk about the Body? The Normative Dimension of Science Studies', *Body & Society*, 10 nos. 2–3 (2004), 211; for the research on which Latour bases his remarks, see Geneviève Teil, 'Devenir expert aromaticien: Y a-t-il une place pour le goût dans les goûts alimentaires?', *Revue de sociologie du travail*, 4 no. 98 (1998), 503–22.

33 Sarah Pink, *Doing Sensory Ethnography* (London: Sage, 2015).

34 For an example, see the material covered in William Tullett, *Smell in Eighteenth Century England: A Social Sense* (Oxford: Oxford University Press, 2019), pp. 43–7.

35 Erin Springsteen, 'Stanford Humanities Students Cook Up Julia Child's Recipes, Study History', *Stanford News*, 8 April 2016, https://news.stanford.edu/2016/04/08/kitchen-french-chef-040616 (accessed 17 April 2023).

36 The best work in this area comes from Nigel Thrift and Paul Glennie, *Shaping the Day: A History of Timekeeping in England and Wales 1300–1800* (Oxford: Oxford University Press, 2011).

37 Catherine Burke and Ian Grosvenor, 'The Hearing School: An Exploration of Sound and Listening in the Modern School', *International Journal of the History of Education*, 47 no. 3 (2011), 323–40; Geert Thyssen, 'Odorous Childhoods and Scented Worlds of Learning: A Sensory History of Health and Outdoor Education Initiatives in Western Europe (1900s–1960s)', *The Senses and* Society, 14 no. 2 (2019), 173–93.

38 Shannon Mattern, 'Resonant Texts: Sounds of the Contemporary American Public Library', *The Senses & Society*, 2 no. 3 (2007), 277–302; Nat Lazakis, '"It Is a Non-Negotiable Order": Public Libraries' Body Odor Bans and the Ableist Politics of Purity', *Journal of Radical Librarianship*, 6 (2020), 24–52.

39 Classen, 'Museum Manners'.

References

Aggleton, J. P. and Waskett, L., 'The Ability of Odours to Serve as State-Dependent Cues for Real-World Memories: Can Viking Smells Aid the Recall of Viking Experiences?', *British Journal of Psychology*, 90 no. 1 (1999), 1–7.

Ahnfelt, Nils-Otto, Fors, Hjalmar and Wendin, Karin, 'Historical Continuity or Different Sensory Worlds? What We Can Learn about the Sensory Characteristics of Early Modern Pharmaceuticals by Taking Them to a Trained Sensory Panel', *Berichte zur Wissenschafts-Geschichte*, 43 no. 3 (2020), 412–29.

Albala, Ken, *Eating Right in the Renaissance* (Berkeley, CA: University of California Press, 2002).

Atkinson, Niall, 'Thinking through Noise, Building toward Silence: Creating a Sound Mind and Sound Architecture in the Premodern City', *Grey Room*, 60 (2015), 10–35.

Beare, Matthew, *The Sensorium* (Exeter: Sam Farley, 1710).

Birdsall, Carolyn et al., 'Forum: The Senses', *German History*, 32 no. 2 (2014), 256–73.

Bjisterveld, Karin, *Sonic Skills: Listening for Knowledge in Science, Medicine and Engineering (1920s–Present)* (Basingstoke: Palgrave Macmillan, 2018).

Boren, Braxton, 'Whitfield's Voice' in *George Whitefield: Life, Context and Legacy*, ed. D. Jones and G. Hammond (Oxford: Oxford University Press, 2016), pp. 167–89.

Buchan, William, *Domestic Medicine* (London: A. Strahan and & T. Cadell, 1790).

Bull, Michael et al., 'Introducing Sensory Studies', *The Senses and Society*, 1 no. 1 (2006), 5–7.

Burke, Catherine and Grosvenor, Ian, 'The Hearing School: an Exploration of Sound and Listening in the Modern School', *International Journal of the History of Education*, 47 no. 3 (2011), 323–40.

Chakkalakal, Silvy, 'The Child of the Senses: Education and the Concept of Experience in the Eighteenth Century', *The Senses and Society*, 41 no. 2 (2019), 148–72.

Chatterjee, Helen and Noble, Guy, *Museums, Health and Well-Being* (Farnham: Ashgate, 2013).

Classen, Constance, 'Museum Manners: The Sensory Life of the Early Museum', *Journal of Social History*, 40 no. 4 (2007), 896–914.

Coffield, F. et al., *Learning Styles and Pedagogy in Post-16 Learning: A Systematic and Critical Review* (London: Learning and Research Skills Council, 2004).

Dugan, Holly, *The Ephemeral History of Perfume: Scent and Sense in Early Modern England* (Baltimore, MD: Johns Hopkins University Press, 2011).

Dyer, Serena, 'Shopping and the Senses: Retail, Browsing and Consumption in Eighteenth-Century England', *History Compass*, 12 no. 9 (2014), 694–703.

Gentilcore, David, *Food and Health in Early Modern Europe: Diet, Medicine, and Society, 1450–1800* (London: Bloomsbury, 2015).

Handley, Sasha, McWilliam, Rohan and Noakes, Lucy (eds), *New Directions in Social and Cultural History* (London: Bloomsbury, 2018).

Harris, Anna, *A Sensory Education* (London: Routledge, 2020).

Hoffer, Peter Charles, *Sensory Worlds in Early America* (Baltimore, MD: Johns Hopkins University Press, 2005).

Jenner, Mark, 'Tasting Lichfield, Touching China: Sir John Floyer's Senses', *The Historical Journal*, 53 no. 3 (2010), 647–70.

Kettler, Andrew, '"Ravishing Odors of Paradise": Jesuits, Olfaction, and Seventeenth-Century North America', *Journal of American Studies*, 50 no. 4 (2016), 827–52.

Kettler, Andrew, 'Delightful a Fragrance: Native American Olfactory Aesthetics within the Eighteenth-Century Anglo American Botanical Community' in *Empire of the Senses: Sensory Practices of Colonialism in Early America*, ed. Daniela Hacke and Paul Musselwhite (Leiden: Brill, 2018), pp. 223–54.

Latour, Bruno, 'How to Talk about the Body? The Normative Dimension of Science Studies', *Body & Society*, 10 nos. 2–3 (2004), 211.

Lawrence, Susan C., 'Educating the Senses: Students, Teachers and Medical Rhetoric in Eighteenth-Century London' in *Medicine and the Five Senses*, ed. W. F. Bynum and Roy Porter (Cambridge: Cambridge University Press, 1993), pp. 153–78.

Lazakis, Nat, '"It Is a Non-Negotiable Order": Public Libraries' Body Odor Bans and the Ableist Politics of Purity', *Journal of Radical Librarianship*, 6 (2020), 24–52.

Mattern, Shannon, 'Resonant Texts: Sounds of the Contemporary American Public Library', *The Senses & Society*, 2 no. 3 (2007), 277–302.

Morris, C., 'Making Sense of Education: Sensory Ethnography and Visual Impairment', *Ethnography and Education*, 12 no. 1 (2016), 1–16.

Norton, Marcy, 'Tasting Empire: Chocolate and the European Internalization of Mesoamerican Aesthetics', *The American Historical Review*, 111 no. 3 (2006), 660–91.

'Pilchards Pits and Postcards' Heritage Lottery Fund, 2015, www.sensorytrust.org.uk/projects/pilchards-pits-postcards.html (accessed 17 April 2023).

Pink, Sarah, *Doing Sensory Ethnography* (London: Sage, 2015).

Porter, Roy (ed.), *Patients and Practitioners: Lay Perceptions of Medicine in Pre-Industrial Society* (Cambridge: Cambridge University Press, 2003).

Powell, Manushag N. and Swenson, Rivka, 'Subject Theory and the Sensational Subject', *The Eighteenth Century*, 54 no. 2 (2013), 147–51.

Rhys-Taylor, Alex, *Food and Multiculture: A Sensory Ethnography of East London* (London: Routledge, 2017).

Schafer, Raymond Murray, *Ear Cleaning: Notes for an Experimental Music Course* (London: Clark & Cruickshank, 1989).

Shapin, Steven, 'Trusting George Cheyne: Scientific Expertise, Common Sense, and Moral Authority in Early Eighteenth-Century Dietetic Medicine', *Bulletin of the History of Medicine*, 77 no. 2 (2003), 263–397.

Shapin, Steven, '"You Are What You Eat": Historical Changes in Ideas about Food and Identity', *Historical Research*, 87 no. 237 (2014), 390–91.

Smith, Mark, 'Producing Sense, Consuming Sense, Making Sense: Perils and Prospects for Sensory History', *Journal of Social History*, 40 no. 4 (2007), 841–58.

Smith, Mark, *The Smell of Battle, the Taste of Siege: A Sensory History of the Civil War* (Oxford: Oxford University Press, 2014).

Smith, Mark, *A Sensory History Manifesto* (University Park, PA: Penn State University Press, 2021).

Sousa Santos, Boaventura de, *The End of the Cognitive Empire: The Coming of Age of Epistemologies of the South* (Durham, NC: Duke University Press, 2018).

Springsteen, Erin, 'Stanford Humanities Students Cook Up Julia Child's Recipes, Study History', *Stanford News*, 8 April 2016, https://news.stanford.edu/2016/04/08/kitchen-french-chef-040616 (accessed 17 April 2023).

Teil, Geneviève, 'Devenir expert aromaticien: Y a-t-il une place pour le goût dans les goûts alimentaires?', *Revue de sociologie du travail*, 4 no. 98 (1998), 503–22.

Thompson, Marie, *Beyond Unwanted Sound: Noise, Affect, and Aesthetic Moralism* (London: Bloomsbury, 2017).

Thrift, Nigel and Glennie, Paul, *Shaping the Day: A History of Timekeeping in England and Wales 1300–1800* (Oxford: Oxford University Press, 2011).

Thyssen, Geert, 'Odorous Childhoods and Scented Worlds of Learning: A Sensory History of Health and Outdoor Education Initiatives in Western Europe (1900s–1960s)', *The Senses and Society*, 14 no. 2 (2019), 173–93.

Tullett, William, *Smell in Eighteenth Century England: A Social Sense* (Oxford: Oxford University Press, 2019).

Tullett, William, 'State of the Field: Sensory History', *History*, 106 no. 373 (2021), 804–20.

Tullett, William, *Smell and the Past: Noses, Archives, Narratives* (London: Bloomsbury 2023).

Chapter 4

Let's talk about sex: 'BAD' approaches to teaching the histories of gender and sexualities

Ruth Larsen

Scholars such as Tony Harland argue that a university education can enable graduates to become 'thoughtful participants in society'.[1] However, Hannah Forsyth and Jedidiah Evans note that 'the way that history is written has been – and often still is – complicit in the perpetuation of empire, heteronormative sexualities, nationalism, patriarchy and forms of white supremacy'.[2] It is therefore important that history degrees have an inclusive curriculum that engages with critical issues. This can include modules that explore histories of gender and sexual identities, their diversities, and how they have been constructed by societies and changed over time. As gender history is also a route into cross-national histories, enabling students to examine how similar ideas were debated in different locations, it is possible to develop a student's ability to become, in Harland's phrase, a 'critic and conscience of society'.[3]

Therefore, although there was resistance to the inclusion of the histories of gender and sexualities in higher education curricula in the early parts of the twentieth century, in recent decades there has been a growing recognition of the importance of these topics in developing a broader understanding the past.[4] The histories of gender and sexuality are especially pertinent for scholars of the eighteenth century. As researchers such as Karen Harvey and Tim Hitchcock have shown, this was a period where there were new ways of discussing sex and sexualities, and gender identities were negotiated and reformed.[5] More recently, there has been an acknowledgement that 'the period's crucial investments in and consolidations of gender and sexual normativity' mean that eighteenth-century studies can be a fruitful arena for the study of queer and trans histories.[6] There is also a diversity of scholarship that means that students have a significant set of historiographical debates that they can engage with and develop their critical understandings of how identities were formed and renegotiated in this period. To support this, there is a wide range of accessible primary sources for students of the eighteenth century, many of them digital such as those available through Eighteenth-Century Collections Online and the Wellcome Collections. This means that students can develop their own voices as historians and chart the development of (and resistance to) shifting social norms and forms of patriarchy.[7]

It is therefore important that we think about how students can be active participants in these modules. This chapter considers strategies that can be employed for encouraging student engagement, with a particular focus on the seminar. In particular, it focuses on an approach which I call, with a certain degree of knowingness, 'BAD' pedagogy. This model stresses the importance of thinking about what happens *before* and *after* each session as a way of encouraging student engagement *during* a seminar. I do not claim that this is a radical way of thinking; it draws on existing pedagogical literature on how to design individual sessions, modules and curricula. In particular, it builds on research that has highlighted the importance of student-centred learning and placing student outcomes, rather than the tutor's desired outcomes, at the heart of teaching.[8] This is the model described by John Biggs as 'constructive alignment', which is focused not on what the teacher does but on what the students do.[9] What I hope this approach does, though, is bring this range of ideas into a simple single model that can be applied to a wide range of different modules in humanities degrees. By looking at case studies of how this approach has been applied to the teaching of the eighteenth-century histories of genders and sexualities to level 5 (second-year) students in a UK university, it highlights how a more holistic approach can help to encourage greater engagement within seminars and enable students to derive long-term benefits from their learning by supporting them to be articulate and critical thinkers.

The seminar is an important feature of many history degrees because of its focus on discussion, which is central to exploring the past within higher education settings. Therefore, much of the research on seminars has been focused on approaches that can encourage students to participate.[10] However, the forms that this engagement takes can vary, depending on subjects, modules and individual students. We also need to ensure that we are thinking about the needs of a wide range of learners, as not all students are comfortable in being active learners. In their study of student experiences of classroom discussions, Do and Schallert note that unlike 'the safe context of a lecture, in which a student could hide, to some students, particularly the nontalkers, the discussion was like a jungle with students needing to chart a path through unexpected thoughts, emotions, and actions'.[11] It is therefore important for the staff leading these sessions that they can provide a route map through the sometimes rocky terrain of a seminar.

However, this is not always easy. Many students feel uncomfortable talking, and it is important to remember that discussion-led learning is new to many higher education learners.[12] This discomfort can be exacerbated when a seminar topic is 'difficult', whether in terms of its complexity or due to ideas about social norms or etiquette. This sense of social awkwardness can impact a whole range of themes that historians consider; in discussions about race, religion and genocide, for example, students are often acutely aware of the need for sensitivity. This can mean that some prefer to remain silent, as this can be a way of either expressing tolerance of their fellow students' views or avoiding an argument.[13] Many students feel that it is not culturally acceptable to discuss some topics, such as sexuality, in open forums, and those students who have strong and/or divergent opinions about what is acceptable or unacceptable regarding sexualities may find it difficult to share these with fellow students.[14] This tendency towards self-censorship has been noted by lecturers in a wide range of disciplines who teach gender and sexuality at university.

This has led to a growing focus on strategies for teaching these subjects. For example, in their edited collection Murphy and Ribarsky include models of best practice including debates, role play, source analysis exercises and assessment strategies.[15] However, these learning and teaching texts have primarily focused on contemporaneous beliefs, experiences and representations of gender and sexuality rather than placing these into wider historical contexts. The challenge, and benefit, of teaching history can be the distance; it is easier for it to feel less personal, especially for periods before 1900. However, it is important to ensure that students do not fall into Whiggishness in their understanding of gender relations, and that they are guided in understanding the complexities of continuity and change. It can also be a challenge when using eighteenth-century sources that employ language and visual imagery that is not always in line with modern sensibilities. There can also be a strong tendency towards heteronormativity, both in terms of seminar contributions and in scholarly literature, and so it is often difficult to highlight that there were queer lives and queer experiences in the period.[16] So how can a historian overcome these challenges? I would suggest that thinking about the student experience *as a whole* and not just on the individual module is crucially important.

Therefore, we need to start with the *before*. This should not just be the week before an individual session but can include thinking about what happens before they start the module, and even the programme, as a whole. This can help to set into place the relationships and expectations which mean that students are ready to have complex discussions and debates about challenging subjects, such as sexuality. Induction activities can really help students to understand what is expected of them at tertiary level. There can sometimes be an expectation that many learners, especially those who can be described as 'traditional' students, know what is required of them at university. However, as Grace Sykes has shown, the old model of 'traditional' and 'non-traditional' student is not helpful, and programmes and modules need to be designed to support a wide range of different learners.[17] Research, such as that of Gibson et al., has stressed the importance of university-wide induction activities in helping a new starter to 'become a student', as it should not be presumed that they necessarily know what this means.[18]

This is also true of becoming 'a historian', and so ensuring that students are made aware of the expectations as early as possible is important. This can be delivered through activities based around research tasks, such as history-based treasure hunts or co-working with fellow students in undertaking a shared task, as well as the more traditional discussion of the expectations that staff have of students and, crucially, vice versa. The process of induction, whether it is at programme or module level, can also help in the formation of positive staff–student relations, which may be through activities such as study trips, informal gatherings such as coffee mornings or one-to-one tutorials early in a module. Inclusivity should be at the heart of these induction activities, in terms of reflecting both the diversity of the student cohort and the histories that they will cover.

Providing a welcoming learning environment along with effective communication and a shared understanding of learning expectations can really help everyone to learn effectively, as well as supporting student retention by increasing students' sense of 'belongingness'.[19]

Another element which is important to consider when thinking about the *before* is the relationship of an individual module within a student's programme of learning. This is because curriculum design can also help to make students more engaged. Effectively designed programmes can ensure that student learning is scaffolded in order to support students to become more engaged and effective independent learners throughout their degree, and to achieve the intended learning outcomes.[20] By moving away from a focus solely on individual modules and towards programme learning outcomes, staff can be aware of how each module fits within a wider programme of learning.[21] This will usually include building student knowledge and skill-sets as they go through each level, through effective assessment and learning content design. In doing this, by taking a 'Universal Design to Learning' (UDL) approach, the diverse needs of students can be anticipated *before* they start a module, meaning that student support is built into the curriculum and module rather than being retrofitted.[22] Ideally, all staff teaching on a programme will be engaged with this process of curriculum design. Therefore, all colleagues, including those on fixed-term contracts, should be made aware of how the modules they are teaching fit with the wider programme so they can design their sessions accordingly. For example, if you are aware that students have already studied modules where source analysis was central to their learning but have not had to present formally to their peers, you can shape the content of your early sessions to draw on existing strengths in order to build new ones.

Supporting students to be engaged learners can also be driven by what comes *after*. This too should shape curriculum design; it is important to think about graduate attributes and how these are scaffolded through the degree as a whole. In relationship to effective seminars, strong oral communication skills can really enhance a student's employability, as well as giving them the confidence to explore key historical ideas and debates.[23] Providing opportunities for critical reading of primary and secondary materials, scholarly writing and effective reflection can also be an important element of developing skills that will support them through their degree and after graduation. These can therefore be incorporated into effective assessment design, and modules on the histories of gender and sexuality can be central in developing these skills.

There is increasing concern that students are 'outcome driven' in their learning, and this is often seen as problematic as it can reflect surface rather than deep learning.[24] However, understanding the strategic mindset and using it as motivation can have positive outcomes. Discussing with students why they are engaging in specific activities, and the benefits of doing so, can enable wider engagement. Part of this can be about long-term outcomes, such as enhancing their post-degree life opportunities; for example, an understanding of gender histories can be important in developing social awareness and interpersonal skills that are especially valued by many employers. This can help students realise that they are not just doing activities to pass modules but that the processes and skills they will develop in doing the work, as well as the knowledge they gain, could have lasting benefits. Therefore, encouraging students to be reflective learners can be important; encouraging students to think about their journey on the programme can help them to understand how they learn, what they have learned and how to continue to develop their own skills and knowledge.[25] This can be about not only what comes after the degree but also what comes next in the programme of learning (or in the immediate module). Helping students to understand how their engagement with an individual session can help them with future sessions and future modules, and encouraging students to reflect on this, can make learning more meaningful.

Thinking about the programme level *before* and *after* can help to shape the *during*. Below I set out how this 'BAD' pedagogy approach can be applied to teaching the histories of gender and sexualities. It draws on my experiences of teaching level 5 students in a UK university on a series of different modules that explored the interrelationships between men and women in the long eighteenth century. This academic material can be challenging, as it is very interdisciplinary in nature, and it often questions traditional ideas about gender norms by highlighting how they changed and were constructed over time. As with other modules on the degrees, these gender history modules were developed with the wider programme learning outcomes in mind, and the discipline-specific skills were mapped to levels and modules. Therefore, as a module leader, it was important for me to be aware of what students had studied before coming to these modules, and what the next steps were going to be.

This meant that these gender history modules not only focused on delivering key content but also developed students' skills in reading and critiquing primary sources, in addition to building their confidence in engaging with historiographical debates. They had been introduced to these ideas and approaches at level 4 (first year), but because these are key skills for history undergraduates, they needed to be reinforced at level 5 so that students were able to apply these effectively in their final-year extended projects or dissertations.

Over the ten years that I taught these modules, seminar-based learning was at the heart of the teaching strategy. Goodman et al. argue that the 'discussion-based classroom serves to foreground the relationship between talk and the production of knowledge'.[26] This knowledge was focused not only on critical understandings of gender history but also on historical methodologies. However, for these seminars to be effective, it was important to ensure that the students were prepared for each session. Providing clear frameworks for expectations and empowering students to become knowledgeable enough about key ideas or debates can facilitate effective classroom discussions.[27] The responsibility for student preparedness should not just fall on the students; academic staff can play a crucial role in giving students guidance and support in being prepared. Within history, there is a long tradition of encouraging students to read before sessions, and most lecturers will know that if students have properly prepared for sessions, it can be hugely beneficial during discussions and debates. Preparing for a session does not have to be just reading; other activities such as watching a pre-recorded lecture, engaging with other audio-visual materials or undertaking a research task can all give students more confidence in advance of a taught session. This approach, when also supported with post-session activities, has often been described as an 'inverted' or 'flipped' classroom.[28] One of the key benefits of this can be that students have more control over when, how and what they learn, which in turn strengthens their conceptual understandings.[29] In terms of these modules specifically, it was again important for me to think about the *before* and the *after* when developing individual sessions. I used a virtual learning environment to give students access to electronic journals and digitised extracts from key books for their set preliminary reading, which helped students to build their knowledge and expertise of the current debates that shape this discipline area. These texts were selected while thinking about their journey through the module as a whole, not just a single session, and with an awareness of the wider programme that they were studying. This meant that the students were able to build up their knowledge and understanding through a scaffolded approach.

This focus on reading and discussion-based teaching shaped the assessment model used, thus connecting the *before* with the *after* and the *during*. In order to encourage students to engage on a module, it is important to not only prepare students for learning but also to consider why they are doing it: what are they preparing for? While being ready for an individual session is of course important, the longer-term impact of the preparation should also be considered, as well as what might be motivating the students, which is often completing an assessment. There has been considerable discussion about the importance of assessment strategies that help students to learn as well as enabling tutors to measure their knowledge and understanding.[30] This is embodied by the assessment for learning approach, which has, at its heart, the goal that all assessments should help students to learn.[31] Ramsden argues that deep approaches to learning are encouraged by 'teaching and assessment methods that foster active and long-term engagement with learning tasks'.[32] For history students, engaging with research activities as part of their learning, which are then assessed, can also help them to develop their ability to engage with independent historical inquiry. This can be through an individual essay and/or through being assessed for their seminar participation, including leading a seminar as part of a group. This approach encourages a co-creation of knowledge, as they form communities of inquiry where they share research, ideas and debates, which in turn helps them to develop a depth of understanding for the topic and also enhances their transferable skills.[33]

These modules assessed students through both the submission of an individual essay and through the assessment of a seminar presentation and ongoing participation in the sessions. In terms of the seminar presentation, students were put into groups and each group selected which of the weekly seminar topics they were going to lead. The sessions that they led were usually between 90 and 120 minutes long. As part of these seminars the students were expected to encourage discussions about key secondary literature, which I set as the module leader, as well as leading wider debates based on their own research. As all students were assessed not just on the seminar they led but also on their engagement in seminars across the module as a whole, the 'presenters' were encouraged to ensure that there was a high level of interactive and discursive learning opportunities for their fellow students. While I facilitated these sessions, making appropriate interventions and encouragements as necessary, they were primarily shaped and led by the students.

For some students this was a challenge; while they had some experience of leading seminars at level 4, they did find it difficult, especially when talking about some of the more complex and/or socially difficult topics. Therefore, to help students develop the skills to be proactive leaders of and participants in discussions, I led the first four seminars. In these I modelled good practice; I designed the sessions so that they were focused on debating and analysing primary and secondary source materials through active learning. This is what I wanted the student groups to do when they led their seminars, and so it was important for them to see it in practice. Writers such as Alan Booth and Geoff Timmins et al. have explored ways in which history can be taught through active learning, including the use of discussion groups, role play, structured debates and so on.[34] Active, or student-centred, learning can help students gain a greater depth of understanding and bring closer together academic research and the student experience.[35] This can then, in turn, encourage students to be more engaged with the process of learning about the past. Enabling students to select their own primary sources for discussion means that they can develop their own understandings of key ideas and topics.

As Elaine Carey found in her teaching in the University of Detroit Mercy, the process of students selecting, presenting and discussing their own primary sources means that they gain a more in-depth understanding of key theoretical and conceptual ideas as they have directly engaged with historical research that they have *led*.[36] I regularly saw this in the sessions my students designed. For example, one group, who led a seminar on gender and empire, brought to the seminar a wide range of primary sources connected to the ways in which gender was understood by the British in India during the late eighteenth and early nineteenth centuries. This included both written and visual sources on the subject of *sati* ('suttee' or 'widow burning') that the students had been able to access through various digital databases. By bringing these materials together, the students leading the seminar were able to encourage the wider class to think about how ideas about race were shaping ideas about gender, and to discuss the similarities and differences between the constructions of 'British' and Hindu femininities. Many of the points raised by the students were sophisticated ideas, which built on both the set secondary reading and their own independent research about the histories of race. This shows how, through working collectively as a class, students were able to develop their own understandings and knowledge of the subject. This focus on students shaping their own learning means that they can become independent thinkers and so gain, in Kreber's phrase, their own 'authenticity'.[37] In order to gain these benefits, they needed to see it in practice, and that is what I was able to demonstrate in the first few weeks.

Another benefit of leading these first sessions was that it also enabled me to get a better understanding of how the students worked together. There was already a good working relationship in place; as there had been programme-level induction activities for these students at both levels 4 and 5, they had already got to know each other and me. However, these first few weeks meant that we could re-establish these connections within the context of the module. It is important that a good relationship between the tutor and the students is formed to enable high levels of engagement. As Hardman notes, 'students' attitude towards cooperative learning is highly dependent on how the tutor promotes and manages the dialogue and discussion arising from the student-to-student interactions'.[38] This meant that they were also able to form relationships with one another before they began to lead the sessions themselves. Do and Schallert note that the social culture of the seminar has a considerable impact on the feelings of the learners.[39] Therefore, if a relaxed learning environment can be developed, the degree of anxiety can be reduced, and the willingness to work with other students can increase. This is especially important when teaching the histories of gender and sexuality. Part of creating this positive social culture was developing a collective understanding of what made a good seminar. We discussed this openly, and in the weeks before the first student-led seminars we formed a 'mock contract' about what was required from the people leading the seminar, the tutor and the rest of the student group in order for a session to be a success. Collaborative learning can lead to a greater depth of understanding if staff and students engage with it fully and recognise that both groups need to play a role in creating a supportive and active learning environment.

Part of the shared agreement about what makes a successful seminar was for all parties to be prepared. This included doing the pre-session (the *before*) work. To support this, an element of the assessment was the completion of a seminar participation form. These forms, which also use the *before*, *during* and *after* approach, were first devised at the University of

Derby by my colleague Professor Ian Whitehead and are used on a number of different modules throughout the history and English programmes. In the forms the student logs what they read in advance of the session, and their critical responses to the texts. This means that they can prepare some key notes and ideas about the materials, which can help some of the more nervous students to contribute more effectively, and to try and reduce the degree of anxiety that some students feel when making a point.[40] They also formally note what contributions they make during sessions, and how they are connected to their wider research. This means that, when grading student participation, it is possible to move away from quantity to quality, as some of the most engaged students may make relatively few contributions to in-class discussions. Research has suggested that the number of utterances made by an individual student does not necessarily reflect the quality of their critical understanding.[41] Participation forms can therefore allow the quieter but more critically engaged student to shine, and can be especially supportive to students who have different learning styles. This is especially important in modules where there are some topics under discussion where some students may self-censor. Finally, students reflect on their engagement after each session on the participation form, as well as completing a longer reflective piece about their engagement on the module as a whole. This encourages them to take ownership of their own learning and to develop strategies for future sessions and modules. This means that students identify that they are on a journey through the programme, and how the before, after and during all interconnect.

These seminar participation forms therefore not only formally capture students' preparation and participation but also encourage them to become active and engaged learners. Gehring and Nicholson have found that students welcome the use of participation forms. While, at first, they can find them time-consuming to complete, they commented that this form of assessment means that more students engage within discussion and debates and that they are more likely to prepare for the sessions.[42] I have found this to be the case for these modules. Since adopting these forms, it is clear how much more engaged students have become, and it encourages them to be more engaged learners. It also enhances the quality of the student-led seminars. Because they are doing the weekly reading, and writing about it, they are more able to make interconnections between different critical ideas. It also encourages them to move away from some of the 'lazy' assumptions about gender and sexuality, and so can prevent ill-informed presumptions about past experiences and discourage heteronormative approaches. Students are also very aware that while they only lead one seminar, they are being assessed throughout the semester. This helps them to recognise that they have a crucial role in making seminars work every week. While researchers have found that some students can see student-led sessions as problematic, as they prefer to be taught by the tutor rather than hear the possible misunderstandings of their fellow learners, it is important that we confront the idea that university learning is a passive experience.[43] This ongoing assessment encourages this more active learning approach, and can mean that students have the confidence to talk about complex topics which may need a degree of sensitivity to discuss effectively. The fact that, during my ten years of teaching these modules, most students fully engaged reflects the real benefit of effective module design, delivery and the integration of assessment for learning into the teaching, using the notion of constructive alignment.[44]

The 'BAD' pedagogy approach can have a positive impact on the way in which students engage with their learning throughout a history degree. Creating, at both module and at programme level, a student-centred curriculum that considers where students are starting from and where they are going can impact on both their studies and their long-term opportunities. Pedagogic research suggests that students are more likely to engage with 'deep' learning when studying a topic that is of particular relevance to them, which can then have a direct impact on their attainment; gender history can be one of those 'relevant' topics.[45] A student-centred approach also encourages students to be researchers and co-producers, and the depth of sources and materials on the histories of sexuality in the eighteenth century allows students to develop their own voice as historians. It is not just about the past; it can also help the students' future too, as well as enabling life-long learning.[46] Student-led seminars are one way to do just this as they encourage a co-creation of knowledge which is supported by the depth of learning facilitated by the seminar participation forms.[47] However, as Hardman argues, it is important that we do not solely place the responsibility for learning and engaging with the students: the tutor also plays a crucial role by ensuring that the seminars are dialogical, thus encouraging engagement.[48] It is also important not just to focus on an individual seminar; lecturers need to consider how single sessions fit within the module and the programme as a whole. This can help tutors to employ strategies to engage students by showing them how they are on a wider programme of learning. I would also argue that the way the seminars are set up, using the 'BAD' pedagogy model can also help to produce a strong tutor–students relationship that can enable them to engage fully in the sessions. This can mean that students feel more capable of discussing the complex, and sometimes socially difficult, subjects that they will encounter on a history programme and develop their own confidence to discuss a wide range of topics, including talking about sex.

Notes

1 Tony Harland, *University Challenge: Critical Issues for Teaching and Learning* (London: Routledge, 2020), p. 89.

2 Hannah Forsyth and Jedidiah Evans, 'Authentic Assessment for a More Inclusive History', *Higher Education Research & Development*, 38.4 (2019), 750.

3 Harland, *University Challenge*, chapter 5. For an elegant discussion about how female contributions to Enlightenment discussions in Spain can be incorporated into modules exploring either Enlightenment or gender histories, see Catherine M. Jaffe, 'Spanish Feminist Texts in Interdisciplinary Courses on the Eighteenth Century: Decentering the Teaching of Gender and the Enlightenment', *Dieciocho: Hispanic Enlightenment*, 44.2 (2021), 373–82.

4 Krassimira Daskalova, 'Women's and Gender History in the Balkans: Looking Back over 50 Years of Teaching and Research', *Clio. Women, Gender, History*, 48 (2018), 191–200; Becki L. Ross, '"The Stubborn Clutter, the Undeniable Record, the Burning, Wilful Evidence": Teaching the History of Sexuality', *Atlantis* 25.1 (2000), 28–38.

5 Karen Harvey, 'The Century of Sex? Gender, Bodies, and Sexuality in the Long Eighteenth Century' *The Historical Journal*, 45.4 (2002), 899–91; Karen Harvey, 'The History of Masculinity, circa 1650–1800', *Journal of British Studies*, 44.2 (2005), 296–311; Tim Hitchcock, 'The Reformulation of Sexual Knowledge in Eighteenth-Century England', *Signs: Journal of Women in Culture & Society*, 37.4 (2012), 823–32. The scholarship on this topic is extensive, but other key works include Julie Peakman (ed.), *A Cultural History of Sexuality in the Enlightenment* (London: Bloomsbury Academic, 2011); Amanda Vickery, 'Golden Age to Separate Spheres? A Review of the Categories and Chronology of English Women's History', *Historical Journal*, 36 (1993), 383–414.

6 Kirsten T. Saxton, Ajuan Maria Mance and Rebekah Edwards, 'Teaching Eighteenth-Century Literature in a Transgendered Classroom' in *Heteronormativity in Eighteenth-Century Literature and Culture*, ed. A. de Freitas Boe and A. Coykendall (Farnham: Ashgate, 2014), p. 169; Julia Ftacek, 'Jonathan Swift and the Transgender Classroom', *Journal for Eighteenth-Century Studies*, 43.3 (2020), 303–14.

7 Ross, 'The Stubborn Clutter', pp. 32–3.

8 For example, ideas discussed in the following texts have especially shaped this model: John Biggs and Catherine Tang, *Teaching for Quality Learning at University: What the Student Does*, 4th edition (Maidenhead: Society for Research into Higher Education, 2011); Holly Buckland Parker, 'Learning Starts with Design: Using Universal Design for Learning (UDL) in Higher Education Course Redesign' in *Transforming Learning Environments: Strategies to Shape the Next Generation*, ed. Fayneese Miller and Anthony H. Normore (Bingley: Emerald Publishing Limited, 2012), pp. 109–36.

9 John Biggs, 'Enhancing Learning through Constructive Alignment' in *Processes Enhancing the Quality of Learning: Dispositions, Instruction, and Learning*,

ed. John R. Kirby and Michael J. Lawson (Cambridge: Cambridge University Press, 2012), pp. 117–36.

10 S. B. Goodman, K. B. Murphy and M. L. D'Andrea, 'Discussion Dilemmas: An Analysis of Beliefs and Ideals in the Undergraduate Seminar', *International Journal of Qualitative Studies in Education*, 27.1 (2014), 1–4.

11 S. L. Do and D. L. Schallert, 'Emotions and Classroom Talk: Toward a Model of the Role of Affect in Students' Experiences of Classroom Discussions', *Journal of Educational Psychology*, 96.4 (2004), 633.

12 Do and Schallert, 'Emotions and Classroom Talk', p. 621.

13 Goodman et al., 'Discussion Dilemmas', pp. 11, 17.

14 Shawn Trivette, 'Sexual Secret Cards: Examining Social Norms and Cultural Taboo around Sexuality' in *Activities for Teaching Gender and Sexuality in the University Classroom*, ed. Michael J. Murphy and Elizabeth N. Ribarsky (Lanham, MD: Rowman & Littlefield Education, 2013), p. 58.

15 Michael J. Murphy and Elizabeth N. Ribarsky (eds), *Activities for Teaching Gender and Sexuality in the University Classroom* (Lanham, MD: Rowman & Littlefield Education, 2013).

16 Robyn Ochs and Michael J. Murphy, 'Beyond Binaries: Seeing Sexual Diversity in the Classroom' in *Activities for Teaching Gender and Sexuality*, ed. Murphy and Ribarsky, p. 63; Ross, 'The Stubborn Clutter', p. 35.

17 Grace Sykes, 'Dispelling the Myth of the "Traditional" University Undergraduate Student in the UK' in *Reimagining the Higher Education Student: Constructing and Contesting Identities*, ed. Rachel Brooks and Sarah O'Shea (London: Routledge, 2021), pp. 79–96.

18 Suanne Gibson, Andrew Grace, Ciaran O'Sullivan and Christie Pritchard, 'Exploring Transitions into the Undergraduate University World Using a Student-Centred Framework', *Teaching in Higher Education*, 24.7 (2019), 819–33; Chris Ribchester, Kim Ross and Emma L. E. Rees, 'Examining the Impact of Pre-Induction Social Networking on the Student Transition into Higher Education', *Innovations in Education and Teaching International*, 51.4 (2014), 355–65.

19 T. Levett-Jones, J. Lathlean, I. Higgins and M. McMillan, 'Staff–Student Relationships and their Impact on Nursing Students' Belongingness and Learning', *Journal of Advanced Nursing*, 65 (2009), 316–24.

20 Biggs and Tang, *Teaching for Quality Learning*, chapter 7.

21 For a discussion of the important of programme-level learning outcomes, see Kent Löfgren, 'Curricular Design and Assessment: Moving Towards a Global Template' in *International Perspectives on Higher Education: Challenging Values and Practice*, ed. Trevor Kerry (London: Continuum, 2012), pp. 127–41 and Julia González and Robert Wagenaar, 'Quality and European Programme Design in Higher Education', *European Journal of Education*, 38.3 (2003), 241–51.

22 For a discussion of UDL, see Parker, 'Learning Starts with Design', pp. 109–36.

23 Geoff Timmins, Keith Vernon and Christine Kinealy, *Teaching and Learning History* (London: SAGE Publications, 2005), p. 202.

24 Biggs, 'Enhancing Learning through Constructive Alignment', pp. 120–1.

25 For a discussion of reflective learning, see Anne Brockbank and Ian McGill, *Facilitating Reflective Learning in Higher Education*, 2nd edition (Maidenhead: McGraw-Hill Education, 2007).

26 Goodman et al., 'Discussion Dilemmas', p. 6.

27 For example, see Shelly Schaefer Hinck and Edward A. Hinck, 'Arguing over Theories of Gender Development' in *Activities for Teaching Gender and Sexuality*, ed. Murphy and Ribarsky, pp. 35–46.

28 J. F. Strayer, 'How Learning in an Inverted Classroom Influences Cooperation, Innovation and Task Orientation', *Learning Environments Research*, 15 (2012), 171–93.

29 Hosam Al-Samarraie, Aizat Shamsuddin and Ahmed Ibrahim Alzahraniet, 'A Flipped Classroom Model in Higher Education: A Review of the Evidence across Disciplines', *Educational Technology Research & Development*, 68.3 (2020), 1044.

30 For a discussion of recent literature, see, for example, Zahra Sokhanvar, Keyvan Salehi and Fatemeh Sokhanvar, 'Advantages of Authentic Assessment for Improving the Learning Experience and Employability Skills of Higher Education Students: A Systematic Literature Review', *Studies in Educational Evaluation*, 70 (2021), doi: 10.1016/j.stueduc.2021.101030; Forsyth and Evans, 'Authentic Assessment', pp. 748–61; Geoffrey Timmins, 'The Future of Learning and Teaching in Social History: The Research Approach and Employability', *Journal of Social History*, 39.3 (2006), 829–42.

31 Kay Sambell, Liz McDowell and Catherine Montgomery, *Assessment for Learning in Higher Education* (London: Routledge, 2013), pp. 3–4.

32 Paul Ramsden, *Learning to Teach in Higher Education* (London: Routledge, 2003), p. 80.

33 Do and Schallert, 'Emotions and Classroom Talk', p. 620; Timmins et al., *Teaching and Learning History*, p. 202. For a discussion of the benefits of communities of inquiry for history undergraduate students, see A. Jones, 'Teaching History at University through Communities of Inquiry', *Australian Historical Studies*, 42.2 (2011), 168–93.

34 Alan Booth, *Teaching History at University: Enhancing Learning and Understanding* (New York: Routledge, 2003), chapter 7; Timmins et al., *Teaching and Learning History*, chapter 5.

35 Jones, 'Teaching History at University', pp. 175–6.

36 Elaine Carey, 'Speaking about Power: Gender, History and the Urban Classroom', *Radical Teacher*, 67 (2003), 8.

37 Carolin Kreber, *Authenticity in and through Teaching in Higher Education* (London: Routledge, 2013), passim.

38 Jan Hardman, 'Tutor–Student Interaction in Seminar Teaching: Implications for Professional Development', *Active Learning in Higher Education*, 17.1 (2016), 64.

39 Do and Schallert, 'Emotions and Classroom Talk', pp. 630–1.

40 Do and Schallert, 'Emotions and Classroom Talk', p. 629.

41 Timmins et al., *Teaching and Learning History*, p. 147.

42 David Gehring and Hannah Nicholson, 'Using Participation Marks as Assessment in History (UK)', *East Midlands Centre for History Learning and Teaching: Funded Project*, 2021, https://eastmidlandscentreforhistorylearningandteaching.education/category/funded-projects (accessed 20 December 2021).

43 Kim J. Herrmann, 'The Impact of Cooperative Learning on Student Engagement: Results from an Intervention', *Active Learning in Higher Education*, 14.3 (2013), 184.

44 Biggs and Tang, *Teaching for Quality Learning at University*, passim, especially chapter 6.

45 Ramsden, *Learning to Teach*, p. 65.

46 Jones, 'Teaching History at University', p. 193.

47 Do and Schallert, 'Emotions and Classroom Talk', p. 620.

48 Hardman, 'Tutor–Student Interaction', pp. 73–4.

References

Al-Samarraie, Hosam, Shamsuddin, Aizat and Alzahraniet, Ahmed Ibrahim, 'A Flipped Classroom Model in Higher Education: A Review of the Evidence across Disciplines', *Educational Technology Research & Development*, 68.3 (2020), 1017–51.

Biggs, John, 'Enhancing Learning through Constructive Alignment' in *Processes Enhancing the Quality of Learning: Dispositions, Instruction, and Learning*, ed. John R. Kirby and Michael J. Lawson (Cambridge: Cambridge University Press, 2012), pp. 117–36.

Biggs, John and Tang, Catherine, *Teaching for Quality Learning at University: What the Student Does*, 4th edition (Maidenhead: Society for Research into Higher Education, 2011).

Booth, Alan, *Teaching History at University: Enhancing Learning and Understanding* (New York: Routledge, 2003).

Brockbank, Anne and McGill, Ian, *Facilitating Reflective Learning in Higher Education*, 2nd edition (Maidenhead: McGraw-Hill Education, 2007).

Carey, Elaine, 'Speaking about Power: Gender, History and the Urban Classroom', *Radical Teacher*, 67 (2003), 4–8.

Daskalova, Krassimira, 'Women's and Gender History in the Balkans: Looking Back over 50 Years of Teaching and Research', *Clio. Women, Gender, History*, 48 (2018), 191–200.

Do, S. L. and Schallert, D. L., 'Emotions and Classroom Talk: Toward a Model of the Role of Affect in Students' Experiences of Classroom Discussions', *Journal of Educational Psychology*, 96.4 (2004), 619–34.

Forsyth, Hannah and Evans, Jedidiah, 'Authentic Assessment for a More Inclusive History', *Higher Education Research & Development*, 38.4 (2019), 748–61.

Ftacek, Julia, 'Jonathan Swift and the Transgender Classroom', *Journal for Eighteenth-Century Studies*, 43.3 (2020), 303–14.

Gehring, David and Nicholson, Hannah, 'Using Participation Marks as Assessment in History (UK)', East Midlands Centre for History Learning and Teaching: Funded Project (2021), https://eastmidlandscentreforhistorylearningandteaching.education/2021/01/06/using-participation-marks-as-assessment-in-history-uk (accessed 20 December 2021).

Gibson, Suanne, Grace, Andrew, O'Sullivan, Ciaran and Pritchard, Christie, 'Exploring Transitions into the Undergraduate University World Using a Student-Centred Framework', *Teaching in Higher Education*, 24.7 (2019), 819–33.

González, Julia and Wagenaar, Robert, 'Quality and European Programme Design in Higher Education', *European Journal of Education*, 38.3 (2003), 241–51.

Goodman, S. B., Murphy, K. B. and D'Andrea, M. L., 'Discussion Dilemmas: An Analysis of Beliefs and Ideals in the Undergraduate Seminar', *International Journal of Qualitative Studies in Education*, 27.1 (2014), 1–22.

Hardman, Jan, 'Tutor–Student Interaction in Seminar Teaching: Implications for Professional Development', *Active Learning in Higher Education*, 17.1 (2016), 63–76.

Harland, Tony, *University Challenge: Critical Issues for Teaching and Learning* (London: Routledge, 2020).

Harvey, Karen, 'The Century of Sex? Gender, Bodies, and Sexuality in the Long Eighteenth Century', *The Historical Journal*, 45.4 (2002), 899–916.

Harvey, Karen, 'The History of Masculinity, circa 1650–1800', *Journal of British Studies*, 44.2 (2005), 296–311.

Herrmann, Kim J., 'The Impact of Cooperative Learning on Student Engagement: Results from an Intervention', *Active Learning in Higher Education*, 14.3 (2013), 175–87.

Hinck, Shelly Schaefer and Hinck, Edward A., 'Arguing over Theories of Gender Development' in *Activities for Teaching Gender and Sexuality in the University Classroom*, ed. Michael Murphy and Elizabeth Ribarsky (Lanham, MD: Rowman & Littlefield Education, 2013), pp. 35–46.

Hitchcock, Tim, 'The Reformulation of Sexual Knowledge in Eighteenth-Century England', *Signs: Journal of Women in Culture & Society*, 37.4 (2012), 823–32.

Jaffe, Catherine M., 'Spanish Feminist Texts in Interdisciplinary Courses on the Eighteenth Century: Decentering the Teaching of Gender and the Enlightenment', *Dieciocho: Hispanic Enlightenment*, 44.2 (2021), 373–82.

Jones, A., 'Teaching History at University through Communities of Inquiry', *Australian Historical Studies*, 42.2 (2011), 168–93.

Kreber, Carolin, *Authenticity in and through Teaching in Higher Education* (London: Routledge, 2013).
Levett-Jones, T., Lathlean, J., Higgins, I. and McMillan, M., 'Staff–Student Relationships and Their Impact on Nursing Students' Belongingness and Learning', *Journal of Advanced Nursing*, 65 (2009), 316–24.
Löfgren, Kent, 'Curricular Design and Assessment: Moving towards a Global Template' in *International Perspectives on Higher Education: Challenging Values and Practice*, ed. Trevor Kerry (London: Continuum, 2012), pp. 127–41.
Murphy, Michael J. and Ribarsky, Elizabeth N. (eds), *Activities for Teaching Gender and Sexuality in the University Classroom* (Lanham, MD: Rowman & Littlefield Education, 2013).
Ochs, Robyn and Murphy, Michael J., 'Beyond Binaries: Seeing Sexual Diversity in the Classroom' in *Activities for Teaching Gender and Sexuality in the University Classroom*, ed. Michael Murphy and Elizabeth Ribarsky (Lanham, MD: Rowman & Littlefield Education, 2013), pp. 62–70.
Parker, Holly Buckland, 'Learning Starts with Design: Using Universal Design for Learning (UDL) in Higher Education Course Redesign' in *Transforming Learning Environments: Strategies to Shape the Next Generation*, ed. Fayneese Miller and Anthony H. Normore (Bingley: Emerald Publishing Limited, 2012), pp. 109–36.
Peakman, Julie (ed.), *A Cultural History of Sexuality in the Enlightenment* (London: Bloomsbury Academic, 2011).
Ramsden, Paul, *Learning to Teach in Higher Education* (London: Routledge, 2003).
Ribchester, Chris, Ross, Kim and Rees, Emma L. E., 'Examining the Impact of Pre-Induction Social Networking on the Student Transition into Higher Education', *Innovations in Education and Teaching International*, 51.4 (2014), 355–65.
Ross, Becki L., '"The Stubborn Clutter, the Undeniable Record, the Burning, Wilful Evidence": Teaching the History of Sexuality', *Atlantis*, 25.1 (2000), 28–38.
Sambell, Kay, McDowell, Liz and Montgomery, Catherine, *Assessment for Learning in Higher Education* (London: Routledge, 2013).
Saxton, Kirsten T., Mance, Ajuan Maria and Edwards, Rebekah, 'Teaching Eighteenth-Century Literature in a Transgendered Classroom' in *Heteronormativity in Eighteenth-Century Literature and Culture*, ed.

Anna de Freitas Boe and Abby Coykendall (Farnham: Ashgate, 2014), pp. 167–88.

Sokhanvar, Zahra, Salehi, Keyvan and Sokhanvar, Fatemeh, 'Advantages of Authentic Assessment for Improving the Learning Experience and Employability Skills of Higher Education Students: A Systematic Literature Review', *Studies in Educational Evaluation*, 70 (2021). doi: 10.1016/j.stueduc.2021.101030.

Strayer, J. F., 'How Learning in an Inverted Classroom Influences Cooperation, Innovation and Task Orientation', *Learning Environments Research*, 15 (2012), 171–93.

Sykes, Grace, 'Dispelling the Myth of the "Traditional" University Undergraduate Student in the UK' in *Reimagining the Higher Education Student: Constructing and Contesting Identities*, ed. Rachel Brooks and Sarah O'Shea (London: Routledge, 2021), pp. 79–96.

Timmins, Geoffrey, Vernon, Keith and Kinealy, Christine, *Teaching and Learning History* (London: SAGE Publications, 2005).

Timmins, Geoffrey, 'The Future of Learning and Teaching in Social History: The Research Approach and Employability', *Journal of Social History*, 39.3 (2006), 829–42.

Trivette, Shawn, 'Sexual Secret Cards: Examining Social Norms and Cultural Taboo around Sexuality' in *Activities for Teaching Gender and Sexuality in the University Classroom*, ed. Michael Murphy and Elizabeth Ribarsky (Lanham, MD: Rowman & Littlefield Education, 2013), pp. 57–61.

Vickery, Amanda, 'Golden Age to Separate Spheres? A Review of the Categories and Chronology of English Women's History', *Historical Journal*, 36 (1993), 383–414.

Chapter 5

Engaging students with political history: citizenship in the (very) long eighteenth century

Matthew McCormack

For a long time, political history dominated the teaching of history in British universities. Certainly until the social history revolution of the 1960s, the type of history that was taught was predominantly political, and was of very particular types. Whig histories focused on English constitutional development, concentrating on the improvement of institutions and lauding the efforts of privileged actors who contributed to this design; and even critiques of this approach tended to be establishmentarian and elitist in their outlook.[1] Following the rise of social and then cultural history, political history became more marginal in the profession, and indeed has often been the type of history that progressive histories have defined themselves against. This chapter will reflect on how best to approach this now less familiar form of history with undergraduates, who often have negative preconceptions about studying it. It will suggest that teaching eighteenth-century politics in terms of 'citizenship' can make it relevant to today's students and will think about some pedagogical strategies that can help to make the experience of learning about it more meaningful and engaging.

Of course, political history has not been static since the 1960s, and has been regularly revitalised by wider developments in the discipline. Social history was often very political in its focus, using Marxist and feminist theory to explore the political life of working men and women, opening up histories of popular politics and protest.[2] And cultural history has enabled new histories of political culture and identity, notably the 'new political history' that focused on the mobilisation of identity categories and the cultural exercise of power.[3] Increasingly, the focus of historians has been away from the state's institutions and personnel and towards the worlds of extra-parliamentary and popular politics. Work on politics in the long eighteenth century in recent years has been notably rich in this respect, including studies of gender, empire, space and material culture.[4]

Even in the light of these shifts, political history can be a tough sell for undergraduate history students. Many will have encountered political history of a fairly traditional type at school:[5] some will have been put off by the experience and come to university with a strong preference for social history; some will be enthusiastic about it but may well have been drawn to politics degrees (or dedicated joint programmes like Manchester's Politics and Modern History) rather than history. Even when they are keen on politics, the political history of the eighteenth century poses particular challenges. From the mid-nineteenth century, British politics settled down into a clear party system that is recognisable to students today, where parties had infrastructures and programmes, and elections had clear outcomes and were fought on national political issues. But the 'First Age of Party' of the late seventeenth and early eighteenth centuries should not be approached with this modern frame of reference, and the subsequent century certainly cannot. Parties were very provisional and were based more upon personal connection and interest than ideology: indeed, most MPs were independents. Elections were mostly uncontested and had much less bearing on the choice of the government: the Lords was more prestigious than the Commons and prime ministers tended to sit there. Much depended on the preferences and personal connections of the monarch, and the exact power relations between the various branches of the political system were complex and constantly debated: everybody talked about the 'constitution' without anybody agreeing what it actually was.

Eighteenth-century politics can therefore be an alien and incomprehensible world. For a long time, the dominant approach to it was that proposed by Sir Lewis Namier in the mid-twentieth century. As a corrective to the presentism and sweeping assumptions of the Whig school, Namier argued that historians should instead embrace its complexity: historians should focus on the detail of high political life, concentrating on the individual motivations and personal connections of its well-documented protagonists.[6] While in some respects this humanised politics, it arguably made it more baffling: its anti-teleological emphasis made it difficult to construct clear explanatory narratives; its dense empirical detail made it inaccessible to the non-specialist; and its elitism made it difficult for most people to relate to. While the world of popular politics has now been opened up to study by subsequent generations of historians, it is still difficult to approach eighteenth-century parliamentary politics without understanding the intricacies of the court, party connections and familial ties. For example, much of the work on women in Georgian politics has been in this Namierite mould, since in practice the women who exercised the greatest political influence in this interconnected familial world – and who left source material – were of the social elite.[7]

Students coming to university will likely not have studied eighteenth-century politics before. This is not in itself a bad thing – and part of the point of a history degree is that students get exposed to new topics – but it does raise the question of how best to approach it in the light of the challenges noted above. Furthermore, if lecturers are running an optional module, then they have to persuade students to choose it or it may not run. This is the task I faced when I moved to the University of Northampton in 2004 and was asked to design a third-year option based on my research interests. With regular updates, it ran most years until 2022. In common with many history degree programmes, the degree at Northampton starts with modules that are quite broad, introductory and often team-taught and concludes with modules that are more specialist, research-driven and individual. Some degrees call such final-year options 'special subjects' and typically offer choice here. How then should I package Georgian politics in a way that assumed no prior knowledge, took into account recent developments in the historiography and was appealing to students?

Political history as citizenship

The module I designed was entitled 'Citizenship and Gender in Britain, 1760–1918'. It was partly designed as a 'long-nineteenth-century' module because of the curriculum I had been employed to cover, but also because of the story I wanted to tell. A key focus of the module was the campaign to reform citizenship rights that started with campaigns for manhood suffrage in the 1760s and concluded with the granting of the vote to women in 1918. Because of the space required to set up the topic, and because

I argued that these two centuries of debate were essentially conducted in terms that were established in the eighteenth century, around half of the module content concerned the Georgian period.

Drawing on my PhD research – which became my first book – I argued that the key political question in this period was: what sorts of people are fit to be citizens? And specifically, who should be granted the parliamentary franchise? Since this political question involved negotiating the boundaries of inclusion and exclusion in social terms, this proved to be a very good way in to political history for students who were more familiar or comfortable with social history. My doctoral research had been influenced by the linguistic turn, thinking about how the language that historical actors used informed their view of the world, and in particular how identity categories were constructed and negotiated.[8] In the module I wanted to connect scholarship on Georgian political discourse with that on the Victorian and Edwardian periods, particularly the work on the Second Reform Act of 1867 by Catherine Hall, Keith McLelland and Jane Rendall. They argued that the Act sought to 'define the Victorian nation' in terms of gender, race and class: the new voters of 1867 were defined as British working men, in distinction to their 'others' represented by foreigners, paupers and women.[9] In tracing a concept over a long period, the module was influenced by my experience as an undergraduate at the University of York, where third-years took a 'Comparative Special Subject' focusing on a theme such as 'heroes' or 'revolutions'. Such modules are demanding and have an important summative function at the end of a degree.[10]

While the module explored various ways of defining the political subject – including national identity, social class, education and property ownership – the key focus of the module was gender. I proposed that this was the key category when negotiating the boundaries of political inclusion and exclusion, and invited the students to disagree with my proposition. In the course of tracing this theme, the module introduced the wealth of work on the political histories of gender, women and masculinity. Although this scholarship is now well established, when the module began in the 2000s it was recent and in some cases controversial: students were asked to consider whether a history of political masculinities was desirable from a feminist point of view, or whether it was just a reassertion of 'men's history' in a male-dominated and traditional field. The focus on gender proved to be a useful entry point for students, who had typically studied women's history before (partly at school but also in a first-year introductory module) but had not necessarily studied politics, and who were often vocal in expressing a preference for social history. It helped them to evaluate an otherwise unfamiliar historiography in terms of current social and political issues. Political history remains a rather 'male' field – both in terms of its practitioners and the people it studies – but enrolments for this module tended to be majority female.

A further reason why 'citizenship' was a relatable focus for students was that it was (and is) a current political issue. Citizenship has been a political buzzword in Britain since the 1990s, and remains so to this day. John Major proposed a 'citizen's charter' of rights and David Cameron focused on the citizen's obligations as part of a 'big society', but it was New Labour who really made it central to their project. Tony Blair introduced citizenship tests for immigrants, which included many questions about history that applicants effectively had to learn by rote (not least because many of the official 'correct' answers were quite problematic).[11] It included questions about popular culture as well as constitutional developments, suggesting that their vision of history was as much about national identity as it was about political education. After the 9/11 and 7/7 attacks, the Labour government focused on fostering a sense of belonging among groups in society who felt disaffected and excluded. This included the introduction of citizenship as a subject in schools. The educationalist Audrey Osler has reviewed Labour's approach to citizenship in their education policy, and notes that there was a fundamental tension between their desire to prescribe 'British' values and their cosmopolitanism. Blair argued that 'democracy, rule of law, tolerance and equal treatment for all' were British values, whereas the foreign secretary Jack Straw noted that these were international values that had developed in a unique way in Britain over the course of its history.[12] It was therefore necessary, Straw argued, that Britons knew their nation's story in order to understand the country they lived in today.

The place of citizenship in education, and the relationship of history education to citizenship, has long been a key political issue in Britain. Peter Yeandle argues that history education was central to citizenship in the late nineteenth and twentieth centuries, but that it was not primarily conveyed in history books themselves but rather in texts such as literacy primers. He further argues that the Victorians sought not to inculcate 'crude' nationalism but rather to foster citizenship and morality: rather than just telling schoolchildren that the empire was a good thing, for example, it emphasised that the English were an 'imperial race' with suitable qualities and a special mission.[13] John Tosh agrees that history has had a special place in citizenship education in Britain. He argues that the purpose of citizenship classes in recent years has been to 'intensify the sense of belonging . . . by anchoring it securely in shared narratives about the past'. History teachers may not have been involved much in delivering the citizenship curriculum, but that is only because history 'is still regarded as a course in citizenship in all but name'.[14] If this was true of New Labour, it is even truer of the Conservatives' reform of the national curriculum for history in the 2010s. The education secretary Michael Gove argued that British schoolchildren should learn their 'island story' in chronological order, so they could value the progression of its political institutions. This distinctly Whig attitude came under criticism from the historian Richard Evans, who argued that history education should foster critical skills rather than be used as a vehicle for identity politics.[15]

Tosh too has taken issue with the way in which history has been appropriated for prescribing models of citizenship, and argues that there are more productive ways for conceiving of the relationship between history education and citizenship. Most historians would agree that their subject 'provides a training in the rational evaluation of evidence and argument'. This is surely a good thing, but history is hardly the only subject that does this. More fundamentally, it provides a historical perspective, which 'enhances the citizen's capacity to make informed judgements about the issues of the day, to participate in public discourse, and to make intelligent use of the vote'. Approaching the present in this way – 'thinking with history' – enables students to illuminate current issues and to think about what is distinctive about the past.[16] A key justification for the value of history should therefore be that it makes its learners informed, critical citizens.

These questions were addressed directly in the module. Education is a key theme in feminist history, since Georgian feminists such as Mary Wollstonecraft and Hannah Wheeler saw deficiencies in women's education as a cause of their subordinate condition and education reform as a means of improving it. Another week focused on Victorian debates about education with respect to the moral qualities educators were supposed to foster, such as 'character' and 'independence'. We discussed the role of education in preparing children for citizenship, and how the introduction of compulsory education was explicitly linked to the widening of the parliamentary franchise. As the Liberal Robert Lowe argued in 1867, it was necessary 'to prevail on our future masters to learn their letters'.[17] This session was of particular interest to the students taking the module who were seeking careers in teaching, and in successive years more of the students had themselves studied citizenship at school. They were therefore able to reflect critically on that experience and to connect their own knowledge of education and political debates today to the historical context of the eighteenth and nineteenth centuries.

Pedagogic strategies

The design of the module was by no means revolutionary. Indeed, it was organised in a fairly conventional way, but I did employ a number of strategies with a view to enhancing student learning and engagement. The module ran in one term of eleven or twelve weeks, with a weekly workshop of around three hours. This time was used flexibly, with short lectures, discussions, document exercises and other activities. The module size varied from about ten to about thirty: in years when it was larger, I split the group in two in the third and fourth hour to give the students more of a seminar experience. A typical format for the class would be to start with a concept (such as the public sphere or feminism) which we would then put into historical context in the second hour. In the final section we would focus on a case study (such as the Queen Caroline Affair or military volunteering) which we would introduce with a student presentation and then explore in small groups with documents. As Peter Frederick notes, small-group work can provide an 'energy shift' and can empower students to talk about their ideas in a space that may feel safer than a whole class.[18] At the conclusion of the session, we would evaluate the concept in the light of what we had discussed, and set up the learning for the following week.

The first session of the module was entitled 'What is citizenship?' After setting up the practicalities and aims of the module, we explored the concept in detail without necessarily getting into the eighteenth-century context. We began with a brainstorm, getting students to think about what citizenship entailed in terms of rights, duties and attachments. They discussed this in small groups and filled in a grid on a worksheet, which we then fed back to the class to come up with an agreed list on the whiteboard. This was invariably a rich discussion that lasted over an hour. Students discovered that this was actually a tricky concept to define, and the examples they drew upon from ancient history to the present day did not necessarily fit the model consistently: the lesson of the exercise was 'it depends', since citizenship has meant different things in different times and contexts. Along the way, I used various examples and sources to stimulate discussion. Among these was the film *Starship Troopers*, which I had encouraged them to watch as preparation for the module. I showed a clip of the opening scenes where the characters debate the nature of citizenship in a school classroom, before joining the military to fight aliens. Although *Starship Troopers* is on the face of it an unsubtle sci-fi war movie, it is based on a novel by Robert A. Heinlein that advocates a classical republican form of citizenship, where 'citizens' earn their rights through military service and 'civilians' are second-class citizens.[19] The 1997 film adaptation by Paul Verhoeven sends up the fascism of this source material, so is a sharp political satire. The clip led to a discussion about the reciprocal nature of citizenship, and we referred back to it later in the module when examining wartime contexts where political rights were earned through service to the nation, such as during the Napoleonic Wars and the First World War.

The module had a strong focus on primary sources and source analysis, which is appropriate for final-year study. For every session I produced a worksheet with multiple primary sources for students to analyse in class: this was usually on paper, but I used electronic versions during the COVID-19 pandemic for online or socially distanced classes, which worked equally well. Many of these were extracts from texts, which students read individually then discussed in groups, before reporting back for a whole-group discussion. In early classes, these required quite a bit of scaffolding – with context to set them up and direct questions to draw out the analysis – but as the students grew more familiar with the material, they were increasingly able to do this without direction from me. Every week we also used visual sources, particularly satirical prints from the Georgian period and cartoons from later periods. Students often assume that pictures are easier to analyse than texts, but they quickly appreciated that visual satire has a complex language that would have been familiar to contemporaries but can be obscure today. Over the course of the module they therefore learned the lost art of 'reading' a Georgian print, and they became more confident doing this with practice. Students made links between the highly visual political culture of the Georgian period and that of today, which is characterised by video clips and internet memes. In later years I also introduced material sources such as badges and memorabilia, so the evolution of the module reflected my own development as a historian, away from the linguistic turn and towards histories of objects and embodiment.

A further way in which textual source material was brought alive was through performance. In the third week on 'political masculinities', we studied an extract from a political stage play of 1757, *The Fall of Public Spirit*. This introduced the characters of Old Time and Ancient Spirit, who travelled through time from ancient Britain to 1757 – a time of moral panic and military disaster – and were appalled at the immorality and decadence that they beheld.[20] This text is fairly flat on the page, but contemporaries would likely have experienced it in performance rather than through silent reading, so getting the students to recreate it as a performance provided insights into the source. In particular, it brought out the force of the political message and how models of masculinity were embodied and politicised. In the following week on the culture of elections, we studied some election songs from the infamous Westminster Election of 1784. Music was a prominent feature of elections at the time, and new lyrics were written to popular songs of the day to support particular candidates and comment on the political situation. Since we know the tunes to which they were set, it is possible to perform them. I played an audio clip of the sea shanty 'Roast Beef of Old England', then led the group in a rendition of 'The Female Patriot: Or, The Devonshire Duchess', which had been set to this tune.[21] Singing is a very accessible form of musical performance that does not necessarily require equipment or training. Although some students found the exercise slightly embarrassing, taking students out of their comfort zone is a positive experience in the classroom if it is managed sensitively. Discomfort can take you radically out of the present and lead to reflection: in this case, it highlighted the emotion and physicality of singing an election song, leading to insights about what an election would have been like to experience in bodily and sensory terms.

As a 'special subject'-type module, the module involved in-depth work on the historiography, and necessarily had an extensive reading list. Most history modules involve a great deal of reading in order to prepare for classes and to work on assignments. History is not a subject where a set body of knowledge is acquired in a sequential order, and tends not to rely on textbooks or primers to deliver this, preferring to focus on specialist literature.[22] For the most part, history lecturers either set specific reading for a given class or provide a reading list from which students can make selections, and assume that this is going on in the background. As Effie MacLellan cautions, however, undergraduate students in general 'are not proficient readers'. They can of course read, but 'reading to learn' is a distinctive skill that has to be fostered.[23] Reading is fundamental to the learning of history, and is often the start of the learning process, so this is part of our disciplinary practice that needs to be 'decoded' if students are going to get the most out of it.[24]

This module therefore had a very explicit focus on the reading process. In the 2006–7 session I carried out a study within the module, with the intention of gaining a greater understanding of how students read. I also hoped that, in the process, students would think about how they themselves read: sometimes it is useful to have a 'triggering event' to encourage students to reflect on their learning practices.[25] I used a series of anonymous weekly questionnaires that asked students what they had read, how long they had spent on it, whether and how they had taken notes, and what they got out of it. In general, this revealed that the students were not reading as much as I had assumed, but that I could improve the way that I set up the activity to help them to get more out of it. The students reported that they appreciated knowing what to look for in their reading – such as a research question or a theme – which provided a focus for their preparation. This made note-taking more of an active 'research' activity rather than a passive exercise in fact-gathering. Some students revealed that they had quite sophisticated methods of note-taking, which enhanced their understanding of the material. MacLellan advocates 'elaboration strategies' such as paraphrasing and summarising as ways for students to gain ownership of their reading, and to promote deep, active learning.[26] I applied these insights to the module in subsequent years and set up reading activities with much greater care.

The assessment strategy for the module changed over the course of its life, partly due to shifts in departmental and institutional policy. The module was assessed by a combination of essay, presentation and examination: in some years it was all three, and in others it was the essay with one of the other two. Of all the assessments, the presentation was probably the most conducive to active learning. Students were tasked with finding a primary source from the period covered by the module, to deliver a spoken presentation about it in class and to take questions from their colleagues. Students could select a text or an image, and in both cases they drew on the skills in source analysis that we had developed over the course of the module. Presentations on visual images worked particularly well, since students could demonstrate how they were 'reading' the visual elements while displaying the image on a screen. This assessment was therefore set up as a 'research' task, and some students went to considerable lengths to find sources that addressed the module's themes and to research contextual information about them. This demonstrated the benefits of treating students as researchers, and the possibilities for including research tasks in undergraduate teaching outside of its traditional locations such as the dissertation.[27]

Conclusion

Overall, the module provided an effective way in to Georgian politics for students who had not studied it before. The focuses of 'citizenship' and 'gender' had several benefits. By thinking about the social and cultural nature of the political world, they enabled students to discuss politics using familiar methodologies, and without the need for substantial factual background knowledge. They connected politics in the eighteenth and nineteenth centuries to political and social issues in the present day, and the focus on 'citizenship' in particular highlighted the historical background to many of today's controversies such as immigration, education policy, Scottish independence and Brexit. They also emphasised the importance of historical study to good citizenship, since it is vital to understand the nature of our political system if we are to participate in it in an informed way and make reasoned decisions about political questions. Indeed, both the students and I would frequently switch between discussions of the historical context and the present day. Students often arrive at university with a sense that historians should avoid presentism and bias, but this module demonstrated that a contemporary and personal perspective enriches our understanding both of the past and the present. This strong contemporary focus contributed to the active learning and higher-level understanding that the module sought to promote.

By way of a coda, the module is unlikely to run again as my role at the university has changed. But in a sense it will live on, since I published a book based on the module in 2019.[28] This was explicitly written as a student textbook and a teaching aid, and I hope that it will be used in similar courses elsewhere. Writing the book was also a learning process for me, since I went about it in a very different way to my previous research publications. Rather than being driven by primary research, it was based on my class materials and my experience of teaching. Instead of a lengthy bibliography, each chapter has a brief guide to further reading. The style of writing was intended to be accessible to the non-specialist, and it was challenging to explain big ideas in a clear and readable way. Writing the book forced me to reflect on how public history should be communicated, which was in itself a lesson in good citizenship.

Notes

1 Herbert Butterfield in *The Whig Interpretation of History* (Ann Arbor, MI: Bell, 1931).

2 E. P. Thompson, *The Making of the English Working Class* (London: Gollancz, 1963); Geoge Rudé, *Wilkes and Liberty: A Social Study of 1763 to 1774* (Oxford: Clarendon Press, 1962).

3 James Vernon, *Politics and the People: A Study in English Political Culture, c. 1815–1867* (Cambridge: Cambridge University Press, 1993), p. 5.

4 For example: Kathryn Gleadle and Sarah Richardson (eds), *Women in British Politics 1780–1860: The Power of the Petticoat* (Houndmills: Palgrave, 2000); Kathleen Wilson, *The Island Race: Englishness, Empire and Gender in the Eighteenth Century* (Abingdon: Routledge, 2003); Mark Knights, *Trust and Distrust: Corruption in Office in Britain and Its Empire 1600–1850* (Oxford: Oxford University Press, 2021); Katrina Navickas, *Protest and the Politics of Space and Place, 1789–1848* (Manchester: Manchester University Press, 2015); Joan Coutu, Jon Stobart and Peter Linfield (eds), *Politics and the English Country House, 1688–1800* (Kingston: McGill-Queens University Press, 2023).

5 Marcus Collins, 'Historiography from Below: How Undergraduates Remember Learning History at School', *Teaching History*, 142 (2011), 34–8 (36).

6 Louis Namier, *The Structure of Politics at the Accession of George III* (London: Macmillan, 1929).

7 Elaine Chalus, *Elite Women in English Political Life, c. 1754–1790* (Oxford: Oxford University Press, 2005); Amanda Foreman, *Georgiana Duchess of Devonshire* (London: HarperCollins, 1998).

8 Matthew McCormack, '"The Independent Man" in English Political Culture, 1760–1832' (PhD thesis, University of Manchester, 2002). This became *The Independent Man: Citizenship and Gender Politics in Georgian England* (Manchester: Manchester University Press, 2005).

9 Catherine Hall, Keith McLelland and Jane Rendall, *Defining the Victorian Nation: Class, Race and Gender in the British Reform Act of 1867* (Cambridge: Cambridge University Press, 2000).

10 Tim Hitchcock, Robert Shoemaker and John Tosh, 'Skills and the Structure of the History Curriculum' in *The Practice of University History Teaching*, ed. Alan Booth and Paul Hyland (Manchester: Manchester University Press, 2000), pp. 47–59 (p. 58). They are still a feature of the York history degree, but are now called 'Comparative History Modules'.

11 'Historians Call for a Review of Home Office Citizenship and Resettlement Test': open letter to the journal *History* (21 July 2020), https://historyjournal.org.uk/2020/07/21/historians-call-for-a-review-of-home-office-citizenship-and-settlement-test (accessed 31 January 2023).

12 Audrey Osler, 'Patriotism, Multiculturalism and Belonging: Political Discourse and the Teaching of History', *Educational Review*, 61:1 (2009), 85–100 (86).

13 Peter Yeandle, *Citizenship, Nation, Empire: The Politics of History Teaching in England, 1870–1930* (Manchester: Manchester University Press, 2015), pp. 2, 174.

14 John Tosh, *Why History Matters* (Houndmills: Palgrave, 2008), pp. ix, 125.

15 Robert Guyver, 'England and the UK: Conflict and Consensus over Curriculum' in *Teaching History and the Changing Nation State: Transnational and Intranational Perspectives*, ed. Robert Guyver (London: Bloomsbury, 2016), pp. 159–74.

16 Tosh, *Why History Matters*, pp. 120–1.

17 Quoted in A. Ottway, *Education and Society: An Introduction to the Sociology of Education* (Oxford: Routledge, 1953), p. 62.

18 Peter J. Frederick, 'Motivating Students by Active Learning in the History Classroom' in *The Practice of University History Teaching*, ed. Booth and Hyland, pp. 101–11 (p. 104).

19 Robert Heinlein, *Starship Troopers* (New York: Putnam, 1959).

20 Anon., *The Fall of Public Spirit: A Dramatic Satire in Two Acts* (London, 1757).

21 *History of the Westminster Election, Containing Every Material Occurrence . . .* (London, 1785), p. 494.

22 Contrast, for example, economics: Paul W. Richardson, 'Reading and Writing from Textbooks in Higher Education: A Case Study from Economics', *Studies in Higher Education*, 29:4 (2004), 505–21.

23 Effie MacLellan, 'Reading to Learn', *Studies in Higher Education*, 22:3 (1997), 277–88 (277).

24 David Pace, 'Decoding the Reading of History: An Example of the Process', *New Directions for Teaching and Learning*, 98 (2004), 13–21.

25 MacLellan, 'Reading to Learn', p. 283.

26 MacLellan, 'Reading to Learn', p. 281.

27 Adrian Jones, 'Teaching History at University through Communities of Inquiry', *Australian Historical Studies*, 42 (2011), 166–93 (189).

28 Matthew McCormack, *Citizenship and Gender in Britain, 1688–1928* (Abingdon: Routledge, 2019).

References

Anon., *The Fall of Public Spirit: A Dramatic Satire in Two Acts* (London, 1757).

Butterfield, Herbert, *The Whig Interpretation of History* (Ann Arbor, MI: Bell, 1931).

Chalus, Elaine, *Elite Women in English Political Life, c. 1754–1790* (Oxford: Oxford University Press, 2005).

Collins, Marcus, 'Historiography from Below: How Undergraduates Remember Learning History at School', *Teaching History*, 142 (2011), 34–8.

Coutu, Joan, Stobart, Jon and Linfield, Peter (eds), *Politics and the English Country House, 1688–1800* (Kingston: McGill-Queens University Press, 2023).

Foreman, Amanda, *Georgiana Duchess of Devonshire* (London: HarperCollins, 1998).

Frederick, Peter J., 'Motivating Students by Active Learning in the History Classroom', in *The Practice of University History Teaching*, ed. Alan Booth and Paul Hyland (Manchester: Manchester University Press, 2000), pp. 101–11.

Gleadle, Kathryn and Richardson, Sarah (eds), *Women in British Politics 1780–1860: The Power of the Petticoat* (Houndmills: Palgrave, 2000).

Guyver, Robert, 'England and the UK: Conflict and Consensus over Curriculum', in *Teaching History and the Changing Nation State: Transnational and Intranational Perspectives*, ed. Robert Guyver (London: Bloomsbury, 2016).

Heinlein, Robert, *Starship Troopers* (New York: Putnam, 1959).

'Historians Call for a Review of Home Office Citizenship and Resettlement Test', *History* (21 July 2020), https://historyjournal.org.uk/2020/07/21/historians-call-for-a-review-of-home-office-citizenship-and-settlement-test (accessed 31 January 2023).

Hitchcock, Tim, Shoemaker, Robert and Tosh, John, 'Skills and the Structure of the History Curriculum' in *The Practice of University History Teaching*, ed. Alan Booth and Paul Hyland (Manchester: Manchester University Press, 2000), pp. 47–59.

Jones, Adrian, 'Teaching History at University through Communities of Inquiry', *Australian Historical Studies*, 42 (2011), 166–93.

Knights, Mark, *Trust and Distrust: Corruption in Office in Britain and Its Empire 1600–1850* (Oxford: Oxford University Press, 2021).

MacLellan, Effie, 'Reading to Learn', *Studies in Higher Education*, 22:3 (1997), 277–88.

McCormack, Matthew, '"The Independent Man" in English Political Culture, 1760–1832' (PhD thesis, University of Manchester, 2002).

McCormack, Matthew, *The Independent Man: Citizenship and Gender Politics in Georgian England* (Manchester: Manchester University Press, 2005).

McCormack, Matthew, *Citizenship and Gender in Britain, 1688–1928* (Abingdon: Routledge, 2019).

Namier, Louis, *The Structure of Politics at the Accession of George III* (London: Macmillan, 1929).

Navickas, Katrina, *Protest and the Politics of Space and Place, 1789–1848* (Manchester: Manchester University Press, 2015).

Osler, Audrey, 'Patriotism, Multiculturalism and Belonging: Political Discourse and the Teaching of History', *Educational Review*, 61:1 (2009), 85–100.

Ottway, A., *Education and Society: An Introduction to the Sociology of Education* (Oxford: Routledge, 1953).

Pace, David, 'Decoding the Reading of History: An Example of the Process', *New Directions for Teaching and Learning*, 98 (2004), 13–21.

Richardson, Paul W., 'Reading and Writing from Textbooks in Higher Education: A Case Study from Economics', *Studies in Higher Education*, 29:4 (2004), 505–21.

Rudé, Geoge, *Wilkes and Liberty: A Social Study of 1763 to 1774* (Oxford: Clarendon Press, 1962).

Thompson, E. P., *The Making of the English Working Class* (London: Gollancz, 1963).

Tosh, John, *Why History Matters* (Houndmills: Palgrave, 2008).

Vernon, James, *Politics and the People: A Study in English Political Culture, c. 1815–1867* (Cambridge: Cambridge University Press, 1993).

Wilson, Kathleen, *The Island Race: Englishness, Empire and Gender in the Eighteenth Century* (Abingdon: Routledge, 2003).

Yeandle, Peter, *Citizenship, Nation, Empire: The Politics of History Teaching in England, 1870–1930* (Manchester: Manchester University Press, 2015).

Part III
MATERIAL CULTURE AND MUSEUM COLLECTIONS

Chapter 6

Beyond 'great white men': teaching histories of science, empire and heritage through collections

Alice Marples

In the past few decades, the history of eighteenth-century science and medicine has been transformed. These linked fields of research have, since their inception, been overwhelmingly concerned with the glorification of 'great men', those seen to exist within a canon of intellectual giants and public-minded individuals who forever altered the ways in which we understand our world. Revealing their dogged and supposedly selfless pursuit of enlightened progress was believed by eighteenth-, nineteenth- and many twentieth-century historians to provide a helpful model for Western society and, through aggressive colonisation and imperialist projects, the rest of the world. This has been the essence of such scholarship from the early modern period onwards.[1]

Recently, however, there has been a deliberate move away from studying scientific individuals and their ideas as if they were lone scholars in a study – a philosophical image that has cast a long shadow – and more towards what Nicholas Jardine calls the 'hybrids of scientific knowledge and practice bound up in the worlds of everyday life, culture and politics'.[2] Questions of agency, materiality and epistemology now help scholars explore how various forms of scientific and medical knowledge permeated eighteenth-century life, from urban shops and kitchen gardens to high society and the high seas. It is increasingly clear that objects and skills crossed complex geographical, cultural, material and experiential boundaries, even as the limits of who and what constituted 'science' became more severely drawn across the centuries. Research in this area now interrogates meanings of connoisseurship, invention, appropriation, exploitation, exchange, marketing and mimicry, among much else.

A critical part of this revised approach to the study of scientific and medical knowledge has been the exploration of the many ways in which it was collected in the early modern period and subsequently transformed into 'modern' physical taxonomies during the eighteenth and nineteenth centuries. The history of collecting as a discipline in its own right was established in 1983 as the result of a conference held in the world's first 'public' museum, The Ashmolean in Oxford. This event, and all the work and discussions surrounding it, ultimately kick-started three decades of conversations uniting curators, academics, artists and engagement professionals on how best to explore the tangled histories of collections.[3] Collections of all kinds – from large national institutions and universities to private cabinets and the semi-public ones of voluntary societies – ceased to be seen as neutral spaces of learning or leisure or the benign results of an individual collector's idiosyncrasies. Instead, they began to be understood as valuable repositories of a diverse array of histories, revealing the labours not only of those who had the wealth or power to create them in the first place but also all those whose contributions of knowledge, labour and material, both voluntary and forced, actually constituted them. Exploration of these have reinforced how closely tied histories of collecting are to imperialism, slavery and exploitation, as the lives and remains of non-white individuals were harvested to construct the hierarchies of Enlightenment science and philosophy.[4]

With all this valuable historical work, the question remains: how can we best present such contentious histories within both museum spaces and classrooms? A response to both aspects of this question can be found in the Enlightenment Gallery at the British Museum, which was opened within a recreation of George III's library in 2003. It evokes both the early modern 'Cabinet of Curiosity' and the eighteenth-century encyclopaedic worldview, disrupting assumptions around modern museum conventions by breaking down material and intellectual boundaries and highlighting the pre-disciplinary jumble of strange, mundane and 'exotic' objects. It is deliberately designed to encourage visitor conversation and is regularly used by students and teachers across London and beyond. Visitor enjoyment of this space is supported by frequent guided tours and object-handling sessions which remind students that the modern museum-going experience of 'look-but-do-not-touch' is actually not how things have always been. The gallery is an example of how historical objects and collections can be used to disrupt assumptions regarding the transfer of information from state 'knowers' to public 'learners' and encourage reflection on both embodied experience and institutional representation, past and present.[5]

Such interventions have links with the 'material turn' of historical scholarship and subsequent popularity of incorporating objects into higher education teaching. This also relates to the current vogue for representations of the early modern Cabinet not only in museums but also across the broader art world.[6] However, such approaches have prompted intense debate in wider museological, educational and philosophical scholarship. In a museum context, for example, the category of 'Curious' is understood by some as sanitising, potentially working to purify violent histories of colonialisation and exploitation by removing curatorial responsibility from objects amassed by seemingly 'amateur' eighteenth-century collectors and naturalists. In the classroom, critics similarly worry over the potential promotion of singular, extraordinary objects, partial stories and set hierarchies of expertise or experience conditioned by the kinds of materials that tend to survive. There is a worry that these methodologies seduce by spectacle, and do not adequately support students in interrogating issues of power and control within the structures of appropriation and display that continue to draw a profit from these collections.[7]

Yet these issues are the ones that are at the heart of current research into the history of science and medicine in the eighteenth century and have, in essence, been debated in various ways since the formation of the earliest collections of natural knowledge. Engaging students with these discussions helps them to understand that Western scientific knowledge, despite historic claims by its supporters, was never created in controlled settings separate from society or without the efforts of a vast array of individuals and peoples from around the globe. It also speaks to urgent contemporary debates on the public understanding and institutional representation of this period of European expansion, exploitation and institutionalisation.

The reflections here are the result of many years of research and teaching in the history of early modern science and medicine and the history of collections but are specifically focused on the experience of teaching a first-year undergraduate course at the University of Chester in 2018–19, entitled 'Collecting Nature: From Cabinets of Curiosity to the 21st Century Digital Display'. While this is just one story, and necessarily skewed towards my own research interest, this account is intended to be useful for thinking about how we, as teachers of the eighteenth century, grapple with the material, institutional, intellectual and cultural difficulties of our period of study and its heritage. It argues that the answer ultimately rests in how we can get students to engage with what Alice Procter has called 'the dirt beneath the surface, where the money and power came from, and how these objects came to be chosen [for display] over others'.[8]

This course was first proposed by a permanent academic at the university who was subsequently awarded research leave and needed quick cover for their teaching. I then designed and delivered the course as a very precarious, 'post-postdoc' academic. I was undertaking a short-term, reimbursable research fellowship in one city and administrative work at a university in another, alongside a host of additional forms of employment. It ran for one year, and then both I and the permanent academic moved on to other institutions, and it was unfortunately not run again. This information is included as part of this chapter's broader motivation to encourage focused attention on the practical, material and social contexts of research and learning throughout history. Deeper exploration is urgently required of all the ways in which academic (and student) precarity is affecting research and teaching in UK academia, often deepening existing structural inequalities. As the University and Colleges Union have repeatedly stated in successive strikes since 2018, backed up with a growing body of contemporary data and research: working conditions are learning conditions.[9] In this case, the students on the course were disappointed they were not able to continue developing their interests in these subjects beyond the first year.

Objects across time and space

As this chapter demonstrates, there is a great deal of value in being able to draw students into the long history of collections as pedagogic 'contact zones' – spaces of cultural interaction and negotiation, of both intellectual inspiration and social subjugation, where expertise might be constructed but also, crucially, endlessly contested.[10] Going beyond the singular object or Cabinet to teach the broad-ranging histories as well as local practices of Western collecting and display helps ground students in the inherent subjectivity of knowledge-making and learning at all levels of society and activity. In so doing, this pedagogical approach encourages the active exploration of the eighteenth century's complex contemporary legacies in a dynamic, inclusive and fundamentally self-reflexive way. Throughout the course in question, lectures and seminars explored the historical trajectory of objects and collections-based learning from early modern natural historical inquiry to nineteenth-century public education – essentially, from the Renaissance Cabinet of Curiosity to the 'encyclopaedic' collection and panoramic worldview of the modern world, as well as revisionist and postmodern contemporary criticism involving collections and their histories. This overarching temporal and thematic framework was designed to give students a foundation for understanding how social, economic and political contexts shaped scientific and social knowledge in the past, and allow them to interrogate this further in more dynamic, task-orientated sessions.[11]

Towards the end of the first term, students were asked as a group to use this knowledge to design their own three-room exhibition on early British histories of collecting and collections. They were given twenty-five examples of historical objects and images with varying amounts of accompanying information, including Robert Hooke's 1665 *Micrographia* engraving of a flea; Edward Tyson's pygmy skeleton; a narwhal horn in the collection of Museo Civico Medievale in Bologna; Mary Delany's 'Nymphaea Alba' collage; and Josiah Wedgwood's Cauliflower-ware teapot, as well as a whole host of other curiosities, prints and material (medical and otherwise) that could potential provide a way into the history of collections. Students were asked to conduct research on these items as a group and then select around ten to fifteen for inclusion in their exhibition, according to the narrative that they had designed together. The exhibition the students constructed saw the visitor travel through displays on natural and artificial 'rarities', through to objects of empirical investigation and attempts to systematise and popularise science and, finally, broader cross-cultural collecting and commerce. The students' exhibition prompted discussion about curatorial choice and audience, as well as what objects and stories are excluded from both historical record and museum narratives.

In another session, we discussed Neil MacGregor's BBC Radio 4 documentary, *A History of the World in 100 Objects*, and listened together to the episode about the Hawaiian chieftain's feather helmet or mahiole seemingly obtained by Captain James Cook on his third voyage (1776–80). This is a significant object in the history of exploration and empire, given as a valuable gift from the Hawaiians as an apparent token of esteem only a few weeks before Cook was killed in his attempt to kidnap the ruling chief of the island, Kalaniʻōpuʻu-a-Kaiamamao, in a failed negotiation tactic. MacGregor discusses the value and sacred nature of the materials used in the helmet, and the ways in which materials and meanings may have been translated between the Hawaiians and the Europeans, as well as the significance of the object's historical and contemporary political resonance. While the object discussed by MacGregor is housed in the British Museum, and one of several collected on the voyage, the original feather helmet placed on Cook's head by Kalaniʻōpuʻu was given to the Dominion Museum in Wellington, New Zealand by Baron St Oswald in 1912. It was subsequently bestowed via long-term loan from the Bernice Pauahai Bishop Museum to the Museum of New Zealand Te Papa Tongarewa, demonstrating the power of reconnecting objects of empire with their source communities.[12]

With this awareness of how an object might become transgressive in multiple ways by its movements into and out of collections, the students were then asked to devise similar presentations for assessment on museum objects discovered via engagement with museum websites. They were prompted to detail their original cultural and material values, the processes of their acquisition or display, and their changing meanings as they moved across different spheres of activity. One group, for example, chose The British Museum's platypus holotype with the missing skull. They explained its cultural significance for Aboriginal Australians, as well as how difficult it was for Europeans to categorise the animal: it was only accepted by the Western world as evidence of a real animal in 1799, when the British Museum's keeper of natural history, George Shaw, scientifically described it. The students also reflected on the creature's symbolic role in post-Second World War international relations. Another group chose the ubiquitous 'Feejeean mermaid' – another touchstone in histories of collecting and global exchange – and used it to explore the commercial dimension of collection-making and -showing, from seventeenth-century merchants and coffeehouse-men to 'the greatest showman' and subject of a recent popular film, P. T. Barnum. They also highlighted the prevalence of mermaid myths around the globe, and how monetarily and intellectually profitable it might be to engage with such symbolic histories. In this way, students were encouraged to think about cultural and temporal relativity and resonance when approaching both objects and collections, and they spontaneously situated these within their own ideas and experience.

Individual, local, national, global

Moving from the ideological and practical underpinnings of the collection, transportation and display of individual objects, the course then shifted its examination to the historical and political trajectories of different kinds of collections. Students were encouraged to think about how different collection histories reflect varying attitudes towards science, public education, region and nation, and have been deployed by different groups for different purposes throughout history. This shift was supported through physical visits to multiple collections where students were assisted in identifying and decoding each museum's organisation and architecture and encouraged to think further about the historiographical debates on empire, knowledge and power we had covered in class. Founded in 1839 as the UK's first teacher training college, the University of Chester does not possess its own collection – the highly varied and often unequal relationship between university heritage and resources and access to social and cultural capital will be addressed later on in this chapter – so instead we visited the city's Grosvenor Museum. The focus of this session was the relationship between museum collections and their geographical and social contexts.

Many smaller civic museums were founded with the collections gathered by local amateur societies and clubs in the eighteenth and nineteenth centuries. This means they often represent regional landscape, history and culture in a much more direct way than the collections found in large national museums (often established with the collections of one or more individual rich patrons). Not only that, but they also have different funding streams and relationships with their audiences as well as surrounding institutions of higher education. Learning about and exploring these aspects of the collection helps situate students within their specific localities of learning, and provides an overarching framework for understanding the relationship between the individual and the collective on the one hand, and local and national on the other. This is also something that might be usefully explored with regard to contemporary questions of crowdsourcing engagement activities by museums and, more broadly, the practice of 'citizen science' over time, both dynamic areas of current research.[13]

The changing relationships between museums and peoples was a key theme in this course. At the World Museum Liverpool, the class discussed the city's history as one of a number of wealthy ports built with the profits made through Britain's undeniable and significant involvement with the slave trade. Throughout the eighteenth and nineteenth centuries, Liverpool scooped up the spoils of empire and pumped them into the industrial revolution, the influx of money and power contributing to distinctively rapid urban, social and intellectual development in this city, alongside many others, including Manchester, Birmingham and Bristol. This well-known history is deeply entwined with that of the development of public science and collections in the UK. As one example, the important Manchester surgeon, collector and hospital-builder Charles White was said by his contemporary Thomas De Quincey to have 'by one whole generation run before the phrenologists and craniologists – having already measured innumerable skulls among the omnigenous seafaring population of Liverpool, illustrating all the races of men' (see Figure 6.1).[14] White was an early architect of biological racism.

Like many other northern industrial cities, Liverpool was hit hard with aggressive deindustrialisation by successive Conservative governments from the 1970s onwards, with the resulting devastation at odds with its

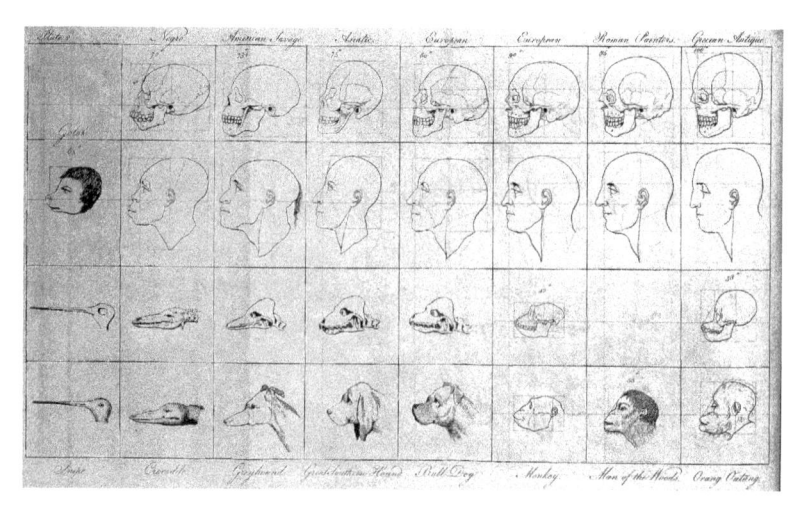

Figure 6.1: Fold-out from Charles White, *An Account of the Regular Gradation in Man, and in Different Animals and Vegetables* (London: Dilly, 1799). Wellcome Collection, Public Domain Mark.

former imperial splendour. This chequered history is evidenced in William Brown Street: named after the nineteenth-century MP and philanthropist who donated the land for the building of a public library and museum, it has recently been transformed by targeted regional renewal schemes, and has specifically benefited from Heritage Lottery funding. Liverpool has become a definitive example of 'culture-led regeneration' policies, where investments into infrastructure and creative economies deliberately combined with targeted public learning, community and arts engagement programmes have essentially transformed the city, its museums and its people. The opening of the International Slavery Museum (ISM) in 2007 is perhaps symbolic of this entwined urban and social history. Beginning life in the aftermath of the Toxteth riots of 1981 as a dedicated gallery space in the Merseyside Maritime Museum in 1994, the ISM has shifted from permanent display to permanent institution through activist projects and working with Liverpool's Black community. The ISM has, under the directorship of Dr Richard Benjamin, led proactive discussions of research and exhibition co-production, community partnership work and institutional articulations of the legacies of slavery and imperialism.[15]

Students were excited by their ability to actively link a museum's past and recent history to its contemporary role in local and national society, which they were able to divine from displays. So, for example, at the World Museum Liverpool, many of its African collections are displayed alongside a series of contemporary 'counterpoint' lino prints by Ghanian artist Atta Kwami, reframing and reworking sketches of some of the artefacts: the Royal Liver Building alongside a similarly shaped African comb, for example, or shapes taken from the Liverpool Docks alongside bright patterns reminiscent of Kente cloth. Students were encouraged to think whether and in what circumstances the inclusion of such artwork should be considered a form of celebration and representation, or a means to augment and, indeed, neutralise and essentially excuse the colonial African materials on display there. One student even connected this back to an earlier seminar on William and John Hunter's collections, the relationship between eighteenth-century science and art (William Hunter was the first professor of anatomy at the Royal Academy of Arts), and the linked investigations into the human body and the question of enlightened aesthetics.

More broadly, the students responded extremely well to the ties between historical themes and contemporary debates or social initiatives. Many of the most fruitful discussions were on diverse issues of inclusivity, representation and engagement. These were all, without exception, driven by the students themselves as they reflected upon syllabus topics using their own knowledge and critical reading of various forms of news media. So, for example, a session on early modern fossil-collecting and the careers of Mary Anning and Gideon Mantell, both important figures in the history of science but barred from formal inclusion and recognition, led to a debate on contemporary barriers to education, funding and advancement for both female and working-class scholars. Another session was on 'Living Bodies to Objects of Scrutiny' and involved the Hunters and their role in the development of collections-based surgical teaching and museum collections. Discussion here focused on the Charles Byrne and Sarah Baartman campaigns to remove their bodies from display, the broader impact of the Human Tissue Act of 2004 on museum ethics and repatriation efforts, and the growing field of disability history, something which excited the students very much.[16] Throughout the course, eighteenth-century issues and topics were demonstrated as linking directly to a variety of important and interesting contemporary cultural, political and ethical discussions, and the relevancy of the period was undeniable.

Breaking down barriers

Teaching in this way invites students to explore and reflect on all the many ways in which tenets of Western science, medicine and society have been constructed and expressed through museums over time, and how this is a key part of understanding broader economic, political and cultural systems and their entwined histories: colonialism and imperialism; slavery and racism; misogyny; class discrimination and working-class education; human zoos, freakshows and spectacles; state-sponsored genocide and the hoarding of human remains; the destruction of the environment; and so on. In doing so, it makes them alert to broader discussions of cultural management and curatorial responsibility in how these histories are either engaged with or ignored: ultimately, how hierarchies of power have been constructed in science and society, and the range of alternative perspectives which interact with them. This kind of teaching encourages critical examination of all outward-facing aspects of collection management and education: accessibility and diversity campaigns, art installations and radical re-readings, public education programmes co-produced with local or source communities, or otherwise created and then presented by the institution in question. Illuminating instances of apparent failure and the reception of criticism alongside more successful ventures, and encouraging conversation about the process, help make it clear that collections are not passive and neutral but active and contested sites, which can – but do not always – allow for the questioning of authority and the sharing of many different forms of expertise. They open up the conversation for students to respond emotionally, on their own terms and with their own prior knowledge, and then to reflect on their reactions, building critical self-awareness and an understanding of many different perspectives in the world around them, while simultaneously honing their ability to analyse and respond effectively to them.

This approach also encourages a greater understanding of the ecosystems of history, heritage and education, the societal forces that unite and divide, the links and the lacks. By exploring such histories, the students are situated within an ever-evolving relationships between museum collections, institutions of higher education and the various publics that engage with them. This reveals how contingent knowledge-making is and always has been; how access to and understanding of collections are subject to issues of geography, funding, audience, policy and politics, community action, and so on. Ultimately, this makes the structures of the world more visible and breaks down some of the real and imagined barriers between institutions of higher education and the world around them, as well as within 'The Academy' itself.[17] It provides explanations as to why some universities have their own museums while others do not, why some towns may have a thriving cultural sector and others do not, why some students appear to have access to greater social capital than others. In this way, intersecting inequalities can be identified and understood, and not merely accepted and thus perpetuated, unthinkingly and ad nauseam.[18]

The impact of this can be measured not only in abstract but also practical terms. For example, towards the end of our course, we travelled to the University of Manchester and were given a tour of the buildings and their histories by a Manchester Museum volunteer, Jemma Houghton, who at that time was also a PhD student at the Centre for the History of Science, Technology and Medicine. Jemma was able to provide an overview of some active curatorial projects and collaborations and facilitate an encounter with the collections she supported, including pedagogical plaster plant models, wet specimens and nineteenth-century microscope slides. In doing this, she provided a direct example of how university hierarchies and structures can be broken down to give undergraduate students a greater sense of academic community and ownership, as well as a broader awareness of local collections (whether human, material or manuscript) and possibilities for their own future and development. At the end of this day, two of the students asked Jemma about volunteering opportunities at the museum (see Figure 6.2).

The individual, social and academic benefits of activities which help build this more holistic experience of research and play a role in personal and professional development are becoming increasingly apparent. There is a growing body of research on the importance of academic work which explores the creation and representation of university heritage, in whatever form that takes.[19] It also reflects broader trends within the Higher Education and GLAM (Galleries, Libraries, Archives and Museum) sectors and the increasing emphasis placed by funding bodies on promoting the movement of knowledge and the transfer of skills across institutions and conceptions of research. The value of this is perhaps exemplified by the success of collaborative doctoral schemes (such as the Arts and Humanities Research Council's Collaborative Doctoral Partnership, launched in 2012)

Figure 6.2: Photograph of Manchester Museum Collections encounter. Image credit: Alice Marples.

and the impact that these former students are having on the structures of historical research and teaching across diverse spaces, highlighting the many opportunities and challenges involved in collaborative research. Teaching the history of collecting in science, medicine and heritage in this way, then, actively places this kind of work in a long view from the early modern period to the present day. This encourages an appreciation of the history of research-driven education, in and of itself. It reinforces an awareness that knowledge has always been a composite of different interests, networks, influences and materials, made up of both formal and non-formal elements across a range of private and public spaces. It also demonstrates how this history has been represented in different ways to tell certain stories about self, society and nation, while excluding others, and asks how this might change in the future.

As well as complementing recent changes in how heritage and academic institutions engage with both their publics and their own workforces, this approach also suits the highly heterogeneous and blended way that most young people learn while directly imparting and promoting the information and digital literacy skills required to navigate contemporary society.[20] It encourages critical engagement with a variety of mediated sources both online and in real life. Sessions held in the IT Lab at Chester that focused on analysing museum websites, online exhibitions and even catalogue platforms were a (slightly surprising) success.[21] Prompting students to explore and articulate the potential objectives behind the participatory strategies of universities and museums, both online and offline, supports the understanding of them as active parts of society. Examining how these institutions engage with local communities and current affairs, and how this shapes their representation, helps demonstrate that learning and styles of learning are not just handed down but constantly being debated, experimented with and altered in response to the times. Similarly, getting students to reflect on their own pedagogical experiences – how they themselves respond to certain campaigns, certain articles, certain objects or displays – allows them to better articulate their needs and advocate for themselves and their ideas, better enabling them to deconstruct the world around them.

Conclusion

At a time when the colonial and imperial legacies of all institutions – museums and universities included – are under intense and extremely vital scrutiny, collections provide a rich ground for the kind of connective research and teaching required to engage students in the study of the eighteenth century.[22] This chapter has made the case that this approach should be a component of all history teaching, from the first year onwards, and not left to the third year, to separate public history modules or to MA studies. As Jim Bennett and many others have said, museums and other scientific collections are never neutral: and it is *because* of this that they are useful not only as objects of study but also as living resources for reflexive knowledge creation and communication across academic, curatorial and public interests.[23]

Notes

1 Ludmilla Jordanova, 'Has the Social History of Medicine Come of Age?', *The Historical Journal*, 36 (1993), 437–49; Nick Jardine, 'Whigs and Stories: Herbert Butterfield and the Historiography of Science', *History of Science*, 41 (2003), 125–40; Anna Maerker, 'Hagiography and Biography: Narratives of "Great Men of Science"', in Anna Maerker, Simon Sleight and Adam Sutcliffe (eds), *History, Memory and Public Life* (London: Routledge, 2018).

2 Nicholas Jardine, 'Reflections on the Preservation of Recent Scientific Heritage in Dispersed University Collections', *Studies in History and Philosophy of Science*, 44 (2013), 737.

3 Oliver Impey and Arthur MacGregor (eds), *The Origins of Museums: The Cabinet of Curiosities in Sixteenth and Seventeenth-Century Europe* (Oxford: Clarendon, 1985); Jim Bennett, 'Museums and the History of Science: Practitioner's Postscript', *Isis*, 96 (2005), 602–8; Rebekah Higgitt, 'Challenging Tropes: Genius, Heroic Invention, and the Longitude Problem in the Museum', *Isis*, 108 (2017), 371–80.

4 Christopher Fox, Roy Porter and Robert Wokler (eds), *Inventing Human Science: Eighteenth-Century Domains* (Berkeley, CA: University of California Press, 1995); Londa Schiebinger, *Plants and Empire: Colonial Bioprospecting in the Atlantic World* (London: Harvard University Press, 2004); Kathleen S. Murphy, 'Collecting Slave Traders: James Petiver, Natural History, and the British Slave Trade', *The William and Mary Quarterly*, 70.4 (2013), 637–70; Alice Marples and Victoria R. M. Pickering, 'Patron's Revies: Exploring Cultures of Collecting in the Early Modern World', *Archives of Natural History*, 43.1 (2016), 1–20; Paul Turnbull, *Science, Museums and Collecting the Indigenous Dead in Colonial Australia* (Basingstoke: Palgrave Macmillan, 2017).

5 Kim Sloan and Andrew Burnett (eds), *Enlightenment: Discovering the World in the Eighteenth Century* (London: British Museum, 2003); Constance Classen, 'Museum Manners: The Sensory Life of the Early Museum', *Journal of Social History*, 40.4 (2007), 895–914; Carin Jacobs et al., 'Beyond the Field Trip: Museum Literacy and Higher Education', *Museum Management and Curatorship*, 24.1 (2009), 5–27; Helen Rees Leahy, *Museum Bodies: The Politics and Practices of Visiting and Viewing* (London: Routledge, 2016).

6 Bruce Robertson and Mark Meadow, 'Microcosms: Objects of Knowledge', *AI & Society*, 14 (2000), 223–9; Colleen J. Sheehy (ed.), *Cabinet of Curiosities: Mark Dion and the University as Installation* (Minneapolis, MN: University of Minneapolis Press, 2006); Karen Harvey (ed.), *History and Material Culture: A Student's Guide to Approaching Alternative Sources* (London: Routledge, 2017); Ulf Johansson Dahre, 'The Return of the Cabinet of Curiosity', in Magdalena Naum and Gitte Tarnow Ingvardson (eds), *Collecting Curiosities: Eighteenth-Century Museum Stobæanum and the Development of Ethnographic Collections in the Nineteenth Century* (Lund: Lund University Press, 2020); Ethan W. Lasser, 'The Return of the *Wunderkammer*: Material Culture in the Museum', in Anne Gerritsen and Giorgio Riello (eds), *Writing Material Culture History* (London: Bloomsbury, 2021).

7 Helen J. Chatterjee and Leonie Hannan (eds), *Engaging the Senses: Object-Based Learning in Higher Education* (London: Routledge, 2016); Suninn Yun,

'Curiosity, Wonder and Museum Education', *Journal of Philosophy of Education*, 52 (2018), 465–82; Sarah Williamson, 'Exploration: Cabinets of Curiosities – Playing with Artefacts in Professional Teacher Education', in Alison James and Chrissi Nerantzi (eds), *The Power of Play in Higher Education: Creativity in Tertiary Learning* (Cham: Springer, 2019), pp. 103–11.

8 Alice Procter, *The Whole Picture: The Colonial Story of the Art in Our Museums and Why We Need to Talk about It* (London: Octopus Publishing Group, 2020).

9 Lindsey B. Carfagna, 'The Pedagogy of Precarity: Labouring to Learn in the New Economy' (PhD thesis: Boston College, 2017); Olivia Mason and Nick Megoran, 'Precarity and Dehumanisation in Higher Education', *Learning and Teaching*, 14.1 (2021), 35–9; Sarah Burton and Benjamin Bowman, 'The Academic Precariat: Understanding Life and Labour in the Neoliberal Academy', *British Journal of Sociology of Education*, 43.4 (2022), 497–512; Jason Arday, '"More to prove and more to lose": Race, Racism, and Precarious Employment in Higher Education', *British Journal of Sociology of Education*, 43.4 (2022), 513–33.

10 Ramesh Srinivasan, Katherine M. Becvar, Robin Boast and Jim Enote, 'Diverse Knowledges and Contact Zones within the Digital Museum', *Science, Technology and Human Values*, 35 (2010), 735–68; Darlene Clover and Kathy Sanford, 'Contemporary Museums as Pedagogic Contact Zones: Potentials of Critical Cultural Adult Education', *Studies in the Education of Adults*, 48 (2016), 127–41.

11 Samuel J. M. M. Alberti, 'Objects and the Museum', *Isis*, 96 (2005), 559–71; Ad Maas, 'The Storyteller and the Altar: Museum Boerhaave and Its Objects', in Susanne Lehmann-Brauns, Christian Sichau and Helmuth Trischler (eds), *The Exhibition as Product and Generator of Scholarship* (Berlin: Max Planck Institute for the History of Science, 2010).

12 Neil MacGregor, *A History of the World in 100 Objects* (London: Allen Lane, 2010); Sean Mallon et al., 'The 'Ahu 'Ula and Mahiole of Kalani'ōpu'u: A Journey of Chiefly Adornments', *Tuhinga: Records of the Museum of New Zealand Te Papa Tongarewa*, 28 (2017), 4–24.

13 David Elliston Allen, *The Naturalist in Britain: A Social History* (Princeton, NJ: Princeton University Press, 1994); Charles W. J. Withers and Diarmid A. Finnegan, 'Natural History Societies, Fieldwork and Local Knowledge in Nineteenth-Century Scotland: Towards a Historical Geography of Civic Science', *Cultural Geographies,* 10 (2003), 334–53; Samuel J. M. M. Alberti, 'Owning and Collecting Natural Objects in Nineteenth-Century Britain', in Marco Beretta (ed.), *From Private to Public: Natural Collections and Museums* (Sagamore Beach, MA: Science History Publications, 2005); Robert E. Kohler, 'Finders, Keepers: Collecting Sciences and Collecting Practice', *History of Science*, 45 (2007), 428–54; Sue Dale Turnbull and Annette Scheersoi (eds), *Natural History Dioramas: History, Construction and Educational Role* (Dordrecht: Springer, 2014).

14 Peter J. Kitson, 'The Strange Case of Dr White and Mr De Quincey: Manchester, Medicine and Romantic Theories of Biological Racism', *Romanticism*, 17 (2011),

279; Alice Marples, 'Scholarship, Skill and Community; Collections and the Creation of "Provincial" Medical Education in Manchester, 1750–1850', *Journal of the History of Collections*, 33 (2021), 505–16.

15 Richard Meegan, 'Urban Regeneration, Politics and Social Cohesion: The Liverpool Case', in Ronaldo Munck (ed.), *Reinventing the City? Liverpool in Comparative Perspective* (Liverpool: Liverpool University Press, 2003); Richard Benjamin, 'The Development of the International Slavery Museum', *African Diaspora Archaeology Newsletter*, 10 (2007), 1–6; Bernadette T. Lynch and Samuel J. M. M. Alberti, 'Legacies of Prejudice: Racism, Co-Production and Radical Trust in the Museum', *Museum Management and Curatorship*, 25 (2010), 12–35; Richard Benjamin, 'Museums and Sensitive Histories: The International Slavery Museum', in Ana Lucia Araujo (ed.), *Politics of Memory: Making Slavery Visible in the Public Space* (New York: Routledge, 2012); Lucia Abbamonte, 'Black Stories Matter: Liverpool's International Slavery Museum and Multimodal Representations of a Controversial Heritage', *ESP Across Cultures*, 17 (2020); Christopher Lawson, 'Making Sense of the Ruins: The Historiography of Deindustrialisation and Its Continued Relevance in Neoliberal Times', *History Compass*, 18 (2020), 1–14.

16 Sadiah Qureshi, 'Displaying Sara Baartman, the "Hottentot Venus"', *History of Science*, 42 (2004), 233–57; Richard Sandell, Annie Delin, Jocelyn Dodd and Jackie Gay, 'In the Shadow of the Freakshow: The Impact of Freakshow Tradition on the Display and Understanding of Disability History in Museums', *Disability Studies Quarterly*, 25 (2005); Elizabeth White, 'Giving Up the Dead? The Impact and Effectiveness of the Human Tissue Act and the Guidance for the Care of Human Remains in English Museums' (PhD thesis: Newcastle University, 2011); Thomas L. Muinzer, 'A Grave Situation: An Examination of the Legal Issues Raised By the Life and Death of Charles Byrne, the "Irish Giant"', *International Journal of Cultural Property*, 20 (2013), 23–48; Roberta Ballestriero, 'The Science and Ethics Concerning the Legacy of Human Remains and Historical Collections: The Gordon Museum of Pathology in London', *Scientiae in the History of Medicine*, 4 (2021), 135–49.

17 Meliha Handzic and Daniela Carlucci (eds), *Knowledge Management, Arts, and Humanities: Interdisciplinary Approaches and the Benefits of Collaboration* (Cham: Springer, 2019).

18 Roy Nash, 'Bourdieu on Education and Social and Cultural Reproduction', *British Journal of Sociology of Education*, 11 (1990), 431–47; Imogen Tyler, 'Classificatory Struggles: Class, Culture and Inequality in Neoliberal Times', *The Sociological Review*, 63 (2015), 493–511; Tom Schuller, John Preton, Cathie Hammond, Angela Brassett-Grundy and John Bynner, *The Benefits of Learning: The Impact of Education on Health, Family Life and Social Capital* (London: Routledge, 2004); Brenda Little, 'The Student Experience and the Impact of Social Capital', in Ian McNay (ed.), *Beyond Mass Higher Education: Building on Experience* (Milton Keynes: The Society for Research into Higher Education and Open University Press, 2006).

19 Zenobia Kozak, 'Promoting the Past, Preserving the Future: British University Heritage Collections and Identity Marketing' (PhD thesis: University

of St Andrews, 2007); P. J. Boylan, 'European Cooperation in the Protection and Promotion of University Heritage', *Les partenariats actifs des musées universitaires* (2003), 30; Marta C. Lourenco, 'Contributions to the History of University Museums and Collections in Europe', *Museologia*, 3 (2003), 17–26.

20 James W. Marcum, 'Rethinking Information Literacy', *The Library Quarterly*, 72 (2002), 1–26; Susie Andretta, Alison Pope and Geoff Walton, 'Information Literacy Education in the UK: Reflections on Perspectives and Practical Approaches of Curricular Integration', *Communications in Information Literacy*, 2 (2008), 5; Thomas P. Mackey and Trudi E. Jacobson, 'Reframing Information Literacy as a Metaliteracy', *College & Research Libraries*, 72 (2011), 62–78.

21 D. Randy Garrison and Heather Kanuka, 'Blended Learning: Uncovering Its Transformative Potential in Higher Education', *Internet and Higher Education*, 7 (2004), 95–105.

22 Kerry Pimblott, 'Decolonising the University: The Origins and Meaning of a Movement', *The Political Quarterly*, 91 (2019), 210–16.

23 Bennett, 'Museums and the History of Science: Practitioner's Postscript', 602–8.

References

Abbamonte, Lucia, 'Black Stories Matter: Liverpool's International Slavery Museum and Multimodal Representations of a Controversial Heritage', *ESP Across Cultures*, 17 (2020).

Alberti, Samuel J. M. M., 'Objects and the Museum', *Isis*, 96 (2005), 559–71.

Alberti, Samuel J. M. M., 'Owning and Collecting Natural Objects in Nineteenth-Century Britain', in Marco Beretta (ed.), *From Private to Public: Natural Collections and Museums* (Sagamore Beach, MA: Science History Publications, 2005).

Allen, David Elliston, *The Naturalist in Britain: A Social History* (Princeton, NJ: Princeton University Press, 1994).

Andretta, Susie, Pope, Alison and Walton, Geoff, 'Information Literacy Education in the UK: Reflections on Perspectives and Practical Approaches of Curricular Integration', *Communications in Information Literacy*, 2 (2008), 5.

Arday, Jason, '"More to prove and more to lose": Race, Racism, and Precarious Employment in Higher Education', *British Journal of Sociology of Education*, 43.4 (2022), 513–33.

Ballestriero, Roberta, 'The Science and Ethics Concerning the Legacy of Human Remains and Historical Collections: The Gordon Museum of Pathology in London', *Scientiae in the History of Medicine*, 4 (2021), 135–49.

Benjamin, Richard, 'The Development of the International Slavery Museum', *African Diaspora Archaeology Newsletter*, 10 (2007), 1–6.

Benjamin, Richard, 'Museums and Sensitive Histories: The International Slavery Museum', in Ana Lucia Araujo (ed.), *Politics of Memory: Making Slavery Visible in the Public Space* (New York: Routledge, 2012).

Bennett, Jim, 'Museums and the History of Science: Practitioner's Postscript', *Isis*, 96 (2005), 602–8.

Boylan, P. J., 'European Cooperation in the Protection and Promotion of University Heritage', *Les partenariats actifs des musées universitaires* (2003), 30.

Burton, Sarah and Bowman, Benjamin, 'The Academic Precariat: Understanding Life and Labour in the Neoliberal Academy', *British Journal of Sociology of Education*, 43.4 (2022), 497–512.

Carfagna, Lindsey B., 'The Pedagogy of Precarity: Labouring to Learn in the New Economy' (PhD thesis: Boston College, 2017).

Chatterjee, Helen J. and Hannan, Leonie (eds), *Engaging the Senses: Object-Based Learning in Higher Education* (London: Routledge, 2016).

Classen, Constance, 'Museum Manners: The Sensory Life of the Early Museum', *Journal of Social History*, 40.4 (2007), 895–914.

Clover, Darlene and Sanford, Kathy, 'Contemporary Museums as Pedagogic Contact Zones: Potentials of Critical Cultural Adult Education', *Studies in the Education of Adults*, 48 (2016), 127–41.

Dahre, Ulf Johansson, 'The Return of the Cabinet of Curiosity', in Magdalena Naum and Gitte Tarnow Ingvardson (eds), *Collecting Curiosities: Eighteenth-Century Museum Stobæanum and the Development of Ethnographic Collections in the Nineteenth Century* (Lund: Lund University Press, 2020).

Fox, Christopher, Porter, Roy and Wokler, Robert (eds), *Inventing Human Science: Eighteenth-Century Domains* (Berkeley, CA: University of California Press, 1995).

Garrison, D. Randy and Kanuka, Heather, 'Blended Learning: Uncovering Its Transformative Potential in Higher Education', *Internet and Higher Education*, 7 (2004), 95–105.

Handzic, Meliha and Carlucci, Daniela (eds), *Knowledge Management, Arts, and Humanities: Interdisciplinary Approaches and the Benefits of Collaboration* (Cham: Springer, 2019).

Harvey, Karen (ed.), *History and Material Culture: A Student's Guide to Approaching Alternative Sources* (London: Routledge, 2017).

Higgitt, Rebekah, 'Challenging Tropes: Genius, Heroic Invention, and the Longitude Problem in the Museum', *Isis*, 108 (2017), 371–80.

Impey, Oliver and MacGregor, Arthur (eds), *The Origins of Museums: The Cabinet of Curiosities in Sixteenth and Seventeenth-Century Europe* (Oxford: Clarendon, 1985).

Jacobs, Carin et al., 'Beyond the Field Trip: Museum Literacy and Higher Education', *Museum Management and Curatorship*, 24.1 (2009), 5–27.

Jardine, Nicholas, 'Whigs and Stories: Herbert Butterfield and the Historiography of Science', *History of Science*, 41 (2003), 125–40.

Jardine, Nicholas, 'Reflections on the Preservation of Recent Scientific Heritage in Dispersed University Collections', *Studies in History and Philosophy of Science*, 44 (2013), 737.

Jordanova, Ludmilla, 'Has the Social History of Medicine Come of Age?', *The Historical Journal*, 36 (1993), 437–49.

Kitson, Peter J., 'The Strange Case of Dr White and Mr De Quincey: Manchester, Medicine and Romantic Theories of Biological Racism', *Romanticism*, 17 (2011), 279.

Kohler, Robert E., 'Finders, Keepers: Collecting Sciences and Collecting Practice', *History of Science*, 45 (2007), 428–54.

Kozak, Zenobia, 'Promoting the Past, Preserving the Future: British University Heritage Collections and Identity Marketing' (PhD thesis: University of St Andrews, 2007).

Lasser, Ethan W., 'The Return of the *Wunderkammer*: Material Culture in the Museum', in Anne Gerritsen and Giorgio Riello (eds), *Writing Material Culture History* (London: Bloomsbury, 2021).

Lawson, Christopher, 'Making Sense of the Ruins: The Historiography of Deindustrialisation and Its Continued Relevance in Neoliberal Times', *History Compass*, 18 (2020), 1–14.

Leahy, Helen Rees, *Museum Bodies: The Politics and Practices of Visiting and Viewing* (London: Routledge, 2016).

Little, Brenda, 'The Student Experience and the Impact of Social Capital', in Ian McNay (ed.), *Beyond Mass Higher Education: Building on Experience* (Milton Keynes: The Society for Research into Higher Education and Open University Press, 2006).

Lourenco, Marta C., 'Contributions to the History of University Museums and Collections in Europe', *Museologia*, 3 (2003), 17–26.

Lynch, Bernadette T. and Alberti, Samuel J. M. M., 'Legacies of Prejudice: Racism, Co-Production and Radical Trust in the Museum', *Museum Management and Curatorship*, 25 (2010), 12–35.

Maas, Ad, 'The Storyteller and the Altar: Museum Boerhaave and Its Objects', in Susanne Lehmann-Brauns, Christian Sichau and Helmuth Trischler (eds), *The Exhibition as Product and Generator of Scholarship* (Berlin: Max Planck Institute for the History of Science, 2010).

MacGregor, Neil, *A History of the World in 100 Objects* (London: Allen Lane, 2010).

Mackey, Thomas P. and Jacobson, Trudi E., 'Reframing Information Literacy as a Metaliteracy', *College & Research Libraries*, 72 (2011), 62–78.

Maerker, Anna, 'Hagiography and Biography: Narratives of "Great Men of Science"', in Anna Maerker, Simon Sleight and Adam Sutcliffe (eds), *History, Memory and Public Life* (London: Routledge, 2018).

Mallon, Sean et al., 'The 'Ahu 'Ula and Mahiole of Kalaniʻōpuʻu: A Journey of Chiefly Adornments', *Tuhinga: Records of the Museum of New Zealand Te Papa Tongarewa*, 28 (2017), 4–24.

Marcum, James W., 'Rethinking Information Literacy', *The Library Quarterly*, 72 (2002), 1–26.

Marples, Alice, 'Scholarship, Skill and Community; Collections and the Creation of "Provincial" Medical Education in Manchester, 1750–1850', *Journal of the History of Collections*, 33 (2021), 505–16.

Marples, Alice and Pickering, Victoria R. M., 'Patron's Revies: Exploring Cultures of Collecting in the Early Modern World', *Archives of Natural History*, 43.1 (2016), 1–20.

Mason, Olivia and Megoran, Nick, 'Precarity and Dehumanisation in Higher Education', *Learning and Teaching*, 14.1 (2021), 35–9.

Meegan, Richard, 'Urban Regeneration, Politics and Social Cohesion: The Liverpool Case', in Ronaldo Munck (ed.), *Reinventing the City? Liverpool in Comparative Perspective* (Liverpool: Liverpool University Press, 2003).

Muinzer, Thomas L., 'A Grave Situation: An Examination of the Legal Issues Raised by the Life and Death of Charles Byrne, the "Irish Giant"', *International Journal of Cultural Property*, 20 (2013), 23–48.

Murphy, Kathleen S., 'Collecting Slave Traders: James Petiver, Natural History, and the British Slave Trade', *The William and Mary Quarterly*, 70.4 (2013), 637–70.

Nash, Roy, 'Bourdieu on Education and Social and Cultural Reproduction', *British Journal of Sociology of Education*, 11 (1990), 431–47.

Pimblott, Kerry, 'Decolonising the University: The Origins and Meaning of a Movement', *The Political Quarterly*, 91 (2019), 210–16.

Procter, Alice, *The Whole Picture: The Colonial Story of the Art in Our Museums and Why We Need to Talk about It* (London: Octopus Publishing Group, 2020).

Qureshi, Sadiah, 'Displaying Sara Baartman, the "Hottentot Venus"', *History of Science*, 42 (2004), 233–57.

Robertson, Bruce and Meadow, Mark, 'Microcosms: Objects of Knowledge', *AI & Society*, 14 (2000), 223–9.

Sandell, Richard, Delin, Annie, Dodd, Jocelyn and Gay, Jackie, 'In the Shadow of the Freakshow: The Impact of Freakshow Tradition on the Display and Understanding of Disability History in Museums', *Disability Studies Quarterly*, 25 (2005).

Schiebinger, Londa, *Plants and Empire: Colonial Bioprospecting in the Atlantic World* (London: Harvard University Press, 2004).

Schuller, Tom, Preton, John, Hammond, Cathie, Angela, Brassett-Grundy and Bynner, John, *The Benefits of Learning: The Impact of Education on Health, Family Life and Social Capital* (London: Routledge, 2004).

Sheehy, Colleen J. (ed.), *Cabinet of Curiosities: Mark Dion and the University as Installation* (Minneapolis, MN: University of Minneapolis Press, 2006).

Sloan, Kim and Burnett, Andrew (eds), *Enlightenment: Discovering the World in the Eighteenth Century* (London: British Museum, 2003).

Srinivasan, Ramesh, Becvar, Katherine M., Boast, Robin and Enote, Jim, 'Diverse Knowledges and Contact Zones within the Digital Museum', *Science, Technology and Human Values*, 35 (2010), 735–68.

Turnbull, Paul, *Science, Museums and Collecting the Indigenous Dead in Colonial Australia* (Basingstoke: Palgrave Macmillan, 2017).

Turnbull, Sue Dale and Scheersoi, Annette (eds), *Natural History Dioramas: History, Construction and Educational Role* (Dordrecht: Springer, 2014).

Tyler, Imogen, 'Classificatory Struggles: Class, Culture and Inequality in Neoliberal Times', *The Sociological Review*, 63 (2015), 493–511.

White, Elizabeth, 'Giving Up the Dead? The Impact and Effectiveness of the Human Tissue Act and the Guidance for the Care of Human Remains in English Museums' (PhD thesis: Newcastle University, 2011).

Williamson, Sarah, 'Exploration: Cabinets of Curiosities – Playing with Artefacts in Professional Teacher Education', in Alison James and Chrissi Nerantzi (eds), *The Power of Play in Higher Education: Creativity in Tertiary Learning* (Cham: Springer, 2019), pp. 103–11.

Withers, Charles W. J. and Finnegan, Diarmid A., 'Natural History Societies, Fieldwork and Local Knowledge in Nineteenth-Century Scotland: Towards a Historical Geography of Civic Science', *Cultural Geographies*, 10 (2003), 334–53.

Yun, Suninn, 'Curiosity, Wonder and Museum Education', *Journal of Philosophy of Education*, 52 (2018), 465–82.

Chapter 7

Teaching eighteenth-century classical reception through university museum collections

Lenia Kouneni

This chapter focuses on the process, challenges and benefits of using physical materials from museum collections of the University of St Andrews to teach eighteenth-century art and its engagement with archaeology and classical culture. The discussion will present the process of designing the module curriculum, the challenges it posed and the responses of the students; it will focus on the different ways museum objects were studied, displayed and utilised in order to enhance learning. This case study is a reflection on the practice of object-based learning (OBL) using museum and special collection objects to promote student engagement and understanding of concepts and ideas around classical reception. The discussion will also address the difficulties and possibilities of an object-based approach in the light of the recent COVID-19 pandemic, considering the use of digital objects through newly developed digital tools.

OBL is a pedagogy based on active or experiential learning using objects to facilitate deep thinking.[1] This student-centred, inquiry-based approach for 'learning about, with and through objects'[2] is used increasingly by many academics across higher education (HE).[3] University College London museums have been leading the field of enquiry into OBL and its particular benefits for university programmes and have developed projects focusing on exploring the ways in which museum collections can enhance learning for HE students.[4] In OBL inquiry is focused on physical materials and sensory experience. Recent scholarly literature has endorsed the value of engaging with objects in making learning real; objects act as multi-sensory 'thinking tools' to inspire discussion and group work, promote lateral thinking, and ultimately deepen students' learning.[5] Objects motivate students to ask questions and to seek answers.[6] Students are generally enthusiastic when presented with real works of art, manuscripts or scientific equipment. They get far more excited and involved in front of real objects than reading a textbook. Objects have the power to create a 'wow' factor, as Kirsten Hardie has argued; they 'surprise, intrigue and absorb' students, adding fun to learning.[7] Research has also illustrated that 'object-handling has a long-lasting effect and relationship with memory'.[8] Haptic engagement with an object triggers emotion and aids memory retention.[9] Students and audiences who engage with actual objects are able to recall knowledge about them and their associated stories better than their peers exposed to digital surrogates.[10] Touching an object is 'a startlingly intimate act and can do more to connect a student with the ancient world than watching a dozen documentaries or sitting through 100 lectures'.[11]

This method forms the basis of my approach to teaching the eighteenth century and its reception of classical culture as part of an art history honours module entitled 'Classicism in Western Art: The Legacy of Greece and Rome'. Running annually, this module considers definitions of the classical, appropriations of classical forms and ideals, as well as changing attitudes to the past and the discipline of classical reception. A large part of the module focuses on the eighteenth century and its broader engagement with archaeology and classical culture. Classes consist of weekly lectures and seminars; the seminars are arranged in small groups of seven to ten students and they provide the ideal setting to experiment with teaching directly from objects. I designed these sessions to complement more formal learning based on lectures in order to create an environment that fosters students' inquisitiveness. These hands-on sessions are centred on specific objects from the museum collections of the University of St Andrews.

Since its foundation in the fifteenth century, the University of St Andrews has amassed collections for the purposes of teaching, research and display, as many British and European universities did.[12] From the second half of the seventeenth century, the university's historic collections were on display in the colleges and shown to visitors as part of a standardised tour.[13] The range of ethnographic, anthropological and natural history material entering the university expanded throughout the late eighteenth and early nineteenth centuries; this expansion relates to intellectual curiosity and to what Matthew Simpson refers to as the 'related culture of British imperialism'.[14] These diverse objects, collectively referred to as 'the Curiosities', were placed in the university library alongside literary tools for their interpretation, such as books on natural philosophy and manuscripts.[15] Their display in such a context emphasised the university's connections with patrons, staff and alumni, and its international links. In 1838, the university and the Literary and Philosophical Society of St Andrews jointly established the first formal museum in the United College buildings.[16] Displays in the Upper Hall in United College showcased the collections of mainly natural historical specimens but also anthropological and archaeological objects (Figures 7.1–7.2). This transfer of the 'Curiosities' collections out of the library context marked an important stage in the history and meaning of the university collections. The modern, rationally ordered displays in United College demonstrate a shift from a culture of 'Curiosities' and wonder to one of scientific inquiry. As Helen Rawson

Figure 7.1: Upper College Hall, North Street, St Andrews, looking east, c. 1910. Courtesy of the University of St Andrews Libraries and Museums, ID: StAU-BPMus-1.

Figure 7.2: Upper College Hall, North Street, St Andrews, looking west, c. 1910. Courtesy of the University of St Andrews Libraries and Museums, ID: StAU-BPMus-2.

has argued, this change is associated with wider cultural shifts related to the Enlightenment and its legacy, British expansionism during the Age of Empire, and the development of modern science.[17]

Throughout the second half of the nineteenth century, there was increasing use of the university collection as a teaching resource for scientific subjects. This is not unique to St Andrews, of course; universities have been informally collecting since at least the mid-sixteenth century in order to support their teaching and research missions.[18] During the eighteenth and nineteenth centuries, university departments accumulated extensive collections, particularly concerning the study of art, archaeology and geology.[19] Many university collections were formed as an instrument to support teaching and were an integral part of student experience in the nineteenth century; they played an active part in explaining, describing and archiving nature and science.

In the early nineteenth century, following the decline of the Literary and Philosophical Society, the university assumed sole responsibility for the museum and its holdings, which in 1912 were transferred to the Bell Pettigrew Museum, funded by Elsie Bell Pettigrew in memory of her husband James Bell Pettigrew, Chandos Professor of Medicine

(1875–1908).[20] The Bell Pettigrew functioned as a university and public museum until the 1950s, when it was reduced to only its zoological collections; it still is today a rare survivor of an Edwardian zoological teaching museum and deeply embedded in departmental teaching. Collecting for teaching and research purposes has continued throughout the twentieth and twenty-first centuries in the fields of zoology, geology, archaeology, art and ethnography, among others. However, during the twentieth century object teaching and use of collections fell from popularity, not only in St Andrews but also around the world. It was only during the late twentieth century that universities and faculties started to look again at their collections with renewed interest.[21]

In the 1990s, the Museum Collections Unit was established in St Andrews with responsibility for all the university's artefact collections, from art, ethnography, archaeology and numismatics to the science collections, including anatomical, geological and zoological specimens. After a long developmental stage, a new museum, MUSA (Museum of the University of St Andrews), was opened to the public in 2008. Today, the university collections consist of about 115,000 objects from art, history, science and medicine, housed in three locations: the Bell Pettigrew Museum and the newly extended and refurbished Wardlaw Museum (the previous MUSA) and a dedicated collections centre. The university actively promotes these collections as 'active, and available for research and teaching'.[22] In addition to these, the university library's special collections hold printed books, manuscripts, photographs and the university archive. As part of a wide consolidation and digitisation project in order to raise the profile and functionality of the collections, a large part of these objects is available online through a dedicated site.[23] Although the rich and diverse range of the collections offer opportunities for teaching and research, the majority of staff and students are not familiar with the nature or extent of the university collections. This is not unique to St Andrews; it has been recognised that one of the main barriers to wider use of OBL in HE is a general lack of awareness by staff and students in institutions of their special collections.[24]

Having worked on the university collections for my research, I was aware of their potential and eager to explore them for use in the classroom. I thus redesigned 'Classicism in Western Art: The Legacy of Greece and Rome' to include seminars that would focus on object-based instruction. It has been a rewarding experience but one that also has had a few challenges. Locating material relevant to the eighteenth century and to the learning outcomes of each session was the first hurdle. As mentioned earlier, the online database does not include all the objects in the collections. It took considerable time to browse and talk to curators in order to come up with a list of objects I could use in my seminars. An institutional circumstance that proved beneficial for my module redesign was the integration of collection data across the university into a single online database, making it easier to locate material. More recently, a re-evaluation of internal governance structures led to the merging of libraries and museums, bringing them together into a new administrative institutional entity with common strategic planning approach and themes. This integration facilitates engagement with library and museum collections across the curriculum and offers more opportunities for contributions to teaching and learning across the university.

The logistical aspects of organising object-led seminars are also important to consider.[25] OBL is a collaborative endeavour requiring support and input from special collections librarians, curators and archivists. There were a number of decisions and preparations to make, from finding suitable rooms and deciding on table arrangements to confirming the availability of curatorial staff to source and transfer the objects. Specialist library and/or museum staff are present in these seminars and introduce students to safe ways to handle objects and historical documents. All seminar sessions take place in rooms where the students can spend time working in small groups of three or four, contemplating an object and sharing their thoughts, responses and ideas (Figure 7.3). Students generally felt that the layout of the room, with the desks set up in a U-shaped configuration, was effective, as they could move around to encounter the objects and their feedback noted 'the fun of being physically active instead of stagnant at desks'. While reading a book or listening to a lecture is a passive way of learning, OBL facilitates a more active encounter with objects.

Moving around the room, students are responsible for leading the sessions. OBL is participatory in principle and a practice based on – but also supporting – inclusive pedagogy. This approach enables a degree of autonomy and agency on behalf of the students, but it also means that as a teacher I had to shift from content expert to facilitator and find effective ways to support students with their enquiries. As one of the students observed, this method 'is more time consuming and less dense in its transmission of information than a standard lecture'. This comment speaks to what I consider to be two of the key challenges of OBL. Multi-sensory

Figure 7.3: Room and desk arrangement. Image credit: Lenia Kouneni.

analysis encourages slow, semi-structured learning; students need appropriate space and time. How as teachers do we fight the prevalent 'content tyranny' that encourages us to push through as much as possible in a session? OBL is not about placing an item in front of students and 'explaining' it to them, nor is it about handing them documents that will do so. Instead, the intention is to strive to engage students' senses and material literacy to draw out the complexities and long histories of objects.

Thus, before providing any information on specific objects, I ask students to talk with each other to attempt to define what it is they see when they look at the object in front of them. Our seminars start with a close looking exercise, examining, describing and sometimes even drawing the physical characteristics of the object, focusing on its materiality. Subsequently, students work together in groups to formulate questions around its use, meaning and interpretation, and they can search the internet for more information, if needed. This process of decoding an object helps students to develop transferable skills such as critical thinking, problem solving and communication.[26] Students recognise the benefits of this approach and their feedback described OBL as an exhilarating and refreshing way to learn that fosters collaboration and improves investigative and reasoning skills.

In order to demonstrate in a more concrete way how I use OBL within my practice and in the context of teaching eighteenth-century approaches to antiquity, I now provide two examples of specific seminar topics and objects. One of the object-based seminars focuses on the concept and experiences of the eighteenth-century Grand Tour. For this session, I brought together objects from the Special Collections and Museum Collections: a display case filled with eighteenth-century cameos collected by Grand Tourists and two travel journals. The case with intaglios is part of a group of six housed in the university collections without much information regarding their provenance (Figure 7.4).[27] The first comments and questions revolved around the physical properties of the wooden case, discussing its potential use. Students examined closely the plaster cameos, noticing their varying sizes and depicted themes and being particularly inquisitive about their modes of production. The discussion then moved to broader issues around eighteenth-century display practices, the relationship between producers and buyers, the reproduction of the material culture and imagery of antiquity for a contemporary audience, and the market for souvenirs.

Alongside these intaglios, students examined another type of 'product' of the Grand Tour: the travel diary. I brought to the classroom two travel journals that recorded the same journey: one written by James David Forbes, a geologist and principal of United Colleges, St Andrews, and one written by his sister, Jane Forbes. Their journals described the long

Figure 7.4: Students looking at impronte (plaster cameos). Image credit: Lenia Kouneni.

continental journey they took between July 1826 and July 1827. Students had an opportunity to examine them, turn their pages and consider them in the context of travel writing. But they also became witnesses to the different approaches and experiences of Jane and James, which prompted a discussion on gender. Even within the restricted time of the seminar, students indicated that Jane's journals present a feminine perspective compared to her brother's diaries, descriptions and drawings. Having the two next to each other, students could look closely at both text and image, and compare the descriptions of a female traveller to that of a male one.

Another seminar takes the form of a case study and centres on a local antiquarian, Lieutenant General Robert Melville (1723–1809). In 1791, General Melville wrote a letter addressed 'To the Rector, Principals and Professors of the University of the City of St Andrews' offering a medallion portrait of himself by James Tassie for display in 'a small space in your Public Library among the more valuable Donations there'.[28] Following a close reading of the letter, students considered Melville's motivations and the way he presented them (including his writing tone), but they were also eager to know more about the display of portraits in the university library during the late eighteenth century. With the assistance of one of the university curators who was present during the seminar, students uncovered the history of the collection of 'curiosities' formed in the university library and its growing pantheon of images of eminent men.

Together with the letter, students examined the medallion portrait created by James Tassie, focusing initially on its style inspired by classical models and its material, Tassie's invention of a new medium, the vitreous glass paste (Figure 7.5).[29] Discussion moved to broader issues around the rise of portraiture in the eighteenth century and patronage. As we delved deeper, students became interested in the life and career of the specific sitter and patron of this portrait. The Fife-born Robert Melville was an antiquarian, interested in the Roman period and a fellow of the Society of Antiquaries, but he was also an army officer, colonial governor and inventor of two types of naval gun, the 'carronade' and 'melvillade'.[30] Melville was governor of Guadeloupe and in 1760 governor to the Ceded Islands (Grenada, Dominica, St Vincent and Tobago); he owned estates, including two large plantations and enslaved people. Thus, the objects of this seminar directed students to consider the colonial context for archaeological collecting, art patronage and antiquarian interest in the late eighteenth century. At the same time, these objects are undisputed manifestations of the imperial and colonial contexts for the collections at St Andrews and the involvement of Scotland (and Fife) in the British imperial project. When Tassie's medallion of Melville was displayed in the library, it was surrounded by weapons of war and a bust of George III, as visual evidence of the success of the Empire and its conquests.[31]

Figure 7.5: James Tassie, medallion portrait of Lieutenant General Robert Melville, vitreous paste, 1791. Courtesy of the University of St Andrews Libraries and Museums, ID: HC982.

Melville's letter and medallion gave students the opportunity to appreciate troublesome and entangled meanings, understand better complex and abstract concepts, such as imperialism and colonialism, and tackle legacies of enslavement and empire.[32] OBL can be a significant tool in disrupting, transforming and even decolonising collections. Teaching with such objects also contributes to the University Museums' Strategic Plan to address colonial histories and institutional legacies.[33] Part of this strategic objective is the project *Re-Collecting Empire*, which explores entanglements of cultures resulting from colonial encounters in the past, and how creative responses can add new dimensions to heritage objects through examining and re-telling their narratives.[34] The inclusion of objects linked to colonialism and empire in teaching not only raises student awareness of such issues but also furthers the university's processes of decolonisation.

When working with any collection, it is imperative that we acknowledge the impact of imperialism and colonisation. Biographies of objects and their interactions with collections are deeply revealing of colonial culture. University collections in Scotland create a space of learning that offers the possibility for revealing the many legacies of empire and slavery present in Scotland's heritage.[35] Placing these objects in front of students and allowing them to interrogate their materiality alongside their origins, meaning and histories is a useful approach in bringing new light to existing collections. Students realise the need to confront imperial legacies within the university collection and wider society. Within the context of growing calls to decolonise institutional spaces, OBL offers an example of how universities and museums can redeploy their cultural assets to support a more democratic, ethical and authentic representation of their collections, their purpose and their origins.[36]

Teaching with university collections often aligns and supports broader university strategies. An interesting aspect that students raised in their feedback is the personal connections that they felt they formed with the history of the university. The University of St Andrews highly values student experience and satisfaction.[37] It is a small university that fosters a sense of community and belonging in its students. Bringing into the classroom objects that are part of the university's heritage provides students with an opportunity to learn about institutional history and feel part of its long tradition. Beyond their didactic value, these objects and collections help form the identity of the university. They provide material evidence of institutional research and tangible proof 'of the evolution in knowledge and teaching which was taking place in the university in the past and continues to this day'.[38] Collection objects are thus central to the creation of a distinctive institutional identity.[39]

Although the University of St Andrews has two museums, the majority of the collections are stored in a collections centre and are currently under-utilised and isolated from student life. Incorporating them into teaching allows them to be released from cabinets and storerooms, to populate tables and student attention, and to play a more dynamic and central role in university experience. Teaching with these objects – investigating, questioning and re-writing their narratives – builds new value and purpose into university collections.

After I organised these hands-on, physical interactions with objects for my seminars and ran them for a year, in spring 2020 I was faced with a challenge that I had not anticipated. The new, pandemic-adjusted teaching structure removed many of the opportunities to engage physically with the collection. This sudden shift affected the planning, organisation and implementation of all teaching activities. Object-based seminars were not possible in the format I had designed, but I was eager to attempt to adapt them to fit the new restrictions and learning realities of the pandemic. The most obvious solution was to employ a digital image. As argued earlier in this chapter, there are clear pedagogical advantages in direct object handling that involves all the senses in comparison to learning through digital surrogates. However, it is also worth noting that there is a long history of mediating objects. The photograph of the nineteenth-century display of the university collections in United Colleges shows objects inside cases that create tangible boundaries between objects and viewers/users. Teaching with these objects was often mediated through glass. In the present climate, the screen replicates the boundaries of glass cases, while enabling a new kind of experience. Discussions of the materiality of digital media have raised interesting issues around the literal, physical and networked qualities of digital artefacts and systems.[40] Digital museum objects have traditionally been described as surrogates and thus as lesser than their physical counterparts; they are, though, objects with their 'own materiality, aura and value'.[41]

Following the pandemic, museums have investigated how best to use online and digital collections in learning and engagement. The curatorial team of the University Museums was eager to explore digital technology as a means to enhance people's experience of the collection remotely and as a way to support teaching and digital delivery. The Director of Libraries and Museums of the University of St Andrews, Katie Eagleton, together with members of the University Museums in Scotland (UMIS) group, initiated a joint research project entitled 'Online teaching with digitised museum collections', supported by funding from the Arts and Humanities Research Council.[42] At the same time, the Museums team and digital technology experts worked together to explore software that would provide an engaging and interactive experience in using museums and special collections digitally. The result was Exhibit, a digital tool that enables anyone to create interactive presentations with digitised material from the university (and other) collections, including 3D models, manuscripts, rare books, artworks and photographs. It is easy to use and can be shared or embedded in PowerPoint, Moodle, Microsoft Teams, WordPress and web pages.

With the support of the curatorial team, students enrolled in the 'Classicism in Western Art' module engaged in digital OBL. They were given links to specific objects from the online catalogue and I employed Exhibit as a teaching tool. For instance, I created a digital storytelling of a Grand Tour journal written in 1822 by Thomas Moody and illustrated with watercolours by Joseph Axe Sleap (1808–59). Exhibit allowed me to annotate passages and zoom in on details of the text and image, drawing students' attention to specific passages, images, techniques and details (Figure 7.6).[43] I also asked students to collaborate in small groups to research individual works and create their own exhibits for a selection of objects in the university collection. They all received training from the Library Application Services Manager on how to use Exhibit and support from the Collections curators. Students engaged with this exercise enthusiastically and reported that it increased their confidence in the use of digital tools to conduct visual analysis and tell stories about individual objects. They also emphasised that it made them feel more comfortable with navigating digital collections and archives and it enhanced their knowledge of the university collections. Moreover, Exhibit challenged them to be creative and write in a different way, prompting them to think about accessibility and communication. Students who participated in these digital object-based seminars engaged with individual objects in an experiential learning environment and acquired both subject-specific knowledge and transferable skills.

My experience during the last few years has shown that digital technologies are a good complement to learning with physical collections

Figure 7.6: Screenshot of Exhibit (https://exhibit.so/exhibits/6YwhPoBWivhGsLXyO2Dw) featuring Thomas Moody, 'Journal of a tour through Switzerland and Italy in 1822', with twenty-four watercolour illustrations by Joseph Axe Sleap. Courtesy of the University of St Andrews Libraries and Museums, ID: msD919.M7E22 (ms229).

and serve as an important tool when access to the physical collection is restricted. Although engaging with physical objects is different to engaging with digital objects, both offer opportunities for learning. Aside from the context of the pandemic, digital images are an alternative to further challenges of OBL, including large class sizes, student-to-object ratio, suitability of classrooms, availability of curatorial staff and access to objects outside of class, to name just a few. Access to high-quality digital objects allows students to study them at their own pace and outside of class time. However, this experience also showed that digital collections and tools cannot replace the tangibility of the physical objects. There are some aspects and benefits of OBL that cannot be achieved through the use of digital images; students, for example, commented upon the value of being able to feel the weight of the object or its tactile details. On the other hand, digital images give students access to a larger number of objects and facilitate a different level of engagement with them; students can study them from home, they can use annotation tools and they can present their work in an engaging and accessible way.[44] Used in conjunction with physical encounters with the objects, digital objects extend the students' experience of the collection. They cannot be touched, smelled or felt in the same way that physical objects can, but it has been argued that they possess some type of matter.[45]

Now, more than ever, we need to think carefully and creatively about course design and delivery. We need to be able to continue to support, inform and enrich the learning of our students. OBL, either through direct engagement with objects, or working with digital images and tools, gives us an opportunity to create a more experiential, interactive experience. It encourages students to participate actively, take control of their learning, learn from one another and foster an academic community. The immersive nature of the OBL experience leads students to explore their own attitudes towards their learning. It also introduces them to the rich history of university collections and fosters future collection advocates.

Notes

1 The bibliography on OBL is extensive; a valuable resource focusing on higher education is *Engaging the Senses: Object-Based Learning in Higher Education*, ed. by Helen J. Chatterjee and Leonie Hannan (London: Routledge, 2015), which brings together contributors from universities and museums across the world and presents a comprehensive exploration of OBL as a pedagogy for higher education.

2 Scott G. Paris, *Perspectives on Object-Centered Learning in Museums* (Mahwah, NJ: Routledge, 2002), p. xiv.

3 In 2013, more than 700 university courses were taught in the United Kingdom using university museum collections: Liz Hide, UMG (University Museums Group) and UMIS (University Museums in Scotland), *Impact and Engagement: University Museums for the 21st Century* (University Museums Group and University Museums in Scotland, 2013), http://universitymuseumsgroup.org/wp-content/uploads/2013/11/UMG-ADVOCACY-single.pdf (accessed 14 June 2022).

4 Helen J. Chatterjee, 'Staying Essential: Articulating the Value of Object Based Learning', *University Museums and Collections Journal*, 1 (2009), 37–42; Chatterjee, 'Object-Based Learning in Higher Education: The Pedagogical Power of Museums', *University Museums and Collections Journal*, 3 (2010), 179–81; Rosalind Duhs, 'Learning from University Museums and Collections in Higher Education: University College London (UCL)', *University Museums and Collections Journal*, 3 (2010), 183–6; Leonie Hannan, Rosaling Duhs and Helen J. Chatterjee, 'Object Based Learning: A Powerful Pedagogy for Higher Education', in A. Boddington, J. Boys and C. Speight (eds), *Museums and Higher Education Working Together: Challenges and Opportunities* (Farnham: Ashgate, 2013), pp. 159–68; Thomas Kador, Leonie Hannah, Julianne Nyhan, Melissa Terras, Helen J. Chatterjee and Mark Carnall, 'Object-Based Learning and Research-Based Education: Case Studies from UCL Curricula', in *Teaching and Learning in Higher Education Perspective from UCL*, ed. by Jason P. Davies and Norbert Pachler (London: UCL Institute of Education Press, 2018), pp. 156–76.

5 Deborah Schultz, 'Three-Dimensional Learning: Exploring Responses to Learning and Interacting with Artefacts', in Stefanie S. Jandl and Mark S. Gold (eds), *A Handbook for Academic Museums, Exhibitions and Educators* (Edinburgh: MuseumsEtc, 2012), pp. 166–89.

6 Pam Meecham, 'Talking about Things: Internationalisation of the Curriculum through Object-Based Learning', in Chatterjee and Hannan (eds), *Engaging the Senses*, pp. 77–94.

7 Kirsten Hardie, *Innovative Pedagogies Series: Wow – The Power of Objects in Object-based Learning and Teaching*. Report from Higher Education Academy, 2015.

8 Devorah Romanek and Bernadette Lynch, 'Touch and the Value of Object Handling: Final Conclusions for a New Sensory Museology', in Helen J. Chatterjee (ed.), *Touch in Museums: Policy and Practice in Object Handling* (Oxford: Berg, 2008), pp. 275–86 (p. 284).

9 Eilean Hooper-Greenhill, *Museums and Their Visitors* (London: Routledge, 1994), p. 145; Judy Willcocks, 'The Power of Concrete Experience: Museum Collections, Touch and Meaning Making in Art and Design Pedagogy', in Chatterjee and Hannan (eds), *Engaging the Senses*, pp. 43–56.

10 Andrew Simpson and Gina Hammond, 'University Collections and Object-Based Pedagogies', *University Museums and Collections Journal*, 5 (2012), 75–81; Rebecca Sweetman, Alison Hadfield and Akira O'Connor, 'Material Culture, Museums, and Memory: Experiments in Visitor Recall and Memory', *Visitor Studies*, 23, no. 1 (2020), 18–45.

11 Anne Tiballi, 'Engaging the Past: Haptics and Object-Based Learning in Multiple Dimensions', in Chatterjee and Hannan (eds), *Engaging the Senses*, pp. 57–75.

12 Ian Carradice, 'Funding and Public Access through Partnership with Business', in Melanie Kelly (ed.), *Managing University Museums: Education and Skills* (Paris: Organisation for Economic Co-operation and Development, 2001), pp. 133–43. St Andrews was Scotland's first university and the third in the British Isles. Teaching began in 1410; full university status was obtained in 1413 with the signing of the Bull of Foundation by Pope Benedict XIII. See Ronald G. Cant, *The University of St Andrews: A Short History* (St Andrews: University of St Andrews, 1992), pp. 1–7.

13 Helen C. Rawson, 'Treasures of the University: An Examination of the Identification, Presentation and Responses to Artefacts of Significance at the University of St Andrews from 1410 to the Mid-19th Century' (unpublished doctoral thesis, University of St Andrews, 2010), pp. 37–44.

14 Matthew Simpson, '"You Have Not Such a One in England": St Andrews University Library as an Eighteenth-Century Mission Statement', *Library History*, 17, no. 1 (2001), 41–56 (51).

15 Matthew Simpson, 'St Andrews University Library in the 18th Century' (unpublished doctoral thesis, University of St Andrews, 1990), pp. 12–15 and appendix 1: List of curiosities in the possession of the St Andrews University Library.

16 William C. McIntosh, *Brief Sketch of the Natural History Museum of the University of St Andrews* (St Andrews: University of St Andrews, 1913); Simpson, 'St Andrews University Library', pp. 11–12.

17 Rawson, 'Treasures of the University', pp. 267–77.

18 Geoffrey D. Lewis, 'Collections, Collectors and Museums: A Brief World Survey', in J. M. A. Thompson (ed.), *Manual of Curatorship* (London: Butterworths, 1984), pp. 7–22; Patrick J. Boylan, 'Universities and Museums: Past, Present and Future', *Museum Management and Curatorship*, 18, no. 1 (1999), 43–56; Marta C. Lourenço, 'Contributions to the History of University Museums and Collections in Europe', *Museologia*, 3 (2003), 17–26.

19 Chatterjee, 'Object-Based Learning in Higher Education'.

20 McIntosh, *Brief Sketch*.

21 Kate Arnold-Forster, '"A Developing Sense of Crisis": A New Look at University Collections in the United Kingdom', *Museum International*, 52, no. 3 (2000), 10–14; Dan Bartlett, Nicolette Meister and William Green, 'Employing Museum Objects in Undergraduate Liberal Arts Education', *Informal Learning Review*, 124 (Jan./Feb. 2014), 3–6.

22 University of St Andrews, 'Collections Centre', www.st-andrews.ac.uk/museums/visit-us/collections-centre (accessed 22 January 2024)

23 University of St Andrews, 'Collections Centre', www.st-andrews.ac.uk/museums/visit-us/collections-centre (accessed 22 January 2024)

24 Jane Thogersen, Andrew Simpson, Gina Hammond, Leonard Janiszewski and Eve Guerry, 'Creating Curriculum Connections: A University Museum Object-Based Learning Project', *Education for Information*, 34 (2018), 113–20; see also Helen J. Chatterjee, Leonie Hannan and Linda Thomson, 'An Introduction to Object-Based Learning and Multisensory Engagement', in Chatterjee and Hannah (eds), *Engaging the Senses*, pp. 1–18.

25 Joe Cain, 'Practical Concerns when Implementing Object-Based Teaching in Higher Education', *University Museums and Collections Journal*, 3 (2010), 197–201 is very useful.

26 Hannan, Duhs and Chatterjee, 'Object Based Learning: A Powerful Pedagogy for Higher Education'.

27 University of St Andrews, 'Plaster Cameos', https://collections.st-andrews.ac.uk/item/plaster-cameos/762806 (accessed 28 April 2023).

28 University of St Andrews, 'Letter from General Robert Melville Presenting a Medallion of Himself to the University', UYUY459/A/20, https://collections.st-andrews.ac.uk/item/letter-from-general-robert-melville-presenting-a-medallion-of-himself-to-the-university/763068 (accessed 28 April 2023).

29 University of St Andrews, 'Medallion Portrait of Lieutenant General Robert Melville', HC982, https://collections.st-andrews.ac.uk/item/medallion-portrait-of-lieutenant-general-robert-melvill/762581 (accessed 28 April 2023).

30 'A Biographical Sketch of General Robert Melville of Strathkinness: Written by His Secretary With notes by Evan W. M. Balfour-Melville and General Robert Melville', *The Scottish Historical Review*, 14, no. 54 (Jan. 1917), 116–46.

31 Simpson, 'You Have Not Such a One', 48–9 discusses the expansion of British trade and the British Empire, and the symbolism of the 'weapons emblematically laid down and inert' in the University Library before the bust of the king and portrait of Melville.

32 On OBL and decolonisation, see Lainie Schultz, 'Object-Based Learning, or Learning from Objects in the Anthropology Museum', *Review of Education, Pedagogy, and Cultural Studies*, 40, no. 4 (2018), 282–304 and Catherine Kevin and Fiona Salmon, 'Indigenous Art in Higher Education: "Palpable History" as a Decolonising Strategy for Enhancing Reconciliation and Wellbeing', in Thomas Kador and Helen Chaterjee (eds), *Object-Based Learning and Well-Being* (London: Routledge, 2020), pp. 60–78.

33 University of St Andrews Libraries and Museums, 'Strategic Plan 2020–2025' (2021), www.st-andrews.ac.uk/assets/university/museums/documents/Musuems%20Strategy%20document%20%C3%A2%C2%80%C2%93%20March%202021%20%C3%A2%C2%80%C2%93%20DU42801.pdf (accessed 28 April 2023).

34 Bond, Emma 'Re-Collecting Empire: Laying the Groundwork'. *Museums Blog: Behind the Scenes at the University of St Andrews Museums* (2021), https://museumblog.wp.st-andrews.ac.uk/2021/08/03/re-collecting-empire-laying-the-groundwork (accessed 28 April 2023).

35 Emma Bond and Michael Morris (eds), *Scotland's Transnational Heritage: Legacies of Empire and Slavery* (Edinburgh: Edinburgh University Press, 2023) outlines some of the many legacies of empire, trade and slavery and offers a range of practical and intellectual methods to help diversify the stories we tell about those legacies.

36 See also Garth Benneyworth and Lourenço C Pinto, 'Sol Plaatje University as a Case Study for Decoloniality: Object-Based Learning as Applied to Heritage Studies', *South African Museums Association Bulletin*, 4, no. 1 (2019), 1–9 and Christina J. Hodge, 'Decolonizing Collections-Based Learning: Experiential Observation as an Interdisciplinary Framework for Object Study', *Museum Anthropology*, 41 (2018), 142–58.

37 University of St Andrews, 'Student Experience at St Andrews', www.st-andrews.ac.uk/study/why/experience (accessed 28 April 2023).

38 Zenobia Kozak, 'The Role of University Museums and Heritage in the 21st Century', *The Museum Review*, 1, no. 1 (2016), https://themuseumreviewjournal.wordpress.com/2016/12/12/vol1no1kozak (accessed 31 January 2024).

39 Andrew Simpson, 'Rethinking University Museums: Material Collections and the Changing World of Higher Education', *Museums Australia Magazine*, 22, no. 3 (autumn 2014), 18–22 discusses effectively how university heritage collections support the development of an institutional narrative.

40 Johanna Drucker, 'Performative Materiality and Theoretical Approaches to Interface', *Digital Humanities Quarterly*, 7, no. 1 (2013).

41 Nicôle Meehan, 'Digital Museum Objects and Transnational Histories', in Bond and Morris (eds), *Scotland's Transnational Heritage*, pp. 171–84.

42 University of St Andrews, 'About the Project', https://collectionteaching.wp.st-andrews.ac.uk (accessed 28 April 2023).

43 You can find the Exhibit at this link: www.exhibit.so/exhibits/6YwhPoBWivhGsLXyO2Dw (accessed 31 January 2024).

44 Olivia C. Frost, 'When the Object Is Digital: Properties of Digital Surrogate Objects and Implications for Learning', in R. Parry (ed.), *Museums in a Digital Age* (Abingdon: Routledge, 2009), pp. 72–85.

45 Paul M. Leonardi, 'Digital Materiality? How Artifacts without Matter, Matter', *First Monday*, 15, no. 6 (2010).

References

'A Biographical Sketch of General Robert Melville of Strathkinness: Written by His Secretary With notes by Evan W. M. Balfour-Melville and General Robert Melville', *The Scottish Historical Review*, 14, no. 54 (Jan. 1917), 116–46.

Arnold-Forster, Kate, '"A Developing Sense of Crisis": A New Look at University Collections in the United Kingdom', *Museum International*, 52, no. 3 (2000), 10–14.

Bartlett, Dan, Meister, Nicolette and Green, William, 'Employing Museum Objects in Undergraduate Liberal Arts Education', *Informal Learning Review*, 124 (Jan./Feb. 2014), 3–6.

Benneyworth, Garth and Pinto, Lourenço C., 'Sol Plaatje University as a Case Study for Decoloniality: Object-Based Learning as Applied to Heritage Studies', *South African Museums Association Bulletin*, 4, no. 1 (2019), 1–9.

Bond, Emma, 'Re-Collecting Empire: Laying the Groundwork'. *Museums Blog: Behind the Scenes at the University of St Andrews Museums* (2021). https://museumblog.wp.st-andrews.ac.uk/2021/08/03/re-collecting-empire-laying-the-groundwork (accessed 28 April 2023).

Bond, Emma and Morris, Michael (eds), *Scotland's Transnational Heritage: Legacies of Empire and Slavery* (Edinburgh: Edinburgh University Press, 2023).

Boylan, Patrick J., 'Universities and Museums: Past, Present and Future', *Museum Management and Curatorship*, 18, no. 1 (1999), 43–56.

Cain, Joe, 'Practical Concerns When Implementing Object-Based Teaching in Higher Education', *University Museums and Collections Journal*, 3 (2010), 197–201.

Cant, Ronald G., *The University of St Andrews: A Short History* (St Andrews: University of St Andrews, 1992).

Carradice, Ian, 'Funding and Public Access through Partnership with Business', in Melanie Kelly (ed.), *Managing University Museums: Education and Skills* (Paris: Organisation for Economic Co-operation and Development, 2001), pp. 133–43.

Chatterjee, Helen J., 'Staying Essential: Articulating the Value of Object Based Learning', *University Museums and Collections Journal*, 1 (2009), 37–42.

Chatterjee, Helen J., 'Object-Based Learning in Higher Education: The Pedagogical Power of Museums', *University Museums and Collections Journal*, 3 (2010), 179–81.

Chatterjee, Helen J. and Hannan, Leonie (eds), *Engaging the Senses: Object-Based Learning in Higher Education* (London: Routledge, 2015).

Chatterjee, Helen J., Hannan, Leonie and Thomson, Linda, 'An Introduction to Object-Based Learning and Multisensory Engagement', in Chatterjee and Hannan (eds), *Engaging the Senses*, pp. 1–18.

Drucker, Johanna, 'Performative Materiality and Theoretical Approaches to Interface', *Digital Humanities Quarterly*, 7, no. 1 (2013).

Duhs, Rosalind, 'Learning from University Museums and Collections in Higher Education: University College London (UCL)', *University Museums and Collections Journal*, 3 (2010), 183–6.

Frost, Olivia C., 'When the Object Is Digital: Properties of Digital Surrogate Objects and Implications for Learning', in R. Parry (ed.), *Museums in a Digital Age* (Abingdon: Routledge, 2009), pp. 72–85.

Hannan, Leonie, Duhs, Rosaling and Chatterjee, Helen J., 'Object Based Learning: A Powerful Pedagogy for Higher Education', in A. Boddington, J. Boys and C. Speight (eds), *Museums and Higher Education Working Together: Challenges and Opportunities* (Farnham: Ashgate, 2013), pp. 159–68.

Hardie, Kirsten, *Innovative Pedagogies Series: Wow – The Power of Objects in Object-Based Learning and Teaching*. Report from Higher Education Academy, 2015.

Hide, Liz, UMG (University Museums Group) and UMIS (University Museums in Scotland), *Impact and Engagement: University Museums for the 21st Century* (University Museums Group and University Museums in Scotland, 2013), http://universitymuseumsgroup.org/wp-content/uploads/2013/11/UMG-ADVOCACY-single.pdf (accessed 14 June 2022).

Hodge, Christina J., 'Decolonizing Collections-Based Learning: Experiential Observation as an Interdisciplinary Framework for Object Study', *Museum Anthropology*, 41 (2018), 142–58.

Hooper-Greenhill, Eilean, *Museums and Their Visitors* (London: Routledge, 1994).

Kador, Thomas, Hannah, Leonie, Nyhan, Julianne, Terras, Melissa, Chatterjee Helen J. and Carnall, Mark, 'Object-Based Learning and

Research-Based Education: Case Studies from UCL Curricula', in Jason P. Davies and Norbert Pachler (eds), *Teaching and Learning in Higher Education Perspective from UCL* (London: UCL Institute of Education Press, 2018), pp. 156–76.

Kevin, Catherine and Salmon, Fiona, 'Indigenous Art in Higher Education: "Palpable History" as a Decolonising Strategy for Enhancing Reconciliation and Wellbeing', in Thomas Kador and Helen Chatterjee (eds), *Object-Based Learning and Well-Being* (London: Routledge, 2020), pp. 60–78.

Kozak, Zenobia, 'The Role of University Museums and Heritage in the 21st Century', *The Museum Review*, 1, no. 1 (2016). https://themuseumreviewjournal.wordpress.com/2016/12/12/vol1no1kozak (accessed 31 January 2024).

Leonardi, Paul M., 'Digital Materiality? How Artifacts without Matter, Matter', *First Monday*, 15, no. 6 (2010).

Lewis, Geoffrey D., 'Collections, Collectors and Museums: A Brief World Survey', in J. M. A. Thompson (ed.), *Manual of Curatorship* (London: Butterworths, 1984), pp. 7–22.

Lourenço, Marta C., 'Contributions to the History of University Museums and Collections in Europe', *Museologia*, 3 (2003), 17–26.

McIntosh, William C., *Brief Sketch of the Natural History Museum of the University of St Andrews* (St Andrews: University of St Andrews, 1913).

Meecham, Pam, 'Talking about Things: Internationalisation of the Curriculum through Object-Based Learning', in Chatterjee and Hannan (eds), *Engaging the Senses*, pp. 77–94.

Meehan, Nicôle, 'Digital Museum Objects and Transnational Histories', in Bond and Morris (eds), *Scotland's Transnational Heritage*, pp. 171–84.

Paris, Scott G., *Perspectives on Object-Centered Learning in Museums* (Mahwah, NJ: Routledge, 2002).

Rawson, Helen C., 'Treasures of the University: An Examination of the Identification, Presentation and Responses to Artefacts of Significance at the University of St Andrews from 1410 to the Mid-19th Century' (unpublished doctoral thesis, University of St Andrews, 2010).

Romanek, Devorah and Lynch, Bernadette, 'Touch and the Value of Object Handling: Final Conclusions for a New Sensory Museology', in Helen J. Chatterjee (ed.), *Touch in Museums: Policy and Practice in Object Handling* (Oxford: Berg, 2008), pp. 275–86.

Schultz, Deborah, 'Three-Dimensional Learning: Exploring Responses to Learning and Interacting with Artefacts', in Stefanie S. Jandl and Mark S. Gold (eds), *A Handbook for Academic Museums, Exhibitions and Educators* (Edinburgh: MuseumsEtc, 2012), pp. 166–89.

Schultz, Lainie, 'Object-Based Learning, or Learning from Objects in the Anthropology Museum', *Review of Education, Pedagogy, and Cultural Studies*, 40, no. 4 (2018), 282–304.

Simpson, Andrew, 'Rethinking University Museums: Material Collections and the Changing World of Higher Education', *Museums Australia Magazine*, 22, no. 3 (autumn 2014), 18–22.

Simpson, Andrew and Hammond, Gina, 'University Collections and Object-Based Pedagogies', *University Museums and Collections Journal*, 5 (2012), 75–81.

Simpson, Matthew, 'St Andrews University Library in the 18th Century' (unpublished doctoral thesis, University of St Andrews, 1990).

Simpson, Matthew, '"You Have Not Such a One in England": St Andrews University Library as an Eighteenth-Century Mission Statement', *Library History*, 17, no. 1 (2001), 41–56.

Sweetman, Rebecca, Hadfield, Alison and O'Connor, Akira, 'Material Culture, Museums, and Memory: Experiments in Visitor Recall and Memory', *Visitor Studies*, 23, no. 1 (2020), 18–45.

Thogersen, Jane, Simpson, Andrew, Hammond, Gina, Janiszewski, Leonard and Guerry, Eve, 'Creating Curriculum Connections: A University Museum Object-Based Learning Project', *Education for Information*, 34, (2018), 113–20.

Tiballi, Anne, 'Engaging the Past: Haptics and Object-Based Learning in Multiple Dimensions', in Chatterjee and Hannan (eds), *Engaging the Senses*, pp. 57–75.

University of St Andrews, 'About the Project', https://collectionteaching.wp.st-andrews.ac.uk (accessed 28 April 2023).

University of St Andrews, 'Collections Centre', www.st-andrews.ac.uk/museums/visit-us/collections-centre (accessed 22 January 2024).

University of St Andrews, 'Letter from General Robert Melville Presenting a Medallion of Himself to the University', UYUY459/A/20, https://collections.st-andrews.ac.uk/item/letter-from-general-robert-melville-presenting-a-medallion-of-himself-to-the-university/763068 (accessed 28 April 2023).

University of St Andrews, 'Medallion Portrait of Lieutenant General Robert Melville', HC982, https://collections.st-andrews.ac.uk/item/medallion-portrait-of-lieutenant-general-robert-melvill/762581 (accessed 28 April 2023).

University of St Andrews, 'Plaster Cameos', https://collections.st-andrews.ac.uk/item/plaster-cameos/762806 (accessed 28 April 2023).

University of St Andrews, 'Student Experience at St Andrews', www.st-andrews.ac.uk/study/why/experience (accessed 28 April 2023).

University of St Andrews Libraries and Museums, 'Strategic Plan 2020–2025' (2021), www.st-andrews.ac.uk/assets/university/museums/documents/Musuems%20Strategy%20document%20%C3%A2%C2%80%C2%93%20March%202021%20%C3%A2%C2%80%C2%93%20DU42801.pdf (accessed 28 April 2023).

Willcocks, Judy, 'The Power of Concrete Experience: Museum Collections, Touch and Meaning Making in Art and Design Pedagogy', in Chatterjee and Hannan (eds), *Engaging the Senses*, pp. 43–56.

Index

active learning, 95, 119
activism, 8, 119
Anning, Mary, 136
archaeology, 153, 155
archives, 6, 21, 24
art, 151
Arts and Humanities Research Council (AHRC), 138, 164
Ashmolean Museum, 128
assessment, 2, 6, 20, 37, 43, 92, 94, 98. *See also* dissertation, essay, presentations
    criteria, 28, 45
Australia, 3, 10, 38, 48, 132

Baartman, Sarah, 136
Biggs, John, 88
Blair, Tony, 113
body, 67, 73
Booth, Alan, 2, 95
Brexit, 119
British Museum, 128, 132
British Society for Eighteenth-Century Studies (BSECS), 19, 29
Burney Collection of Newspapers, 40–1, 69
Byrne, Charles, 136

Cameron, David, 113
Carey, Elaine, 95
Caroline of Ansbach, 30
Caroline of Brunswick, 115
Charlotte of Mecklenburg-Strelitz, 30
Cheyne, William, 71
chronology, 68, 111
citizenship, 109–20
class, 38, 48, 112, 136
colonialism, 1, 8, 11, 48, 73, 87, 110, 127–8, 139, 154, 160
    decolonised curricula, 8, 162
Conservative Party (UK), 113–14, 134
Cook, James, 132
COVID-19 pandemic, 6, 23, 53, 116

cultural history, 3, 109–10
curriculum design, 91

Delany, Mary, 131
digital history, 5, 11, 19–36, 37–58
    digital skills, 41
    digitised sources, 6, 40, 57, 163
disability, 8
discomfort, 7, 89, 117
dissertation, 39, 119

ecology, 1, 47
Eighteenth-Century Collections Online (ECCO), 5, 34n1, 40, 69, 88
eighteenth-century studies, 1
emotions, 1, 8, 67, 89
empathy, 10
empire. *See* colonialism
English literature, 26, 30, 97
Enlightenment, 4, 52, 128
equality, diversity and inclusion, 9
essay, 37, 43
evaluation, 53–4, 162
Evans, Richard, 114
external examining, 42

feedback, 45
feminism, 109, 112, 115
Forbes, David and Jane, 158–60
Foundling Hospital, 6
Frederick, Peter, 115

gender, 87–99, 110, 112, 119
George II, 31
George III, 23, 25, 31, 48, 128, 160
George IV, 23, 31
Georgian Papers Programme, 6, 20–33
Glassie, Henry, 6
Gove, Michael, 114
Grand Tour, 158, 164
group work, 20, 26, 47, 152

Hardie, Kirsten, 152
Hardman, Jan, 96, 98
Harland, Tony, 87
Harvey, Karen, 87
Higher Education Academy (UK), 2
history
  as branch of the arts, 3
  discipline of, 2–3, 5, 39, 92, 109
  historiography, 67, 69
History UK, 2, 6
Hitchcock, Tim, 87
Hooke, Robert, 131
Hyland, Paul, 2

impact, 24. See also public history
inquiry-based learning, 35n10
Institute for Historical Research (IHR), 19
interdisciplinarity, 1, 7, 19, 29, 92

Jardine, Nicholas, 127
joint degrees, 4, 110

Kwami, Atta, 135

Labour Party (UK), 113–14
Latour, Bruno, 75
lecture, 43, 77, 89, 152
Liverpool, 134–5
Lowe, Robert, 114

MacGregor, Neil, 131–2
MacLellan, Effie, 118
Mantell, Gideon, 136
marketisation, 1
Marsden, Samuel, 47–8
Marxism, 109
masculinity, 112, 117
material culture, 1, 7–8, 69, 110, 116, 129
medicine, 71–3, 136
  history of, 127, 129
Melville, Robert, 160, 162
Moody, Thomas, 164
museums, 7–9, 74, 78, 127–40, 151–66
music, 7, 117

Namier, Lewis, 110–11
nationalism, 87, 112
New Zealand, 48, 132

object-based learning (OBL), 151–2, 156, 162, 166
Old Bailey Online, 34n1, 40–1, 49, 58, 69
Omohundro Institute, 21
online learning, 6, 13n17

Pace, David, 5
palaeography, 26, 31
patriarchy, 87–8
peer support, 47
philosophy, 26, 30
politics, 38, 109–20
presentations, 27, 118–19
primary sources, 39, 91, 116, 120
Proctor, Alice, 130
public history, 20, 23

race, 7, 25, 48, 73, 89, 95, 112
Rawson, Helen, 153
reading, 72, 93, 117–18
Reform Act of 1867, 112
religion, 47–8, 89
research skills, 16, 20, 37–42, 90, 118–19
Royal Collection Trust, 21–2, 26
Royal Historical Society, 25

satirical prints, 116
school, 24, 110, 113–15
  history curriculum, 1, 4
science, 128, 133, 153
  history of, 127, 129, 136
Scotland, 42, 119, 160, 162
seminar, 88–9, 94–5, 115, 152
  participation forms, 96–7
senses, 7–9, 67–78, 156
sexism, 8
sexuality, 1, 87–99
Shaw, George, 132
Simpson, Matthew, 153
skills, 1–4, 10, 20, 32, 41, 78
  quantitative, 5
  transferable, 5–6, 24, 39, 57, 164
slavery, 48
social history, 109–10, 112–13
Starship Troopers, 116

Straw, Jack, 113
student-centred learning, 9, 88, 98
subject benchmarking, 2-4, 34n2, 39
Sykes, Grace, 90

Tassie, James, 160
theory, 1, 95
Tosh, John, 114
trans history, 88
Tyson, Edward, 131

universities, 1, 68
　Anglia Ruskin, 75
　Chester, 130, 133
　excellence frameworks, 9
　hiring practices, 8, 130
　King's College London (KCL), 20
　Manchester, 137
　Northampton, 111
　St Andrews, 153, 162-3

University College London, 151
Western Sydney (WSU), 37-8, 46-7
York, 112
USA, 2, 3, 33, 76

video, 45
vocational education, 3

Wedgwood, Josiah, 131
Wellcome Collection, 88
Wheeler, Anna, 114
Whig history, 90, 109-10, 114
Whitehead, Ian, 97
Wilberforce, William, 47-8
Wollstonecraft, Mary, 114
women's history, 112

Xerte software, 27

Yeandle, Peter, 113